# CREATIVE AGGRESSION

Dr. George Bach and Dr. Herb Goldberg

# CREATIVE AGGRESSION

## The Art of Assertive Living

ANCHOR BOOKS
ANCHOR PRESS/DOUBLEDAY
GARDEN CITY, NEW YORK

Grateful acknowledgment is made to the following for permission to use selections from their publications:

Excerpt from "Do not go gentle into that good night" from *The Poems of Dylan Thomas.* Copyright 1952 by Dylan Thomas. Reprinted by permission of New Directions Publishing Corporation and J. M. Dent & Sons Ltd. and the Trustees of the late Dylan Thomas. From "The use of aggression in psychotherapy" by Carl A. Whitaker, *Proceedings,* Ninth Annual Conference, Group Psychotherapy of Southern California, Inc., edited by George R. Bach.

Library of Congress Cataloging in Publication Data

Bach, George Robert, 1914–
Creative Aggression.

Includes bibliographical references and index.
1. Aggressiveness (Psychology)   2. Anger.
3. Assertiveness (Psychology)   I. Goldberg, Herb,
1937–            II. Title.
BF575.A3B3   1983      152.4      82–45621
ISBN 0-385-18442-5

TO THOSE WHO REFUSE
TO PAY THE PRICE OF
BEING "NICE"

# Acknowledgments

We are grateful to those professional colleagues who over the years have worked with our ideas and techniques independently in their own seminars and therapeutic work and discussed their experiences with us. They include Dr. Roger Bach (Salt Lake City), Dr. Lew Engel (San Francisco), Dr. David Lowry (New York City), and Dr. Lee Pulos (Vancouver, British Columbia).

Among our European colleagues who have utilized aggression techniques in their settings abroad we wish to thank Professor Guido Groeger (Berlin), Dipl. Psych. Herman Latka (Munich), Dr. Herman Paula and Dr. Udo Derbolowsky (Hamburg), and Professor Adolph Daümling (Bonn). Their work has reassured the authors that our approach is not culturebound or limited to the American scene.

Mr. Ed Monsson and his staff at the University of California, Los Angeles, have provided us with a hospitable setting where, over the past ten years, we have been able to try out and refine many of our techniques on an intelligent, normal adult population.

We are also indebted to the laboratory leaders on our staff whose work with us has been important in communicating the spirit and essence of our approach to the public. They include Dr. Eric Field, who has been highly instrumental in the development of office aggression techniques. Claudia Bach and Luree Nicholson have developed a special expertise utilizing aggression techniques with children in school and family settings. Catherine Bond, Yetta Bernhard, Joan Hotchkis, Sandra Burton, Alex and Johanna Vilumsons, and Sascha Schneider regularly teach our techniques in various educational settings. We also wish to thank Connie Grippo and Judy Black for providing many useful illustrations on the effects of indirect and repressed aggression in work settings.

Certain professional colleagues have been especially important to us through their own therapeutic and theoretical work and have given us helpful insights during the course of many conversations. They include Dr. Seymour Feshbach (UCLA), Dr. Robert W. Zaslow (Los Gatos, California), Dr. Carl Whitaker (Wisconsin), Dr. Zev Wanderer (Los Angeles), Dr. William C. Schutz (Esalen), and the late Dr. Eric Berne and Dr. Alvirdo Pearson.

For giving us personal encouragement and for providing a congenial environment in which the two independent and not always agreeing coauthors could "fight it out" creatively, we acknowledge the hostess artistry of Peggy and Stephanie Bach and Stephanie Goldberg.

In the actual production of the manuscript we are indebted to Mr. Alex Liepa, the editor who gave relevant encouragement and expert guidance for the direction of this book. Last but not least, Mr. Marvin Moss applied successful pressure where and when needed to meet our deadlines.

# Contents

## PART THREE

### HOW TO LIVE CONSTRUCTIVELY WITH AGGRESSION

# Introduction
to the 1983 Edition

Almost a decade has passed since *Creative Aggression* was first published. At that time it was the hope of the authors that, as a result of the book, the public and the psychological professions would become more aware of the phenomenon and problems caused by repressed and mismanaged aggression—in intimate relationships as well as in the large context of society. Our definition of aggression encompasses its various manifestations, including positive assertion, resistances and their expression, anger, the sharing of direct and honest feedback, the clear presentation of one's self, the process of resolving conflict, initiating communication, and even the expression of rage.

The focal idea, first fully asserted and explained in *Creative Aggression,* was that human aggression had important, even vital and life-sustaining functions. It was the denial, suppression, and repression of aggression, to the point where it produced destructive and hostile confrontations, as well as a continual, largely invisible yet insidious seepage of unexpressed anger that contaminated relationships, that caused aggression to be feared, avoided, and perceived as destructive and dangerous.

In this book, we set about to define and explore ways of recognizing and articulating this "underbelly" of human relationships in a way that might allow it to be constructively and creatively handled. We created learning games, "rules," and rituals that could act as safe vehicles for the release of aggression, so that this aspect of each relationship could be modified and expressed in constructive ways.

While the psychological professions had placed great emphasis on the role of repressed sexuality, childhood trauma, and developmental fixations in the creation of personal and relationship problems, they too had minimized, ignored, even perhaps had a "blind spot" for the existence of aggression and its repressed manifestations *in all of us*. All of us had been socialized and educated in a society whose ethos mandated being "nice" and avoided any verbal expressions or behaviors that were "not nice." None of us escaped the endless pressures to measure up to this standard. The result was that, for many, even a simple matter as saying "No," or asserting that "I want to be left alone," or "That makes me angry," became traumatic. In addition, shyness—a painful result of the repression of aggression—afflicts a very high percentage of the population.

Aggression, from the academic perspective, had generally been theorized to be the indirect result of frustration. Once all frustration was removed, supposedly aggression would disappear also. Our position and premise was, to the contrary, aggression was a major, necessary ingredient in the development of authentic cooperation, compassion, and bonding between people. The "nice" people in relationships, we explained, would inevitably come to feel disillusioned and alienated from each other as their repeated attempts to fulfill romantic fantasies of "harmony" and achieve conflict-free relationships repeatedly failed.

In the past, when relationship problems occurred, the psychological and psychiatric professions tended to place the blame for their origin on individual neurotic problems, unresolved hostility toward parents and other significant people of one's past, etc. That all relationships were at least grossly limited, if not doomed to failure, by the fact that their aggressive aspects were not constructively managed, and that, in addition, aggression was inevitably present whenever two human beings sought to have an intimate relationship, was not dealt with and often overlooked.

After years of working with individuals in groups, with couples involved in intimate relationships, and with people in business and educational settings to create methods in which to deal with their aggression in constructive ways, the following seemed clear to the authors. *The ability to define and communicate one's resistances and reservations honestly, to acknowledge and communicate anger, to ask directly and clearly for what one wanted, to resist intrusions by others in the form of mind reading or unrequested analysis, and to do all of these things without guilt or labels of being "inappropriate," impolite, or hostile, was crucial to both individual growth and healthy, realistic, and satisfying bonding.*

We were mindful of the age-old "love-hate" paradox—accepted in both romantic fiction and folklore—where supposedly love and hate were invariably coexistent. This "love-hate" paradox, we strove to explicate in our book, could be resolved if the necessary, inevitable, and creative aspects of aggression could be appreciated and dealt with. *Without doing this, however, relationships would be fragile and volatile and people would become victims rather than conscious managers of their relationship experiences.* In addition to a major obstacle to intimacy being present, repression would also cause personal symptoms such as "nervousness," sundry physical ailments, sexual resistances, depression, and destructive eruptions of rage.

The publication of *Creative Aggression* seemed to both herald and partially trigger a wave of popular and academic literature, seminars, research, ongoing programs, and social philosophies that promoted assertiveness, the management of anger, learning to say "No," and the many other aspects of being creatively aggressive. The authors felt both delighted and validated when, on September 20, 1981, the Los Angeles *Times* selected our book as one of the "100 American Books for the Contemporary Person," a list based on all books published since 1946. Among their criteria for selection was "importance to contemporary understanding . . . intellectual influence and extreme popularity."[1] Our gratification, more than anything else, was the awareness that our work and ideas had begun to penetrate and have an impact (and perhaps the rigid ethos of always having to be "nice" as the ultimate standard was giving way).

In the past decade, teaching people to be assertive in many dimensions of life's experience became a particularly popular and widespread phenomenon. While we feel that these courses and "systems" have contributed to people's ability to have greater positive control over their lives, the unfortunate side effect of some of this training has too often been to generate an insensitive, egocentric attitude and orientation which inadvertently encouraged the manipulation of others. While temporary satisfaction, gain, or "victory" would result, the end point would be alienation and self-defeat. It would enclose and isolate individuals from each other, rather than facilitate a more satisfying connection.

The philosophy and teaching of the various forms of assertion training also tended to promote an orientation of "I've been a victim and I'm not going to take it anymore" and, therefore, indirectly also fostered a more defensive climate. Too often, people emerged militant about "protecting their space" and "doing their thing," while refusing to take responsibility for their influence on others. (*"I'm* not making you feel that way, *you're* making yourself feel that way.")

"Creative aggression," is not a philosophy and set of techniques that simply teaches people how to get what they want. Rather, it is based on instructing individuals on how to have impact and constructive dialogue, how to get close to others without falsely accommodating and denying important parts of themselves, and how to resolve conflict fairly and rationally. We are a part of a human environment that is presently not in need of newer and better forms of one-upmanship. Rather, what is needed are tools for a full, authentic, and nondestructive communication, in order to create a more conscious, intimate reality, and the ability to impact with one's loving and caring side devoid of a contaminating, aggressive undertow.

There were many other outgrowths of the past decade which pleased and excited us because they created or expressed an orientation that was creatively aggressive. The 1970s saw an explosion of openness and authenticity in matters of sexuality. In our "creative aggression" workshops, we strived to foster a climate of honest communication between men and women about their sexual needs, attractions, "turn-offs," false notions, distortions and stereotyping, and sharing of fantasies. The widespread transformation of a once largely taboo matter into one that could be openly, candidly, and enthusiastically discussed has represented an enormous stride toward placing sexuality into its rightful perspective, such that it will be neither exaggerated, minimized, nor made a matter of haunting obsession or destructive impulse.

Women have learned to assert and express their sexual needs and work through their conditioned inhibitions, while men are learning to humanize their responses and attitudes and break through a conditioning that was severely damaging and limiting. Their sexual experience, because it had equated masculine self-worth with performance, had caused them to be goal-obsessed, out of touch with their emotional, sensual, and caring side, while causing them to be goal-fixated and frightened of the labels of "impotence" and "premature ejaculation." Worst of all, women were transformed into objects or "nonpersons."

The sexual revolution has failed and produced more stress and dehumanization because of an overemphasis on trying to live up to mythical ideals of performance and the pursuit of some never-ending, never-realized ecstasy. Sex has also often been part of a destructive interaction wherein it becomes a tool for hidden and indirect aggression. Men and women alike may be knowingly or unwittingly using sex in the service of power or release of rage. The result is more alienation and tension, rather than the facilitation of intimacy. In their book *Stop! You're Driving Me Crazy,* Dr. George R. Bach and Ronald M. Deutsch explore the ways in which passive and indirect aggression ruin sexual relationships.[2]

Along with the recent revolution of sexual consciousness is the emergence of a conscious acknowledgment and development of the aggressive and power strivings of women—a phenomenon which the "women's movement" has had significant influence in facilitating. We believe that this is an enormously helpful and exciting development toward aiding the management of conflict and aggression between men and women, and thereby making authentic intimacy genuinely possible. "Creative aggression," its use and potential, is optimal when power dimensions between partners are equalized and when neither perceives the other as threatening because they are deeply dependent on them for underlying needs and insecurities. That is, the balancing of power between the sexes allows men and women to choose partners based on *want* rather than *need,* meaning who the person is and how he or she makes one feel, rather than choice of partner and attraction based on the symbols of the other or what they can do to compensate for one's own insecurities and inadequacies.

Women are increasingly taking responsibility for their economic autonomy, as well as for the development of a clearly defined, separate identity. Women today are successful and comfortable participants in even the most aggressive of sports. They are learning the skills of psychological and physical self-defense. As a result, the arbitrary dominance and control of the male has been significantly reduced.

The primary negative or destructive element we see in the "women's revolution," an element we believe presents a major obstacle to the process and potential of "creative aggression" between the sexes, is the lingering tendency to blame—and attempt to define who is at fault for what. The male is still being accused by women of being a destructive oppressor, while the woman is accused by men of exploiting and manipulating the male.

This lingering tendency is a serious block to the potential for authentic intimacy between the sexes. It damages the ability to constructively manage aggression between the sexes through a mutual acknowledgment of responsibility for the problems and growth of these relationships. Conflict resolution, facilitative and constructive impact, and growth via "creative aggression" can only take root and flourish in an atmosphere of "goodwill." Men and women have both been equal victims in their own ways of a damaging conditioning that has prevented the development of healthy intimacy. The responsibility for change needs to come from both sides.

In spite of the latter problem, it is a far healthier man-woman climate we live in today. Women no longer need to respond from a "powerless" position and accommodate the "controlling" male while building up intense hidden resentment. Men no longer need deny their vulnerabilities, weaknesses, and fears. This portends a unique adventure in the male-female relationship potential and the capacity for the sexes to become friends and companions without hidden motives and the repression of their total selves. In the future, they may be able to support each other's growth without fearing that the development of one will be a threat to the security of the other.

"Creative aggression" in the service of the growth of both sexes will mean the mobilization of energies toward the full development of men and women as balanced, complete people—able to recognize and resist the destruction of their expressiveness, life choices, relationship styles, and behavior due to pressures to conform to constricting definitions of masculinity and femininity. These are the kinds of stereotyping our "creative aggression" workshops have sought to break down in the past two decades. We are therefore delighted with this emerging powerful trend toward moving beyond sex-role expectations.

There are other significant advances that involve the emergence of a constructive and creative expression of aggression. They can be seen, for example, in the fields of education and health.

The late 1960s and the early 1970s were periods of liberation for the university student. During this time, there was a demystification of academic authority figures and a breaking down of the alienation that had resulted from the arbitrary authority of instructors who had been allowed to hide behind masks of infallibility. This concomitantly had produced a falsely accommodating and sycophantic posture of students.

These changes are not a matter of sanctioning student disrespect. Rather, it has meant that teachers will be held accountable for their performance, evaluations of students, and the student's right to a person-to-person dialogue in the matters of his or her future. Educators have become sensitized to the needs and reality of the world of the students and we salute this as one of the most significant manifestations of an era of "creative aggression."

Likewise, dramatically significant changes have taken place in the health consciousness of the many people who have gone beyond a passive-submissive orientation vis-à-vis physicians and other health specialists. In the past, doctors, even more than educators, have been allowed to bathe in an aura of infallibility and mystification and have been distorted and placed on a pedestal and given permission to put themselves beyond the questioning, confrontations, and resistances of the patients they serve.

There is an ever-growing awareness that each of us is, more or less, an active participant in the creation of our own states of diseases and health. Concomitantly, repressed or distorted aggression, autonomy, sexuality, and assertiveness are all significant factors in the creation of illnesses, along with nutritional, ecological, and other physical factors. The blind faith that existed in many people regarding physicians is giving way. In its place, there is emerging a new consciousness which involves a more active and responsible patient participation in recovery from illness, and a search for alternative forms of treatment or even self-healing via an alteration of physical and environmental factors.

One vital dimension in a "creative aggression" orientation in these matters is the rejection of intimidating labels such as "health nut" or "health fanatic" by those who are concerned with and actively monitoring the health facets of their lives. At the same time, there is emerging an assertive recognition and resistance toward those pressures and people who would undermine the quest to understand and follow through on one's own sensibilities regarding the power of one's body to respond in a self-healing or self-corrective way when unimpeded by destructive emotional and physical factors.

The passive-"victim" orientation toward health in the past involved endless searching for labels to put on one's body states and external or "magical" treatments to "cure" illnesses in ways that meant nothing in the patient's life needed to be changed. Only the right "cure," externally imposed, needed to be found.

The new assertive orientation toward health that many are beginning to assume involves the recognition that we are all part of the total fabric of nature, capable of being and remaining healthy and facilitating our own recovery from illness through a full physical self-awareness and the presence of an assertive-aggressive capacity to take responsibility for one's health. As part of this consciousness, there is also the emergence of a new breed of physicians and health professionals who are increasingly assuming the role of teacher and partner in illness prevention, rather than in assuming a godlike posture.

Similarly, in the practice of psychology and psychotherapy, there has been a movement away from past tendencies to endlessly analyze the traumas and fixations of one's past. This represented a passive-ruminative approach toward changing oneself. Instead, the focus has moved toward a greater emphasis on the present and the recognition of how we avoid taking responsibility for making our lives feel good and improving our relationships.

Increasingly, the armamentarium of psychotherapy has included encounter and group therapeutic techniques that use confrontation and growth exercises and includes an active, authentic dialogue between patient and therapist. We believe that the principles of traditional psychotherapeutic counseling created an inauthentic, growth-retarding climate for the client. In *Creative Aggression,* we explore the problems of the "nice therapist" and the dilemmas and problems faced when attempting to work within the humanly impossible strictures of transcending the aggressive dimensions of the therapist-patient relationship.

In reference to the emotional problems of individuals in our society, one could say that we are all "neurotic" insofar as we have all had significant aspects of our developing, healthy humanness and expressiveness repressed and distorted in the name of being "nice," or even of being appropriately "masculine" or "feminine." Sooner or later, people seeking to change the quality of their lives or their relationships must begin the threatening process of breaking down rigidly conditioned "comfortable" responses that block them in the "here and now." This requires calling forth the aggressive energy in oneself to resist the criticisms of those who put the mandate to be "appropriate" above all else. Also, it means resisting those elements and "movements" in our society that offer quick "solutions" and "formulas" for change. These hide the fact that we are all in a similar, arduous, and threatening process of changing patterns and responses that interfere with our total expressive humanness and there are no easy, quick ways to do it.

Dr. Bach has had a pioneering influence in approaching the psychotherapeutic process by taking a strong stand against the damaging tendency to use psychological and psychiatric labels as a way of boxing people in and, in the process, intimidating them. Also, his active-interventionist approach to therapy has represented a resistance to the tendency to endlessly and passively analyze and ruminate about problems, rather than risk the process of growth.

On a broader level the contemporary movements to break down ethnic, racial, age, gender, and physical disability stereotypes—and the antinuclear, antiwar, and ecology preservation movements—are exciting manifestations of aggression in the form of constructive impacting. The increasing resistance to granting arbitrary power over our lives to politicians who place winning and supremacy over everything is also a gratifying one.

The element of these movements that does not fit our model of "creative aggression" is the continuing tendency to create "good guy-bad guy," "black-and-white" dichotomies and interpretations of problems, rather than focusing on those elements in all of us that need to be acknowledged and dealt with in order to change that which we abhor. Those who are ultimately most helpful and will have the greatest constructive impact in remedying matters are those who avoid blaming and victim-oppressor dichotomies, while coming to grips with the total realities of each of these issues.

In regard to the destructive stereotyping of any minority group, we admire and appreciate those who reject the wholesale labeling or "thinging" of *any* person or persons. One of the precursors and necessary elements in war and other forms of violence is the depersonalization of people into symbols, objects, or "nonpersons." Each individual or group who resists such stereotyping by displaying his or her unique and separate humanness moves us all that much closer to a healthier, more manageable world.

On the negative side, countercurrents or trends and traumatic social problems resulting from the mismanagement or distortion of aggression are still with us in significant measure.

The increasing presence of gurus, fanatical religious groups who would mandate the behavior of others, communication hucksters, and organizations who would set themselves up as being more righteous and enlightened are a threatening evidence of the increasing numbers of people who are intrinsically passive and paralyzed in their capacity to chart their own visions and courses. They are unconsciously seeking to give up responsibility for recognizing and dealing with the difficult and contradictory realities we live with, at the same time believing there are those who exist who have "answers" and will guide us to a better life if we only believe in and give ourselves over to them.

Those who portray themselves as enlightened leaders of morality, righteousness, and the path to a "correct life," *whatever* their persuasion, we believe, would be found to be hypocrites and manipulators were their true inner feelings and thoughts only known. They have acquired their "powers" by a finely honed ability to mystify, mask, and manipulate. Even those who seem to do good are feeding on the passive-submissive posture and fears of their followers. This phenomenon is, we believe, inexorably dangerous and destructive to the quest for greater humanness and continued survival.

Those who do most for the process of human growth and the making of a truly human world are, we believe, those who are willing to risk transparency, vulnerability, and the uneven struggle to become more fully and "sanely" human. Those with fixed philosophies involving the dichotomies of "good-bad," "right-wrong," etc. are running away from the conflict-full struggle of life.

High degrees of crime, spouse violence, child abuse, and rape are other manifestations of the mismanagement or distortion of aggression.

Abuse between spouses often involves the inability or refusal to see one's partner as a person and the avoidance of displaying one's own total humanness openly. Spouse abuse will be significantly reduced when the "creative aggressive" path of growth has led to the full development of men and women into separate people who can choose each other as partners based on a motive of "want" rather than the dependent "need" to be rescued, fulfilled, taken care of, or validated by the other. This will allow them to see each other realistically as people, without initially needing to falsely place them on pedestals, only to tear them down later. The essence of a workable new man-woman relationship has been defined in a recent book by Dr. Herb Goldberg.[3]

Similarly, rape is partially an outgrowth of the conditioned perception of woman as "sex object" and "nonperson." Training in aggressive self-defense, and women's awareness of their strengths, and the concomitant growth of men to the point where women are seen as complete people and not just bodies will result in significant breakthroughs in these problems.

Likewise, child abuse is more likely to be present in the homes of "immature" couples, where children have been conceived on the wave of unrealistic romantic fantasy, rather than on the readiness and conscious desire of the parents involved. Recent studies on child abuse reveal that young parents are significantly more prone to being violent toward their children than older parents.[4] A book describing the implementation of "creative aggression" techniques with children, titled *How to Fight with Your Kids and Win!,* was published in 1978.[5]

We salute those parents of today who have resisted the pressures to have children early, who instead waited until their thirties, and who, as "late parents," are discovering that raising a child is a joyful, relatively stress-free process, rather than a "burden" or "responsibility" that creates intensely hostile feelings toward the child.

The most difficult challenge in facilitating "creative aggression" in today's society is the creation of a context of "goodwill" that will make it attractive and desirable to be authentic in the "not-so-nice" dimensions of aggression. We submit that our approach, as detailed in this book, fails when it is used manipulatively and in the presence of "ill will"—meaning the uncommunicated desire to harm, control, exploit, or triumph over the other person. We continue in our work and writing to probe and root out the underlying dimensions that will create and promote the context of "goodwill." Our research led to new ways of actively developing, rather than passively expecting, goodwill. These findings are published in Dr. Bach's and Laura Torbert's latest book, *A Time for Caring*.[6]

Those operating from a posture of "ill will" can be recognized by their orientation of blaming, pretending to a lack of anger or aggression, and posturing moral righteousness while creating an atmosphere in others of "walking on eggshells" lest a wrong word be said.

We also acknowledge that, for some, the use of "creative aggression" techniques may backfire or make matters seemingly worse. This is true when there is an absence of "goodwill," the presence of an unreal "romantic" bond that prevents an authentic communication, or in the hands of deeply distrustful, paranoid, hostile individuals who are unaware of or out of touch with themselves and see the expression of their feelings as a license to be destructive.

"Creative aggression" was never intended to provide permission for rudeness, irrational outbursts, unsolicited and hostile feedback, and the lopsided, cathartic discharge of rage and negativity. Rather, it is the mutual exchange of one's aggressive side by permission and with a motive of getting closer or clarifying and improving the process of a relationship that is involved. "Creative aggression" is designed to facilitate constructive impact and *not* to grant a license for self-indulgence in the acting out of one-sided hostility.

In the original edition of *Creative Aggression,* we dedicated the book to "those who refuse to pay the price of being 'nice.'" We continue to applaud and commend those who are committed to authenticity via constructive confrontation and the rejection of the phony "niceness" that deadens and poisons the human atmosphere.

We know of the resistances and rejection that some experience as they seek to create an atmosphere of honest, constructive confrontation or the aggressive side of the human experience. We hope that this book provides individuals with the courage to venture into these domains with emotional sustenance, support, and appreciation.

LOS ANGELES, CALIFORNIA
OCTOBER 1, 1982


GEORGE R. BACH, PH.D.
DISTINGUISHED PROFESSOR OF PSYCHOLOGY,
PROFESSIONAL SCHOOL OF HUMANISTIC STUDIES,
SAN DIEGO, CALIFORNIA


HERB GOLDBERG, PH.D.
PROFESSOR OF PSYCHOLOGY
CALIFORNIA STATE UNIVERSITY
LOS ANGELES, CALIFORNIA

PART ONE

# The "Nice" People

# CHAPTER 1

# The Myth of the "Nice" Guy

Joe Michaels was a "nice" guy. People took a liking to him right away because he always had a ready smile and something pleasant to say. Friends could almost always get him to do what they wanted, because, as he'd say, "I can enjoy almost anything." Nobody ever heard Joe get nasty, argue, or even disagree very vigorously; as he put it, being negative wasn't his style.

When his friends heard that Joe's wife, Nina, had a nervous breakdown, they were shocked. It was only then that they found out she'd been seeing a psychotherapist for the previous seven months.

During her therapy Nina had trouble defining what was wrong with her marriage. She felt guilty as hell, because everyone told her how lucky she was to be married to such a "nice" guy. And, yet, *she* knew the relationship was driving her up a wall. Her husband, Joe, was so placid and even-tempered that whenever there was trouble she felt it was her fault. For example, she yelled at the kids because Joe wouldn't. After a while she began to feel like a "bitch on wheels." The kids would insult her, and run to Joe for protection. He'd usually take their side. Their eighteen-year-old son, Michael, was doing poorly in school. He had no direction. He either sat around listening to records or went out riding on his motorcycle. Joe never said much about it, and so Nina wound up having to stay on Michael's back. After some more months in therapy, Nina began to realize that the only way she could maintain her sanity was to get a divorce. A number of friends advised against it, and blamed her for expecting too much. But when she asked them to help her understand Joe better, they admitted that they didn't know too much about him, except that he was a real "nice" guy.

Nina confronted Joe about a divorce, but he didn't even seem to care very much, and he hardly reacted when he was served with the papers. Shortly after the divorce Joe remarried, and almost never came over to see the children. His new wife didn't want him to, he said. The children became withdrawn and sullen.

## THE "NICE" AMERICANS

Mysterious? No. The "nice" guy is as American as jazz, apple pie, and baseball. He is well liked just because his major concern seems to be being liked by everybody. More than anything else, he reflects the typical American fear of aggressive interaction in a personal relationship. He is by no means a pacifist or a coward. It is only in personal relationships that he fears being aggressive. He may have no hesitation about killing in a war situation, for example.

The "nice" guy is very preoccupied with his image, and part of that image involves being a friendly, well-liked person. His behavior, however, is primarily a way of manipulating people and situations. In this way he avoids strong emotional encounters, which he dislikes. Nor will he have to worry whether others are saying bad things about him.

Behind his "niceness" he is well guarded. He permits few, if any, including his family, to come close enough to really get to know him. His "nice" guy behavior is a path of least resistance because it requires minimal emotional involvement and interpersonal commitment. His "niceness" is also an indirectly aggressive manipulation. It is impersonal, and designed to get him ahead. He is liked by others not because they know him well, but because he does not threaten their own aggression control systems by confronting them, asserting himself or getting openly angry.

There are many variations of the "nice" guy. Among those that will be discussed here are the "nice" mommy, the "nice" daddy, the "nice" children, the "nice" parents, the "nice" boss, the "nice" employees, the "nice" teacher, the "nice" students, the "nice" therapist, the "nice" patients, the "nice" sport, the "nice" traveling companions, and the "nice" lovers.

Each of these will be described as types. Undoubtedly no one person embodies all the characteristics in any of these types. However, there are many characteristics common to all of them. That is, the aggression is present and powerful, but is always disguised and indirect, and, therefore, does not *seem* to be aggression. In fact, to casual observers "nice" behavior appears to be highly appropriate, virtuous, and even loving. Only through its impact on others do we see its aggressive meanings. The "nice" person is especially destructive emotionally, because his impact is so elusive and indirect. Being aware of him, and understanding him for what he is, is therefore particularly important in developing a knowledge of what aggression is really about.

Each type will be described in terms of the outward behavior, the personality underneath that behavior, the "reward," or what the person gains from the behavior, and the "price," meaning its damaging effects.

## THE "NICE" MOMMY

The "nice" mommy does everything for everybody in the family, and rarely asks for anything in return. She works herself "to the bone," even when she's feeling sick, which is fairly often. The house is kept immaculately clean and there is always a favorite goodie cooking on the stove or sitting in the refrigerator. The "nice" mommy worries a lot about everybody: whether they've eaten enough, are at home on time, or are dressed properly. She rarely buys clothing, because she doesn't like to spend money on herself. She is a good listener, particularly to tales of woe and misfortune.

Every once in a while, more frequently as the children grow older, the "nice" mommy goes into vicious outbursts. She screams, threatens, calls people ungrateful, and makes everybody feel guilty. There's no talking to her during these rages. But afterward she calms down and becomes "nice" again. As her children grow older, and the prospect of their leaving home arises, the "nice" mommy often acts as if she may be on the verge of a nervous breakdown.

THE PERSONALITY UNDERNEATH The "nice" mommy comes from a strict, moralistic background, where as a child she was told to be seen but not heard. When she became openly angry she was immediately punished for being disrespectful. She was brought up to believe that being a wife and mother were the most important things she could do, and that "good" women always loved their husbands and their children. She wasn't allowed to develop a mind of her own, or to live independently. She married fairly young, and never really broke the ties with her parents. At marriage she was emotionally still a child.

Secretly, she envies her friends who broke away from family ties and experimented, sexually and with freer lifestyles. She feels deprived, and is inwardly very resentful of being a wife and mother. But she has a strong conscience, and would never fully admit this resentment to herself. To keep these feelings in control, and to prove to herself and to others what a good mother she really is, she works herself "to the bone." Every once in a while, however, her resentment comes pouring through. She says she overprotects her children because she cares so much, but the underlying motive is more to control them, and prevent them from becoming too strong and free.

The "nice" mommy feels inadequate, because she was never allowed to develop her potentials. Therefore, she gets attention and importance through her illnesses, aches, and pains. She is unable to gain attention and importance directly, because she is afraid of being directly assertive and saying "I want." Instead, like a child, she expects to be given to.

THE REWARD   The "nice" mommy is told by everybody what a fine person she is, and this reassures her somewhat. She rules the house, and basically everyone is afraid of her, because she makes them feel constantly in debt to her. By always doing things for others, particularly her children, she makes them dependent and keeps them under control. Family problems can always be blamed on somebody else, because her motives are so "pure." Her being so busy all the time is a permanent excuse for not having to be involved in outside social activities. These would frighten her, because she avoids situations where she is not in complete control.

THE PRICE   The "nice" mommy is emotionally very destructive. She gives off confusing indirect messages of "I love you" and "I hate you." Every time her children show signs of independence, she makes them feel selfish and guilty. After all, "nice" mommy is working so hard. How could anyone even think of abandoning her?

She is a powerful tyrant who skillfully utilizes indirect aggression. Her controlling tools are guilt, illness, and "morality." Even daddy becomes merely a passive shadow who gives up, because there's no way of winning against "nice" mommy.

## THE "NICE" DADDY

"Nice" daddy is a soft touch. He can always be persuaded to say "Yes" after mother has said "No." He never screams or yells, because, as he has said many times, all he wants is "peace." He finds it behind the newspaper, or in front of the television set. He lets mother do the disciplining of the children.

When the kids bring home bad grades from school, "nice" daddy says something like "Try harder," or "Don't show it to your mother." The kids feel sorry for him, because mother bosses him around. The only times they really get upset at "nice" daddy is when he forgets one of their names, mixes up their names, or forgets how old they are.

THE PERSONALITY UNDERNEATH  "Nice" daddy is passive and detached. He got married and had children because it was the thing socially acceptable men were supposed to do. But basically he is just going through the motions. "Nice" daddy is afraid of feelings, his own and those of others. He is also afraid of losing control. His own upbringing was repressive, and he was not permitted to raise his voice or talk back. He learned to control aggressive feelings by withdrawing. He becomes very threatened by angry feelings, because he doesn't know what to do with his own, and is afraid of what he might do if he let go. He worries about what people think of him, even though he doesn't let anybody get very close.

THE REWARD  The "nice" daddy can avoid taking responsibility for the things that go wrong in the family environment. He makes others seem to be the villains, because he is always so "nice," with his "live and let live" philosophy. He also spares himself considerable amounts of wear and tear, as he manages to stay above the fray. His style serves him well, particularly in terms of retaining his image of self-control, fairness, and "niceness."

THE PRICE    "Nice" daddy expresses his aggression by not getting involved. He starves his wife emotionally. He forces her into the role of "bitch," and he comes out smelling like a rose. His lack of support when she disciplines the children undermines his wife's authority. By being "nice" when the kids do poorly in school or misbehave, he indirectly demonstrates a lack of concern. He fails to provide his children motivation or standards to strive for. They learn that it doesn't really matter to him if they succeed or fail. This is particularly hurtful to his sons, because his shadowy, passive nature prevents them from making a strong masculine identification. His "even-tempered" behavior eventually becomes irritating and boring. It's really his indirectly aggressive way of saying to those around him, "You don't exist," and "I can't be bothered."

## THE "NICE" CHILDREN

Grownups love "nice" children because "nice" children are charming and eager to please, and they act so "adult." Grownups say they wish all children were that polite and well-mannered. The "nice" child is also the teacher's pet, because he or she is so willing to help out, and never presents a discipline problem.

The only fly in the ointment is that "nice" children don't get along with other children. Their peers see them as acting superior, and untrustworthy because, as allies of the adults, they might tattle-tale. "Nice" children are also not much fun to be with, because they don't really enjoy peer group activities, which they consider boring.

THE PERSONALITY UNDERNEATH    "Nice" children are manipulators, who see being loved and accepted by all adults as most vital to their survival. Because their parents are status seekers who are more interested in having a perfect status symbol to show the world than in having a real child, "nice" children are always performing for them in order to get their love.

Basically, the "nice" child is a rejected child, treated like an object rather than a person. "The "niceness" does not stem from genuine warmth or caring but is instead a survival technique designed to please adults. The charm hides underlying feelings of resentment, rejection, and rage that the child feels at being manipulated into a status symbol, and of not being allowed to be a child.

THE REWARD   "Nice" children receive compliments and attention from grownups. This allows them to feel superior to other children, and very special. Because of their "charm," adults give them things, and allow them to participate in adult activities in which other children would not ordinarily be permitted.

THE PRICE   The "nice" child is a manipulator with little genuine human empathy. As an adult, he will be prone to using and discarding people very casually. Anger will be acted out behind a smile and a smooth manner, and many disappointed and hurt victims will be left behind. The "nice" child eventually becomes an alienated, lonely adult, unable to establish an involved, caring relationship.

## THE "NICE" PARENTS

These good guys are "liberal" in attitude. They smoke pot with their kids, outfit their teenage daughter with a diaphragm, and identify themselves heavily with their children's activities and causes. They maintain a laissez-faire attitude toward their children's school performance. Discipline is always on a rational and reasonable basis, with an avoidance of any kind of fighting, loud voices, or "pulling rank." Their children's friends love to come over, because there's always food, pot, privacy, rock music, and "good vibes" while they're "doing their thing." The "nice" parents work hard at being liked and accepted by their children's friends.

THE PERSONALITY UNDERNEATH   The "nice" parents are image-oriented. They need to see themselves as youthful, and so they unconsciously deny their age, and their role as parental guides and authorities. Their "let them blossom" attitude toward their children really represents a denial of their parental responsibilities, and their fear of being openly aggressive and assertive. They feel inadequate as adults and parents, and develop a "hip" approach to avoid commitment and responsibility.

THE REWARD   The "nice" parents are admired by their children's peers, who see them as "groovy." This allows these parents to feel special and youthful.

THE PRICE   The rejection of their roles as adults and parents also implies a rejection of their children. In fact, they turn their children into parent figures for themselves. This creates an unreal sense of power and omnipotence in their children, that will ultimately result in a crisis when they have to live independently. At that point they will have grandiose feelings of being too special to work in one direction, or to be confined within the limits of a job.

## THE "NICE" BOSS

Mr. Mike Andrews, the division manager of a large, successful eastern accounting firm, would certainly qualify as being a "nice" boss. He keeps a large calendar on his wall on which he circles the birthdays of every employee in his office; from his top accountants to his secretaries and receptionists. He then sends flowers, perfume or candy to the women, and sporting equipment, liquor, or smoking accessories to the men.

He gives two major parties each year to which everybody is invited. The Christmas party is for the employees only, without their spouses. At this party Mr. Andrews becomes "one of the boys." He gets happily drunk, kisses the ladies in a friendly but "correct" manner, and keeps telling everybody to "have a ball." On July fourth, he gives his annual barbecue. This affair takes place at his home, where he plays the role of friendly host and master chef. Food is in abundance, and the liquor flows.

At work Mike Andrews keeps his office door open at all times, smiles, and says, "How're things going?" as people walk by. He is eager to be the "nice" guy and help others out. For example, late one afternoon he sat around helping to stuff and seal envelopes that needed to go out that day while his own work sat waiting on his desk.

In general, Mr. Andrews hesitates to ask an employee to do anything out of the ordinary, such as to work late or carry an extra assignment. He secretly shudders at the thought of giving orders. He never gets openly angry and studiously avoids criticizing anybody. To the contrary, he always looks for the positives and goes out of his way to find something nice to say about everybody's work. Nobody ever gets fired once they've been with the office more than three months. He himself is the very model of a hard worker, frequently at his desk well past 7:00 P.M., and often coming in to work on Saturdays. But if anybody in his office looks overtired, he is quick to tell the person to take the rest of the day off. Clearly, nobody would call this "gentle soul" who never yells, criticizes, or makes demands on anybody, anything but "nice."

THE PERSONALITY UNDERNEATH    The "nice" boss is terrified of being disliked or of being seen as a bad guy. Open conflict upsets him, and he goes to great lengths to avoid it. To him, conflict means that somebody will be badly hurt emotionally, and he doesn't want to be responsible for that.

It makes him uncomfortable to be confronted with the frustrations or anger of others. He hopes therefore that by being constantly "nice" others won't make demands or bring him into the middle of their office fights, because he hates taking sides in a dispute. Someone is sure to wind up angry at him, he feels.

Mr. Andrews has periods where he is raging mad inside himself, but he never shows it. During these moods, which increase over the years, he sees himself as a victim, being used, abused, and neglected by others. "I go around helping everybody, but nobody gives a damn about me," he tells himself. Particularly when things seem to be falling apart in the office because the work is late or not being done properly, he rages secretly over the fact that the burden of responsibility is always being placed on his shoulders. However, he never tells anybody how he feels because it upsets him and makes him feel guilty to think of himself as having these feelings of resentment.

THE REWARD   The "nice" boss does manage, by and large, to avoid being involved in the conflicts, or disharmony around him. Employees smile when they're around him, rarely raise their voices, nor make anything but positive, happy-type conversation with him.

Those who quit their jobs to go elsewhere never tell him the truth about their real sources of discontent or frustration. He therefore is never made to feel that personnel dissatisfaction has anything to do with him. The behavior of others around him allows him to see himself as a person who creates an atmosphere of peace, love, and harmony around him. This self-image is very satisfying to him.

THE PRICE   The heaviest price the "nice" boss pays at work is that he loses his best employees. This happens for several reasons. Since he is loath to criticize or be disliked by anybody, he does not really discriminate between an excellent performance and a lesser one. The genuinely talented, productive, and creative employees begin to feel that it's not worth extending themselves. They begin to feel stagnant and unchallenged. Eventually, they become so bored and frustrated that they quit. Over the years, as the best people leave, the "nice" boss finds himself increasingly surrounded by the clingers, the lesser competent, and the sycophants, who can't really produce well but who feel safe and protected because they can survive by smiling and playing the game of being "nice." The more manipulative employees begin to see that they can get away with anything and so they take more and more liberties: long coffee breaks, coming to work late, and leaving early. Consequently the quality of work steadily declines.

Inside himself the "nice" boss is also chronically tense, worried, and prone to psychosomatic problems such as ulcers and hypertension. Because he carries so much unnecessary responsibility on his shoulders, it also has a particularly disastrous effect on his home life. He arrives there in the evening totally exhausted. He rarely, if ever, makes love to his wife. His excuse is that he's tired. Often when he tries he finds himself barely able to get an erection. In turn, his wife starts to gain weight, drink, and feel increasingly unattractive and unloved.

His children suffer too, because he has no energy or time to get involved with them, and so they begin to function poorly. Eventually, everything in his life begins to feel meaningless and empty. He doesn't understand why, with all of his good intentions, he feels so lonely, friendless, and neglected. Eventually this plummets him into a chronically depressed attitude and/or escape through alcoholism.

## THE "NICE" EMPLOYEES

Whether they be female or male, the behavior pattern of this kind of "nice" employee runs a similar course. They try to ingratiate themselves to the boss by being always ready and eager to help out. They offer to take on additional tasks that are not really a part of their responsibilities. Though often overburdened and exploited because of this extreme willingness to cooperate,

they never complain or get angry. They may walk around looking exhausted and unhappy, but when asked if anything's wrong
they are quick to answer that "everything is just great!"

They zero in and thrive on their employer's weak areas
and get a sense of security and indispensability by offering to do
things for him that he tends to do poorly himself. That is, if their
employer tends to be forgetful, they become his reminders. If he
drinks too much or acts rude, they cover up or apologize for
him. They also try to protect him against any people who would
confront, challenge, or criticize him.

THE PERSONALITY UNDERNEATH    Insecurity and a desire
for power that they do not feel adequate enough to obtain directly for themselves are the major motivations of the "nice"
employees. Being always helpful and covering for their boss's
weak areas allows them to feel secure and important. They get
their sense of strength by feeding on their employer's dependency.

"Nice" employees feel basically inferior to others and are
also frightened of failure. By being "nice" they lessen these fears
of failing, and they even stand a chance of becoming successful
and powerful by making themselves indispensable to their boss.
Their underlying hostility shows through in the way they will
mistreat and even sabotage those who are in lesser positions. This
is particularly true if they sense challenge or competition with
their own ambitions.

THE REWARD    Through their "nice" behavior, this kind
of employee often does manage to work his way into a special
relationship with the boss. They may eventually become his con-
fidants; they are let in on everything, and this allows them to
feel increasingly secure and powerful. In addition, even though
they themselves feel unable to assert themselves, or to achieve or
succeed independently, they are able to get some of the power
they crave by letting the boss do their aggressing for them. He
brings in the business and fights the important battles, and they

can reap the benefits without taking the risks simply by remaining in his shadow and being "nice" to him.

THE PRICE    The "nice" employee never grows up. He or she remains basically a child in the work situation—a dependent sycophant who thrives by accommodating to someone else's needs. Because the boss is "daddy," they can never feel genuinely independent or successful in their own right.

Eventually, the "nice" employees lose all of their own unique creative potential as they become increasingly preoccupied with their status, promotions, and manipulations. At the same time, however, there is always the gnawing realization that if the boss leaves, gets sick, or dies, they might be nowhere. This creates a constant sense of vulnerability and self-doubt.

The boss also pays a price for the "nice" employee's behavior. Because he is covered up for, and his weaknesses and dependencies are being exploited, he is lulled into feeling he doesn't have to improve or change. For example, if he is tactless, abrupt, an incipient alcoholic, careless, or whatever, he doesn't realize his impact on others because his "nice" employees cover for him. Therefore, he feels no pressure to alter his self-destructive patterns. Consequently, his behavior is bound to deteriorate, and both he and the "nice" employees will pay the consequences for this.

## THE "NICE" TEACHER

Little or no homework, lots of rapping in class about "feelings," no required attendance, and easy exams are the hallmarks of the "nice" teacher. He or she tries to be everybody's friend, and runs a "hang loose" class.

"Nice" teachers can be easily manipulated by a tale of woe. They promise everything to everybody. "Nice" teachers will align themselves with student causes, and may even let the students decide themselves on what grade they want.

THE PERSONALITY UNDERNEATH "Nice" teachers have an underlying resentment toward authority figures, and dislike casting themselves in that role. Underneath that reluctance, however, often lurks a hard-core authoritarian that they try to suppress, but that pops up whenever any student becomes aggressive enough to say he doesn't like the way the class is being run. Suddenly, the "nice" teacher is not so nice.

THE REWARD "Nice" teachers can see themselves as special heroes, and martyrs to the establishment. Students "dig" them, and they get lots of compliments and flattery.

THE PRICE Most of the time, it's the students who pay the price. "Nice" teachers provide students with an unreal model of the competitive world of education, from which the teacher has benefited, and which the students may someday need. Because they don't set meaningful standards and are equally "nice" to all students, the "nice" teacher's grades and letters of recommendation eventually become worthless. By not providing the necessary course content, their students are also that much less prepared for future courses. Because they promise everything to everyone, they often disappoint students when they either forget, or don't have time to fulfill the promises. Their behavior then is an act of indirect hostility toward the students, an act that allows the teacher to look like a "good guy," while in the end the students pay the price. The student who is disgruntled and speaks out in favor of more course structure stands to be made to feel "unhip" and "uptight."

## THE "NICE" STUDENTS

They sit toward the front of the class taking careful notes, asking "sincere" questions, smiling, and nodding affirmatively in the direction of the teacher. They often stay after class, crowding the teacher's desk to continue the discussion. They identify themselves with the teacher more than with the students.

THE PERSONALITY UNDERNEATH "Nice" students are very ambitious and highly manipulative. Their smiling and nodding in class is indiscriminate, and is, in fact, a conning of the teacher. They give all teachers the same worshipful response. They are basically frightened of authority, hungry to please, and insecure about their own talents and abilities. Their insincere reactions represent their desperate need to achieve. They relate poorly to peers, because they are secretly extremely competitive, and will not be derailed from their achievement goals by "time-wasting" peer relationships.

THE REWARD  Their techniques usually work, and they often get high grades, teacher approval, and good letters of recommendation. With even a fairly good basic intelligence, they stand a better chance of academic success than the quiet, less manipulative student of equal intelligence.

THE PRICE  "Nice" students treat teachers as objects to be used. Their hostility is seen in their indiscriminate manipulation of authority figures and their disdain for the attempts of fellow students who use individuality to make their education and lives more relevant. When they graduate and take on the role of a teacher themselves, they will tend to function in the hard-core authoritarian fashion, again with a disregard for individual needs.

## THE "NICE" PSYCHOTHERAPIST

The "nice" psychotherapist is totally accepting, supportive, and "loving" with his patients. His therapy hours are fun, and he makes people "feel good." He will readily reduce his fee, not push bill collection, and run his hour over the usual fifty-minute limit.

THE PERSONALITY UNDERNEATH  The "nice" psychotherapist is as dependent on his patients as they become on him. Basically his "niceness" serves his needs, not his patients', for he is
equally "nice" to all of them. He himself is uncomfortable with
anger and aggressive feelings and prefers the "loving" approach.
Beneath his "niceness," however, there is considerable resentment and distance from people. His "niceness" is a "head trip"
that protects him against feeling the anger that lies underneath.

THE REWARD  The "nice" psychotherapist is loved by his
patients, builds a big practice, and has patients who stay with
him a long time. He feels godlike and important to them.

THE PRICE  Because of his own needs, the "nice" psychotherapist tends to nurture his patients' dependencies and keeps
them coming for years and years. To accommodate their therapist the patients change little, if at all, though they always tell
him how much they've changed. His own fear of anger and aggressive, assertive behavior sets a poor role model for his patients,
who come to believe that they will someday be "cured" strictly
by their doctor's "lovingness." The psychotherapist's indirect aggression comes through as he duplicates the role of the over-
protective mother by nurturing dependency and stifling assertive,
aggressive behavior.

## THE "NICE" PATIENTS

The "nice" patients are more interested in having their
doctor like them than in getting better. They always tell the doctor how wonderful he is and never resist his authority. Their illnesses often drag on for years.

THE PERSONALITY UNDERNEATH  The "nice" patients are
hungry for attention and unable to find appropriate ways of obtaining it directly by self-assertion. They have a large stake in

their illness and the concern and attention of their doctors. It provides them with a sense of importance and love. The "nice" patients are childlike personalities wanting to be taken care of. At the same time they are controlling in their dependency and will quit a doctor who doesn't confirm their "sick" self-perception. They are incapable of real interpersonal pleasure experiences and, instead, get their pleasure by suffering and the indirect benefits of care and attention.

THE REWARD  The "nice" patients get the attention they are seeking, and this allows them to feel special. The confirmation of their illnesses gives them a ready rationalization for not asserting themselves or competing successfully in the everyday world. They are often told that they are "very good patients" by their doctors, and this makes them feel very important. By being sick and, therefore, helpless, they get lots of attention and are given to without being required to give in return.

THE PRICE  The "nice" patients use their illnesses as tools to control their families. Therefore, they can't afford to really ever get better. Becoming healthy is a frightening prospect, because it may throw them back on their own feelings of failure and inadequacy. They must, therefore, remain sick to validate their existence.

A heavy price is also paid by the other family members. The "nice" patients' illnesses are weapons by which they can generate guilt and abort the emotional growth of family members who want to free themselves from the involvement with this person.

## THE "NICE" TRAVELING COMPANIONS

"Let's not spoil the vacation by arguing" is the major motto of the "nice" traveling companions. On the surface they are totally cooperative and compliant. They're always happy to do what you want to do and to go where you want to go. When they don't like something they usually say nothing. At worst, they become quiet. When things go badly they never complain.

They make no demands, and in hotels they allow you to choose a bed first and let you decide who will sleep by the window. They'll always try the restaurant you want to go to. Their role is being the "helpful" one, and so they warn you not to eat certain foods, tell you not to go to certain places because they're dangerous, make sure no suspicious-looking people steal your money, and have an instinct for keeping you away from people who don't look "nice." Otherwise, everything is usually "marvelous," according to them.

THE PERSONALITY UNDERNEATH   The "nice" traveling companions are basically very dependent and passive, readily following the lead of others, and needing their support. They are fearful of any conflict or aggressive emotion that will threaten the relationship and possibly disturb their dependency.

They are also fearful of taking responsibility and resistant to making decisions. Because they suppress their assertiveness, they are in many ways identityless in that they have few clearly defined preferences or enthusiasms. Though they go along with things, they rarely, if ever, really get into things or get very much pleasure out of them.

On trips their repressed aggression emerges in indirect ways. For example, they become easily fatigued and readily ill.

THE REWARD   The "nice" traveling companions manage to avoid the open conflict that they fear and to get polite and "friendly" reactions from others. When an argument or fight erupts they can always take comfort in the fact that it was started by the other person.

When things get bungled up or an experience is boring, they do not have to feel responsible, because they did not make the decisions.

Because they're so "nice," others tend to feel guilty about leaving them on their own and going off to pursue a personal interest. When the "nice" traveling companion is tired everyone goes to bed, and when they're ill there's always someone around to take care of them. Through their "niceness" they manage to exert a great deal of control over the freedom and spontaneity of others.

THE PRICE Everyone on the trip pays a price for the aggression-fearful company of the "nice" person. The vacation readily becomes monotonous and deadening. Everything is always "marvelous," but there is no genuine feedback and no sense of being with another real person. Anything spontaneous or in the least bit risky is avoided. Because the "nice" traveling companions are always so socially appropriate, they tend to make others feel self-conscious for letting go in a spontaneous way. Traveling with the "nice" companion can be so numbing it becomes equally meaningful to put the vacation money in the bank and look at slides of the vacation spot in one's living room.

## THE "NICE" SPORT

Bob Richmond was in Phoenix, Arizona, for a computer sales convention. He was known in his field as a mathematical genius. In addition, Bob was an excellent sportsman.

His wife received an emergency phone call from Bob at two o'clock one afternoon. Bob was in the hospital. It seemed that he had spent the morning playing tennis and had been winning every set. At the end of the final one his rattled and bumbling opponent accidentally smashed a ball into Bob's eye as Bob was walking toward the net to shake hands. The damage was severe and required an operation.

In a subsequent discussion with Bob over what happened, it became clear that during the entire morning's play Bob's partner was making one stupid play after another. Bob never said a word nor criticized his partner's play. He was too "nice" to do that. Instead, he'd look for any spark of decent play and lavishly praise him with comments, such as "great shot."

This was the second sporting accident that Bob had been the victim of. On another occasion he had gone pheasant hunting with his brother. His brother, who was an inferior hunter in comparison to Bob, was missing shots frequently. The hunting dogs were also being ruined in terms of their effectiveness, because Bob would always let his brother take the good shots and so as not to be "offensive" or "insulting" would not shoot as a backup when his brother missed. His brother was missing so often that the dogs couldn't do their job of retrieving. One Saturday afternoon his brother's sloppiness resulted in an accidental gun discharge that wounded Bob in the arm.

THE PERSONALITY UNDERNEATH   In part Bob is a product and a victim of a socialization process that makes it taboo for one to openly and publicly exult in one's own abilities or criticize a partner unless one is specifically asked for help. One is fearful of being labeled arrogant or a braggart and to be wished the worst by the other players. "Nice" sports only look for positive things to say.

Bob knew he was good, but felt embarrassed about openly acknowledging this fact. He bent over backward fearing that he'd be disliked for being "too good." He was, therefore, always supercautious about not saying anything to make the other players feel inferior.

THE REWARD   By being supportive of all his coplayers, even when they performed poorly, Bob could feel comfortable that he wasn't offending anybody and could enjoy his reputation as a "great" guy and a "great" sport. He was also always being sought after to play, because he was a challenge, but never made anyone feel inferior. Being a "nice" sport also had other side benefits. He was quickly promoted at work to an executive position, and he brought the company lots of business.

THE PRICE  Because he never critiqued his partners, they never learned. In this way, he was indirectly aborting their development. Their sloppiness and lack of development continued until Bob finally became the victim of it.

The "nice" guy sports ethic also has other prices. Because it is taboo to criticize another player, the person who is playing poorly is left to feel furious at himself and to rage inwardly in angry self-attacks. The aggression that could be mobilized by being critiqued and prodded by the other is lost. Being supported by comments such as "nice try" when one is playing poorly can be an immensely frustrating experience, one that can readily generate considerable self-hate. It is one of those crazy paradoxes of athletic competition that though players go all-out to win, they are not supposed to exult over their triumphs or criticize another's play or mistake. It is not good sportsmanship. One is only permitted to freely and continually get angry at one's own flaws.

## THE "NICE" LOVERS

Alan and Sylvia are "nice" lovers. They've been with each other for five months and nine days and came together to one of our marathon therapy groups to work on their relationship.

Both are "sensitive" people, so within their relationship they're been very gentle with each other. When Alan does little things that annoy her, Sylvia won't mention them to him because she doesn't want to hurt his feelings or cause him to feel rejected. When Alan thinks that Sylvia's clothes are unattractive or when she cooks something for him that he doesn't like, he never mentions it. On the contrary, he'll purposely flatter her taste in clothing and "build up her ego" by eating the food he doesn't like with "gusto." He does this because he feels Sylvia lacks self-confidence and he wants to give her tender loving care, unconditionally. Besides, he doesn't want to be like his father, who was always criticizing everything about his mother.

Weekend planning often gets bogged down because Sylvia will ask Alan what he wants to do. His usual reply is, "It doesn't really make any difference to me. Anything you want to do will be O.K." Then they go round and round on it. Sylvia finds this bothersome to her, because when they really wind up doing what she likes, such as going to a classical music concert, Alan, who had been enthusiastic about the idea, will be dozing before midconcert. Sylvia then feels guilty about her choice. Alan reacts similarly to Sylvia's edginess when they go to the football games.

When they have sex Alan always asks Sylvia with great concern whether she's had an orgasm. He's always supergentle and patient with her in bed. Secretly, Sylvia would much prefer it if Alan would be rougher and more aggressive. Inwardly, she also gets quite annoyed at his preoccupation with her orgasms, because it makes her feel like a medical case. She doesn't mention these bothersome things, because she feels Alan's motives are really kindly and "nice," and she doesn't want to kill this "sensitivity."

Recently, Alan and Sylvia have been delving into psychology. Their mutual philosophy has become "do you own thing" and "don't lay your trips on the other person." This has increased their cautiousness around each other, particularly in regard to setting expectations or making demands. They came to our marathon therapy group because the relationship seemed to be going stale. Alan was complaining of feelings of boredom and deadness and had begun to show interest in other girls. Sylvia had been having crying spells and the "bluesies," which she said made her want to sleep all the time.

THE PERSONALITY UNDERNEATH  Alan and Sylvia's great sensitivity with each other is a reflection of an underlying, exaggerated fear of anger, assertiveness, and confrontation. They are both really individuals with considerable aggression, but they hold these feelings in. They have learned to equate "niceness" with fight avoidance. Each fears they'll somehow crush the other if they make demands or level about their feelings. When he was a boy Alan's mother used to tell him that if he raised his voice to her she would get sick and maybe even die. Then he'd be sorry! Sylvia's mother used to tell her that only tramps talked loudly or got openly angry. Consequently, both Alan and Sylvia are afraid of real closeness because they're afraid of losing control over their aggressive feelings. Instead of experiencing these feelings directly, Sylvia gets anxiety attacks and crying spells. Alan gets feelings of boredom and deadness. Their "do your own thing" philosophy is an excuse to keep distance and avoid aggressive interaction.

THE REWARD   The "nice" behavior allows both Alan and Sylvia, who are very sensitive to rejection and criticism, to feel comfortable and accepted during the early stages of the relationship. Their early reaction to each other was that they'd finally found someone who was very special and who understood and accepted them as they "really were." They could also avoid the hassling and conflicts that only get both of them uptight. When the relationship finally breaks up they can both go on feeling it was just part of life. Both have done their own thing, and this, according to Alan and Sylvia, is what relationships are really all about.

THE PRICE   The "nice" lovers always watch their "ideal" relationships come to a crashing halt. Both then continue their search for another person they can really "groove" with. However, both will be left feeling that they didn't really get to know each other. In fact, they didn't. As they go from relationship to relationship, they will continue their pattern of initial euphoria, followed by slowly developing feelings of boredom and deadness, and a breakup. Then the search for a new partner will begin again. Each relationship, however, will only produce a deeper sense of alienation, cynicism, doubt, and fear about ever really "making it" with another person.

## LIVING WITH THE "NICE" PERSON

Coping with the disengagement and indirect aggression of the "nice" person, in the various patterns described in this chapter, are among the more complicated interpersonal negotiations in our society. That is, invariably the "nice" person induces guilt in the person confronting him. After all, how can you get angry toward someone who's only trying to be "nice"? The most common defense on behalf of the "nice" person one will encounter is "Why don't you leave him alone? He's not hurting anybody." Or "Just do your thing and let him do his." It is, therefore, important for one's emotional self-protection to be aware of the negative or destructive impact of the "nice" person's behavior on yourself before you engage him directly.

A primary question to ask oneself in trying to deal with the "nice" person is "What needs of mine are being served by his 'niceness'?" Invariably individuals who get closely involved with the "nice" person are protecting their own aggression-phobic tendencies. That is, they are attracted to this kind of person because they are left alone and never confronted. Individuals who tend to involve themselves with "nice" people are, therefore, really saying the following important thing about themselves: "I am attracted to the 'nice' person because he lets me get away with my hangups, spoiled behavior, and fear of strong involvement." The unspoken agreement between the "nice" person and those he involves himself with is "You don't make any demands on me and I won't make any demands on you."

In a recent marathon therapy session coconducted by Dr. Bach and Dr. Goldberg a married couple participated, in which the husband was the classic "nice" guy. Initially, everybody in the marathon liked him because of his complimentary, "sensitive" style. Everyone, that is, except his wife. She felt she was being driven crazy by his inability to take a firm stand, and express anger and other strong emotions directly. She couldn't stop his phony "adoring" behavior of her, which she felt was only smothering her and making her feel guilty whenever she sought to function independently of him. The wife of this "nice" guy would scream in frustration, but her husband would do little more than get slightly uncomfortable and say "I don't understand what you want of me."

Eventually, this passivity began to drive the group crazy too, once they had tired of his constant pleasantness and flattery. However, with the encouragement of the therapists the "nice" guy husband made a breakthrough and began to come on stronger. At this point the group made an important discovery. As he became strong, his wife tried to seduce him back into being "nice." It soon became increasingly clear that his "nice" guy behavior was allowing her to remain a demanding, self-indulgent, uncontrolled "baby." Though she had pleaded for more strength from him, when it finally came, she didn't really like it and tried to sabotage it. The primary question to be asked then is "What needs of both parties are being served by the 'nice' person's behavior?" Basically, only aggression-phobic people will find the "nice" person's behavior anything but stagnating, boring, and emotionally intolerable.

Once having become less afraid of one's own aggression, dealing with the "nice" person becomes a simpler matter. The "nice" person will recognize by your directness and assertiveness that you will not buy his essentially phony or manipulative behavior, and he will either change or leave the relationship. In general, "nice" behavior is only temporarily comforting to aggression-phobic individuals. In very little time this behavior becomes limiting and very dull to be around, not to mention all of the destructive side effects it has. The directly aggressive person may be initially less comfortable to be with, but he recharges relationships and social situations with an activating energy that is indispensable to staying involved and emotionally healthy.

Children having to live with the "nice" mommy or "nice" daddy will have a considerably more difficult time of it. Without professional or sophisticated adult intervention they will probably not be able to impact and change this behavior. However, close friends and relatives of the family, alert to these patterns, can be helpful in alleviating some of the guilt and the binds in which the child is enveloped by relating to him and his parents in directly aggressive ways. This modeling, which the child sees, can have a very therapeutic impact.

## THE PRICE OF "NICE"

"Nice" behavior eventually has a "price" for both the "nice" guy and the person or persons involved with him. It is alienating, indirectly hostile, and self-destructive because:

1. The "nice" guy tends to create an atmosphere such that others avoid giving him honest, genuine feedback. This blocks his emotional growth.

2. "Nice" behavior will ultimately be distrusted by others. That is, it generates a sense of uncertainty and lack of safety in others, who can never be sure if they will be supported by the "nice" guy in a crisis situation that requires an aggressive confrontation with others.

3. "Nice" guys stifle the growth of others. They avoid giving others genuine feedback, and they deprive others of a real person to assert against. This tends to force others in the relationship to turn their aggression against themselves. It also tends to generate guilt and depressed feelings in others who are intimately involved and dependent on him.

4. Because of his chronic "niceness," others can never be certain if the relationship with a "nice" guy could endure a conflict or sustain an angry confrontation, if it did occur spontane-

ously. This places great limits on the potential extent of intimacy in the relationship by placing others constantly on their guard.

5.   "Nice" behavior is not reliable. Periodically, the "nice" person explodes in unexpected rage and those involved with him are shocked and unprepared to cope with it.

6.   The "nice" guy, by holding his aggression in, may pay a physiological price in the form of psychosomatic problems and a psychological price in the form of alienation.

7.   "Nice" behavior is emotionally unreal behavior. It puts severe limitations on all relationships, and the ultimate victim is the "nice" person himself.

# CHAPTER 2

# The "Nice" Mother and the "Nice" Father

*Rock-a-bye-baby on the tree top,*
*When the wind blows the cradle will rock,*
*When the bough breaks the cradle will fall,*
*And down will come baby, cradle and all.*

How many mothers, while reflexively singing this lullaby, are aware of its lyric content and the hostile fantasy it contains? Its content is undoubtedly in sharp contrast to what most mothers are consciously experiencing as they lull their babies to sleep. Most mothers would, in fact, become extremely disturbed at the suggestion that they do harbor such resentful, destructive feelings and impulses toward their young infants.

Partially because they themselves anxiously overcontrol their own aggressive impulses toward their children, many mothers tend to become upset over any aggressive manifestations coming from their child. Specifically, outbursts of screaming, crying, raging, and thrashing about that normal babies are prone to do, will be distressing to aggression-phobic mothers. Consequently, they will try to suppress these responses.

However, the healthy fusion of aggression with developmental processes is crucial to the child's eventual mastery of the environment and his struggle for survival in a difficult, competitive culture. Particularly in today's world, where achievement and success are prized and usually result from assertive individual enterprise, the capacity to be constructively aggressive is an integral part of a fulfilling life.

Critical aspects of development that require aggressive mobilization include: learning to master physical and intellectual skills; expressing exploratory drives; moving from total dependence in infancy to partial autonomy during school age and eventual independence in the late adolescence; recognizing, expressing, and obtaining satisfaction of one's unique needs; overcoming obstacles that produce frustration; determining vocational and life goals; seeking out and developing satisfying relationships; and successfully expressing one's sexuality.

From conception onward, growth and development are intimately bound up with appropriate aggressive expression. The healthy fetus makes his existence known to his mother by kicking. The very first response of the healthy baby to separation from its mother's body is the aggressive birth cry. This symbolic expression of the "rage to live" has the important biological function of starting the baby's breathing.

During the first few months of life, crying is the only way the baby can assertively communicate his discomfort and need. The quiet baby so often wrongly described as the "good" baby may turn out instead to be physically sick or emotionally disturbed. The healthy hungry baby, for example, from whom breast or bottle is prematurely removed, will cry and thrash about in protest. The so-called "good" baby will just lie there, passively accepting, but not meaningfully or directly communicating or signaling his needs.

## THE INFANT'S AGGRESSIVE ENERGY

During the first year of life, the infant's aggressive energies allow him to move his arms and legs, roll over, pull himself up, propel himself on all fours, and begin to sit up. This aggressive energy, often taken for granted, has been found to be absent in some disturbed infants, in particular those who were raised in institutions without individual mothering attention. Without this appropriate mothering stimulation, orphans may retreat into a state of apathetic withdrawal, a passive nonresponsiveness accompanied by an inability to make human eye contact. This disease, first described in the research literature by Dr. Renee A. Spitz in his study on infants brought up in foundling homes, has been called *marasmus* or *anaclitic depression*.[1] The behavior indeed resembles that of the behavior of a deeply depressed adult.

The vital baby who responds by biting, tearing, and crawling into things is also in the process of developing perceptual coordination and manipulative mastery. If blocked or prohibited from expressing these impulses by expressions of parental disapproval, such as slapping or being isolated, the child learns that spontaneous enjoyment of physical activity and the exploration of the world is "bad." These activities or impulses will then become progressively inhibited in the child. He will narrow his scope and degree of responsiveness and engage only in such activities in the future with inhibition, caution, and guilt.

During the second year of life the child becomes more immediately aware of reality and vulnerable to frustrations. The aggressive behavior becomes increasingly purposeful. The child is becoming aware of specific interferences to his activities and impulses and of who the frustrating agent is. At the same time he begins to lose some of his feelings of omnipotence, that glorious feeling of being the center of the universe, in which gratification is always provided upon demand. As he is learning about reality, he is also beginning to learn purposeful self-assertion.

The time between 1½ and 2½ years of age, for the normal child, is a period of negativism and resistance. During this period the child is learning to say "No!" It is normal for outbursts of anger to appear during this period. These outbursts reach their peak by 2 years, and so-called negative resistance reaches its height by 2½ years of age. As the child becomes increasingly aware of mother as a person, he also becomes possessive and readily aroused to anger because of jealousy. Therefore, at this age children commonly become angry at other children or adults who seem to be taking away some of their mother's love and attention. The extremely passive and compliant child who does not express these negative feelings may have already had some of his developmental vitality diminished.

Even at this young age, behavior that may be the product of extreme repression of overt aggression is manifested by the turning of aggressive impulses against the self. These constricted toddlers may bite themselves or bang their heads in displaced, self-destructive fury. In the older child and young adult these identical, inhibited manifestations will be expressed more subtly. It may take the form of teeth grinding during sleep, nail biting, lip chewing, or scratching at one's skin. In the adult these manifestations become even less obvious. They manifest themselves in the form of being accident or illness prone, being morbidly preoccupied, or by repeated entry into unsatisfying, self-destructive relationships and situations.

Some theorists point to the tendency toward rampant destructiveness against the ecology and violence among people as being at least partially the result of modern Western civilization's tendency to snuff out and inhibit much of the healthy curiosity and exploratory tendencies and aggressiveness in childhood.

The child encounters a constant barrage of "Don'ts!" and "Nos" in contemporary urban settings that he would not have been faced with in more primitive environments. The child's spontaneous exploratory impulses and desires are being frustrated and curtailed at every turn. Out-of-doors the child is endlessly cautioned about the dangers of automobiles and other traffic. Children are taught to be wary of strangers and to not speak with anyone that they do not know. In the home their movements are inhibited through constant warnings about the dangers of electrical appliances, the stove, glass objects, the medicine cabinet, and the many "precious," fragile furnishings that crowd the rooms. The cult of privacy that exists in many homes further means that many rooms and spaces are not to be explored or entered. And of course the heavy emphasis in our culture on neatness, orderliness, and cleanliness further inhibit the child's spontaneous movements.

Once the child comes of school age and enters into relationships with children his own age, the capacity for self-assertion is particularly crucial for gaining peer acceptance and for confronting and overcoming the increasing number of social obstacles and frustrations.

In the school setting, the "nice" passive child may become the teacher's pet, but at the same time becomes a target for scapegoating, bullying, teasing, and being left out of games and social events by other children.

The problem of the aggressively inhibited child will come into particularly strong focus during the stressful period of adolescence. During this stage all the assertive energy the adolescent can muster will be required for the movement toward independent functioning, the determination of appropriate vocational goals, the development of a personally satisfying lifestyle, and relationships of intimacy with the opposite sex. Passive adolescents will find their patterns of passivity, withdrawal, and intellectual rumination intensifying under the pressures of this lifestage. They may seek shelter in drugs, religious cults, esoteric philosophies, or communal homes, all in search of the instant answer or rationalization that would allow them to avoid the difficult and painful assertive efforts demanded of them on the way to becoming self-sustaining, independent, and functioning adults.

During adulthood and old age the maintenance of an aggressive, externally directed response is essential for avoiding the traps of insulation and isolation from changing social realities, and the tendency to retreat behind illnesses during times of stress. The continuing capacity to muster this response may mean the difference in facilitating the ability to adapt, live in the here-and-now, and find creative, personally satisfying alternatives in a society that worships youth and shuns the elderly. Old age for the passive person may become a pathetic replay of childhood, in which he regresses into a dependency and demandingness on others that ultimately results in rejection and despair.

## THE RAISING OF HIDDEN AGGRESSORS

When open aggressive expression or interpersonal encounters are suppressed, either for conscious reasons, such as the desire to be polite or "nice," or for deeper motivations, such as the fear of angry interchanges, these feelings are not lost. Rather, they are driven underground, so to speak, and re-emerge transformed behind socially acceptable masks.

Suppression of the expression of angry feelings may begin a spiral of complicated communication entanglements. For example, a toilet-trained four-year-old is prevented from expressing resentment, jealousy, and rage over the birth of a sibling. The parents keep informing the child of how lucky and happy he *should* feel to have a new brother or sister and how naughty it is to be jealous or selfish. To win the parents' approval, these feelings are repressed. Suddenly, however, the toilet-trained four-year-old begins to wet his bed again. This is an indirect expression of the resentment and anger toward the parent that was blocked from direct, guilt-free expression. The original anger assumes the form of a "medical" problem. It is now a much more complicated phenomenon to deal with, as the child is no longer aware of the original underlying feelings. The child is now also able to aggravate and distress the parents without the risks of an open confrontation and rejection through his "problem." In this way, a simple feeling of blocked resentment becomes a long-term source of difficulty.

## THE TRAGEDY OF THE "GOOD" BABY

As briefly mentioned earlier in this chapter, some of the most severely emotionally disturbed children were originally perceived by their mothers to be model infants. This "good baby" was a very quiet, noncrying, and nondemanding infant.

In some of these instances the "good baby" behavior is an early symptom of the syndrome of autism, a form of childhood schizophrenia. The child is seen as "good" because he does not develop a functionally useful cry. Autism is one of the most severe forms of childhood psychosis, one in which the child shuns and even rebels against human contact and any form of human involvement or control. The child relates comfortably only to objects, not people. He can stare at a washing machine or listen to the same song for hours at a time.

Some psychological studies of the parents of these autistic children have painted a portrait of them as highly intelligent, well-educated, and verbal, but emotionally cold. They are also described as easily threatened by and avoidant of aggressive give-and-take, and overly sensitive to the primitive responses of their infant. The husband-wife interaction tends to be quiet and controlled. These parents become particularly distressed by the anger or rage outbursts of their child, and consequently tend to avoid physical or emotional contact or handling of the child while he is expressing these feelings.[2]

Autistic children will not assert themselves in a direction toward other people. Their aggressive energy is often channeled into self-destructive behaviors. They are known to hit their own faces, bang their heads against walls, bite themselves, and even tear at their own body in self-aggression.

Recently, a technique has been pioneered by Dr. Robert Zaslow of San Jose, California, for the treatment of these autistic children. Briefly, in this therapy that he calls Z-process therapy, he induces a series of rage reactions by cradling the child as if it were a baby and not breaking contact or control over the child until the child finally makes genuine eye contact in a relaxed interaction. Before this is achieved the child will invariably protest and resist in every imaginable way against this human contact. He will emit incredibly intense anger and rage responses in his attempt to break contact. Eventually the child, after discharging these enormous feelings of rage and resentment, sometimes for a period of several hours, will begin to relax and make a genuine and loving eye contact response.

According to Dr. Zaslow, he has been successful in treating many different emotional disorders whose roots are repressed aggression by using this technique. These include hyperkinesis, allergies, and school learning problems. Dr. Zaslow is doing with his technique what the parents were unable to do, namely controlling the child, tolerating the child's aggressive expression, and facilitating this expression and interaction *within* the relationship.

When this Z-process therapy is successfully completed, the child is able to express his anger directly at the therapist and not indirectly and manipulatively. He is able, for example, to punch the therapist's open, inviting hand while making direct eye contact. The child also then becomes capable of showing loving and positive emotions in human interaction, such as affection, smiling, and playfulness.[3]

## THE MYTH OF THE CRUEL CHILD

The widely read book *Lord of the Flies,* subsequently made into a film, depicted the cruel interactions that can occur among children. The traditional myth perpetuated by this film is that children are innately cruel little savages when uncontrolled and left to their own devices.

It is believed by the authors, and has been previously

theorized by other researchers in child behavior, that this cruel response is only a by-product or displaced expression of aggressive feelings that were originally experienced within the family but were inhibited, punished, and repressed.

Aggression-repressive parents who bring up their children by the dictum that children should be seen and not heard, that sparing the rod spoils the child, and that respect means children do not talk back, we believe are indirectly creating a powerful and destructive reservoir of repressed aggression in their child. The child will be prone to seek out other, safe targets for these feelings, such as weaker peers or helpless animals. In fact, the severity and punitiveness of maternal discipline and the use of arbitrary power over the child has been shown to be related to the amount of a child's hostility toward other children and also to his resistance to social influence.

Studies of teasing behavior in children, a behavior often reacted to casually by adults but powerfully traumatic to the young victim of this behavior, suggest that it is significantly more prevalent among children from homes where discipline is severe and authoritarian, contrasted to homes with a tolerance for the open, direct expression of anger and assertiveness. A child who teases is expressing indirect hostility. The teasing is a manifestation of his inability to express aggression in open and direct ways. The teasing child is not reacting to real and immediate annoyances. He is scapegoating and expressing ill will that has been carried over as a result of past suppression of the direct expression of these feelings.

The biblical commandment "Honor thy mother and father" could profitably be altered to read, "Fight fairly with your mother and father." We believe that many of the common forms of displaced aggression such as scapegoating, bullying, prejudice, and cruelty are by-products of aggressive feelings first felt within the family but suppressed. The aggressively constructive family will be the one that not only accepts but energizes itself on the full and direct expression of these feelings in the home as they come up, giving them equal importance and respect alongside feelings of love and allowing them to enhance intimacy and provide useful information.

## BEWARE THE OVERCONTROLLED "NICE" CHILD!

Recent important research on violence by psychologist Dr. Edwin I. Megargee indicates that we have less to fear from the impulsive, openly aggressive child than from the heavily overcontrolled child. Docile passivity and violent potential can be two sides of the same coin. Megargee's research shows that many of the most brutal, senseless murders of the past twenty years have been committed by persons perceived to be mild mannered, inhibited, passive, and overcontrolled.[4] It appears that the chronic repression of aggression created a dangerous boiling kettle. When the controls broke down under stress, the aggression burst forth in a brutal and bizarre way. The chapter "The 'Nice' Killers" in this book describes this phenomenon at greater length.

## THE CHILD MUST DEAL WITH FRUSTRATION

A popular theory regarding the origins of aggression that was originally set forth many years back theorized that the cause of aggression was frustration. Many enlightened parents who desired to raise peace-loving, unaggressive children proceeded to try to do so through a permissive child-rearing style that greatly minimized the frustrations. This approach has in many instances backfired. Many children raised in this fashion grew up to be more aggressive and with more problems than children brought up experiencing considerable frustrations.

This mode of upbringing without frustration had merely served to inculcate in the child an unreal sense of personal omnipotence. Whatever he wanted he got and felt he deserved. Most psychologists now acknowledge that it is only through the experiencing of and learning to deal with frustration that the child develops an ability to cope with reality and to realize and accept his own limitations. Children brought up with a permissive avoidance of frustration also grow up developing little tolerance for it. When they become young adults they manifest much greater difficulty following through on long-range goals and plans. They have never learned to be assertive on their own behalf because they never had to as children. They were catered to and learned to expect that all would be eventually given to them or would be made readily accessible. The victims of this child-rearing style are many of the bright, aimless young people of today who float from job to job and home to home without being able to take hold on an integrated style of life.

Children learn to handle life and to utilize their aggressive energies constructively through parental resistance and opposition. The frustration-aggression theory became so popular in part because it reinforced the fantasy of an aggression-free human being. Parents who are afraid to frustrate their children are unwittingly harming them by not providing real situations, or a real person for the child to resist against. The child is given no opportunity to learn how to assert himself independently. With no overt resistance, the child's aggression may eventually even be turned against himself in the form of self-destructive indulgence in drugs, a tendency toward depression and inactivity, or even suicide. The "nice" guy parent who offers his child no resistance is unconsciously destroying his child's capacity to function and survive.

## THE TRAINING OF DOVES AND HAWKS

The Women's Liberation movement has been very instrumental in forcing a re-examination of the validity of the notion that males are "naturally" more aggressive than females. It has pointed out that much of this difference can be attributed to social conditioning processes that negatively reinforce aggressive behavior in girls while positively reinforcing their passivity, and vice versa for boys.

A study by two Yale sociologists, Louis Wolf Goodman and Janet Lever, discussed in *Ms.* magazine, described this double standard as it is manifested in the selection of toys bought as gifts for children during the Christmas season. In thirty hours of observation in toy departments, no field workers reported a single scientific toy being bought for a girl. Toys purchased for boys were found to be significantly more designed for active, complex social activities. In addition, they were more varied and expensive than the toys for girls. "Feminine" toys were described to be typically of a passive, solitary, and simple nature.

In the marketing of children's costumes, boys were cast in aggressive, prestigious roles such as race car drivers, Superman, Indian chiefs, astronauts, or highway troopers. Girls, on the other hand, were depicted in roles that were significantly less commanding and aggressive, such as fairy princesses, ballerinas, nurses, or brides. In catalogue pictures that illustrated the use of the games and toys, the father was most often seen as the "instructor" or "play companion" to the child. Mother was seen in the role of "spectator" and on at least two occasions was shown in the process of cleaning up.

Toys used for aggressive play such as guns are usually not given to girls. Fashion dolls, which constitute a large percentage of the gifts for girls, seem to encourage the little girls to perceive themselves as mannequins, sex objects, or housekeepers. One doll, called "Bizzie Lizzie," represented a woman with a mop in one hand and an iron in the other, with a feather duster sweeper as optional equipment.[5]

One particularly emotionally destructive aspect of this lopsided socialization of the female to be passively oriented is that as adults some of them are unable to have a constructive, communicative, aggressive interchange within their intimate relationships. Instead they tend to become readily threatened by an aggressive interchange, break easily into tears, and become explosive or withdrawn. Or their aggression only emerges passively and indirectly. Psychological and physiological toll is taken through a vulnerability to disorders such as migraine headaches, neurasthenia, and masochistic interactions. All have as at least one of their root cores, repressed aggression.

It is particularly noteworthy that approximately 3.7 percent of all reported murders in America involve child killings and infanticide. Almost 100 percent of the time the murder is committed by the mother. The authors hypothesize that in some instances the woman who is unable to discharge her rage and frustration directly toward her husband and her role as wife and mother, passively acquiescing to demands, but unconsciously resenting the controls and pressure she faces, may release her murderous fury against her child instead.

The anxiety that mothers have over the greater aggressiveness of their sons and the mothers' tendency to overreact in an attempt to control this aggression may be a critical factor in explaining the statistics that show that major psychological problems such as autism, reading problems, stuttering, and delinquency are significantly more prevalent in boys than in girls. In an attempt to control the dreaded aggressive potential of their sons, these mothers overly inhibit their male child's aggressive behavior. The repressed aggressive feelings of the boy are then instead expressed passively and indirectly through a resistance to learning and socialization.

Equally hazardous to the emotional development of the male child is the mother's tendency to turn the business of disciplining the boy over to the father, thus making the father the "bad" guy. Mother meanwhile solicitously empathizes with the boy's pain and hurt feelings. This produces a greater distance or alienation between the boy and his father than between the boy and his mother. It makes identification with his father more difficult because he is significantly more fearful of him than of his mother.

In major part, thanks to the Women's Liberation movement, aggressive expression in the female will undoubtedly undergo dramatic change and become continually more direct. The authors see this as having an extremely beneficial effect in the liberation of the male as well. Men will no longer need to react toward women in guilt-oriented, overly protective, and solicitous ways. They will no longer have to see themselves as the "heavy," the ogre who callously crushed the fragile feminine flower. Furthermore, it will allow men to move away from their defensive posture of constantly needing to prove to the world that they are the able providers, the capable hunters, warriors, and breadwinners.

## AGGRESSION AND PROTEST

The constructive, growth-furthering use of the freedom to be aggressive can also be seen in the weaning of the young person from physical, emotional, and intellectual dependency on his parents and elders. Many of our neurotic adult patients are still trying to grow up, and their weaning is indeed long overdue. Many of the younger patients (ages twenty-one to thirty) had to literally run away in order to extricate themselves from over-protective, overdirective, dependency-reinforcing environments. For example, California is filled with psychological refugees from parents in the East who were dependency-nurturing and incompetent weaners. Many kept their offspring tied to them by instilling a fear of the "cold, rejecting" world outside.

Aggression and protest is youth's protection against a growth-stunting family and school environment. It takes aggressive resistance to stop dependency reinforcers, crazymakers, and fear evokers. It also takes aggressive energy for a young adult to wrest his psychological self away from rigid role expectations insensitively laid on him by older family members. The earlier children learn to use their freedom to be aggressive creatively, the greater their chances to fully develop their human potential.

## AGGRESSION AND LOVE

The readers who have cats or dogs in their homes know that their animals may be in the midst of a seemingly vicious fight with each other one minute and playing together peacefully or sleeping curled next to each other the next. We feel that children too are potentially capable of intertwining aggression and love in this way in their relationships.

Two kindergarten-age boys were recently observed by the authors in heated struggle for possession of a particular building block, even though several others were available. Before anyone was even able to intervene they were already in each other's arms expressing mutual love.

A writer in a child development journal recounted the following episode. A five-year-old child came to school covered with scratches and explained without ill feeling that he had received the scratches at the hands of his "best friend." To the child the scratches and "best friendness" were not in the least bit contradictory.[6]

Parents may feel foolish when they find themselves about to discipline one child for having been mean to another when suddenly the "victim" comes to the defense of the "offender." The parent himself ends up feeling like the culprit. In the aggression-phobic consciousness of most adults it does not seem possible that two children who care for each other can also vigorously fight with each other. In the adult fantasy one child might kill the other if there was no intervention.

It cannot be stressed too often that feelings of love are not necessarily contradictory or in opposition to aggressive feelings within a relationship Children therefore should not be taught, as they so often are, that they must divide their feelings, with aggressive feelings being reserved for enemies and outsiders and love feelings reserved for the family and friends. For the healthy emotional and physical development of the children, both of these sets of feelings must be allowed equal play within the family's intimate relationships.

# CHAPTER 3

# The "Nice" Spouses

---

*The best guess as to "who did it" is that an intimate of the victim was the culprit. In one-half to three-fourths of the homicide victims reported on in various studies, the murderer and his victim had at least some previous association.*

REPORT TO THE NATIONAL COMMISSION
ON THE CAUSES AND PREVENTION OF VIOLENCE[1]

It is at the same time reassuring yet somewhat frightening that the chances that one will become the victim of a murder or aggravated assault are greater that it will be at the hand of someone we're familiar with than at the hand of a stranger. This fact regarding violent behavior in America is rather startling. We have been conditioned by the media to associate violence with senseless, impersonal brutality. Headlines are filled for days at a time with news about a crazed sniper, a hospital escapee, or a frantic, drug-addicted person who is on a violent spree. These kinds of murderous and assaultive behaviors lend themselves well to outcries about danger in the streets of modern cities, or the need for greater police protection. They also lend themselves well to lofty pronouncements by politicians about "law and order." However, the very high rate of violence among intimates and the widespread ignorance regarding ways to predict, handle, or control this phenomenon is rarely if ever given much attention. In more ways than one it strikes too close to home. Like the facts of death or cancer, it is more comforting to deny that violence is also within our experiential province.

It was with the specific intent of analyzing marital violence to discover patterns and other information that would allow for prediction and control that Dr. George Bach, along with his research assistant, Dr. Roger Bach, interviewed seventy-four spouse killers around the world. Of these, thirty-eight were husbands who had killed their wives, and thirty-six were wives who had killed their husbands. The purposes of this study were several: to develop greater perspective and insight into the causes and management of intimate hostilities, to construct a probability model that would facilitate the prediction of lethal or near-lethal violence in intimate relationships, and to chart some programs or plans for violence-prevention work.[2]

Demographic characteristics of the spouse murderers studied can be found in Table I. All of the spouse murderers interviewed were in prisons at the time, either in the United States of America, England, France, Germany, or Greece.

*Table I*

## SPOUSE MURDER POPULATION

| National Origin | No. | Sex | Racial Origin | Age Range | Data Collection Method |
|---|---|---|---|---|---|
| Greece | 20 | Females | | 22–52 | Grp.* |
| Germany | 1 | Female | | 41 | Ind.† |
| | 3 | Males | | 27–62 | Ind. |
| England | 10 | Males | 7 White | 24–58 | Grp. |
| | | | 3 West Indian | 22–32 | Grp. |
| French (Polynesia) | 1 | Female | Native | 35 | Ind. |
| | 1 | Male | Native | 54 | Ind. |

## U.S.A. (California)

| Sample 1: | 13 | Males | 5 Black | | Grp. |
| | | | 8 White | 25–51 | |
| | 1 | Female | White | 28 | Ind. |
| Sample 2: | 11 | Males | 4 Black | | |
| | | | 7 White | 21–45 | I.A.Q.‡ |
| | 13 | Females | 2 Black | | |
| | | | 11 White | 22–60 | Grp. |

\* Group Interview
† Individual Interview
‡ Intimate Aggression Questionnaires

## Summary

| Male | Female | Age Range | U.S.A. | Foreign | White | Other |
|------|--------|-----------|--------|---------|-------|-------|
| 38 | 36 | 22–62 | 38 | 36 | 58 | 16 |

Interviews centered around the following dimensions of the relationships:

1. Depth and mutuality of the emotional and sexual involvement.

2. Modes of sharing of stressful and joyful experiences.

3. Styles of expressing anger and other forms of aggression.

4. Reconciliation patterns.

5. Expectations and major sources of disappointment.

6. "Love frames" and "hate frames"; behavior that turned love or hate on or off.

7. Individual and mutually shared social lives.

8. Use of alcoholism and drugs.

9. Occurrence of special crises, such as suicide attempts or breakdowns.

Bach's study pointed out one fact that seems particularly noteworthy. Less than 6 percent of these spouse killers could be considered clearly "psychotic" or severely disturbed. The four who were, rather than being impulsive acting-out types, were instead severely overcontrolled and self-hating. They were unaware of and unable to express their hostilities openly. When the dam finally broke over a minor precipitating event, they exploded.

Their self-hate throughout the marriage was intensified rather than calmed by their spouse's attempt to reach out and love them. They were unable to accept this kind of loving intimacy. Instead, they experienced it as an unbearable suffocation and demandingness.

For the other spouse murderers, recurrent patterns emerged. All of the killings involved the motivation to punish a partner for not fitting into a role, image, or situation as defined and wished for by the other. Spouse killers experienced their spouses as "spoilers" of what they had wishfully fantasized would make the relationship fulfilling. This fantasy expectation tended to follow the stereotype of the romantic model of love. It had no room for the presence of conflict and aggressive interaction. The killers had dreams and idealizations about the relationship as something that they felt should be harmonious and beautiful. They were not able to feel it or accept it for what it was until the spoiled expectations loomed too large to ignore.

Spouse murderers also tended to be rigidly fixated on how the other should behave, and what satisfactions should be provided in the relationship. For example, a young divorcee, the mother of two little boys, had secretly sworn to herself before her marriage to her second husband that she would kill any husband who would be mean to her children. Indeed, she killed her husband for just such behavior three years later. Her particular "love turn-off," the behavior that would cause her to hate the man she married, was his open and direct demonstration of hostility toward her children. This is, in fact, a typical hate releaser among second- and third-time married mother-divorcees.

When the murderers began to realize that important expectations were not being fulfilled, they continued to cling tightly to their expectations nevertheless and attempted to manipulate the other person into behaving the way they wanted the person to behave.

## A NARROW BASIS FOR LOVING

Spouse murderers also tended to have an unusually narrow basis for loving. That is, they seemed to require very specific behaviors from their partners in order to feel loving. Many of the murderers confessed the experience of a turning point, a specific behavior on their spouse's part that forever ruined their ability to release love and allow themselves to be loved. They began to set secret traps. "I will test her. If she comes through I will stay. If she fails, I'll leave. If she does not let me leave, I will punish her."

The romantic model of love, the tendency to idealize one's relationship rather than experience it for what it is, is commonly experienced early in a relationship when there is a strong tendency to mutually accommodate to each other's fantasy expectations. If there is a continuing and deep commitment to the fulfillment of one's rigid expectations, there will also be a tendency for the secret buildup of bitterness and rage and then a possible violent explosion.

In one such situation, a dentist had discovered that his wife was having an affair. In fact, she had told him of it herself. His image of her was that she was "pure" and totally loyal. Though other males always picked up on her very seductive manner, he was blind to it. Even after she told him about the affair, he tried to deny her admission of it by telling himself it was something she made up to make him jealous. He continued to insist that she was an innocent babe in the woods. Sometime after that, during a party when he actually saw her physically go off into another room on an involvement, his rage built rapidly, and he knifed both her and her boyfriend. He had rigid expectations as to what she should be like, and denied the reality of who and what she was when he saw it. He finally killed her for being a "spoiler" of the "beautiful thing" he insisted that they had going for them.

Spouse killers were also, on the whole, very secretive. When they felt disappointment they rarely, if ever, shared the depth of their pain or disappointment. On the few occasions when they tried, they were both embarrassed and frightened by the intensity of their hostility.

## THE FORGIVE-AND-FORGET RITUAL

The vast majority of couples in this study abhorred and therefore avoided open conflict and fighting. The majority of the male offenders were accommodating guys, while their female counterparts tended to be caring helpmates. When these couples became frustrated or angry, they would not show it. When an annoyance would momentarily break into an open argument, they would tend to withdraw and give each other the "silent treatment" rather than continuing to work on it.

Then they would soon forget or ignore the fact of the fight and use sexual involvement with each other as a forgive-and-forget ritual. Between most spouse killers and their dead spouses there had been a strong sexual attraction and frequent sexual activity. Sex was used as a strategy for avoiding conflict. After a hassle, the couple avoided talking about what the hostility outbreaks were all about. Thus they never gained or learned from these occasional hostility outbreaks. They did not know how to work toward marital improvement, nor did they even confide their troubles to others on the outside.

The final move toward lethal violence occurred when one

partner in desperation announced a decision to leave. Invariably, the attempt to leave was blocked. At this point, women had more of a tendency than men to shoot their way out in order to get rid of the clinging vine. If the person did succeed in getting away, the loss was so frightening and unbearable to the loser left behind that the loser went after and murdered the leaver. This was especially true if the loser had determined that reconciliation was hopeless.

## THE PATTERNS OF SPOUSE MURDER

The following patterns seemed most characteristic of these spouse-killing relationships:

1. *Conflict evasion.* Aggression phobia and the inability to work for changes openly was the rule. The more guarded partners tended to kill the more overt partners in a ratio of three to one.

2. *Nontransparency of expectations.* There was an unwillingness to indicate disappointment and hurt when it arose.

3. *Making up without change.* Sex was often used as a way to make up and cover up. However, no real changes were made in the process.

4. *Severe power disparities.* One person was often a ruler, while the other person was relatively passive. Interestingly, there were more killers among the passive group than among the tyrannical group.

5. *Extreme disparities in giving and taking.* A frequent pattern in these relationships was that the "taker" was insatiable while the "giver" increasingly felt worn out and unappreciated.

6. *Extreme disparities in outside social contacts.* One mate was invariably more socially oriented than the other. The isolated, withdrawn mate became highly threatened by the social activities of the freer, more popular mate. In the end, however. it was just as likely that the shy, isolated mate would do in the

popular, socializing mate, as it was that the popular mate would get rid of the mate who was seen as blocking the fun.

7. *Malicious premeditation.* The majority of spouse killers, speaking with the promise of confidentiality, admitted that they had thought about killing their mate many times before they actually did it. The killers in this study gave no support to the myth of the spontaneous, passionate killing that supposedly occurs in spouse murders. The seeds of murder were planted long before the actual act occurred.

8. *"Thinging."* The spouse killers had radically altered their concept of their victims, transforming them in their minds from whole persons to dehumanized symbols, "dream spoilers" or "enemies," before they killed them.

9. *Exit blocking.* "I'll never let you go" was often meant literally in the case of these spouse killers. In general, there were more would-be leavers who killed their restrainers than restrainers who lethally punished their deserting partners.

## THE GOAL OF FIGHT TRAINING

There are many things to be learned from studying the most lethal form of intimate violence. These couples are only extreme examples of the potential results of conflict evasion, aggression phobia, and ignorance regarding the handling of emotions of hostility, resentfulness, and anger in intimate involvements.

The goal of fight training is to avoid this development of distorted expectations, to destroy the romantic fantasies of eternal harmony, and to overcome the fears and avoidances of angry encounters. Basic to this kind of training is the willingness to acknowledge the existence of these feelings in oneself and also one's violent potential, latent as it may seem to be. Among the ritual exercises for this purpose, taught to intimates during fight training are:

1. *Expectation exercise.* This requires couples to share their most intense mutual expectations. For example, Molly says to Roger, "I expect that you will never have an affair without

first talking it over with me. I also expect that we will have children and that you will actively share in the raising of them. Finally, I expect that whenever you come home from a long day away from me that you will sit and talk with me before running off to your newspaper, television, or other work." The other spouse is then asked to confirm or deny his willingness to live up to these expectations.

2. *Power disparity exercises.* Because of the inevitability that one partner will have greater physical strength or a more dominating personality, effort is made to find ways of equalizing power disparities in order to allow each spouse to feel free to fully release aggression without the fear of destructive retaliation.

On a physical level we use exercises such as bataca fighting, pushing to the wall, etc., described in the chapter "Aggression Rituals." We train spouses to use physical handicapping in order to even up imbalances. On a verbal level, exercises such as "feedback" are useful in slowing down a more verbal, controlling spouse and thereby equalizing the difference. In teaching the Fair Fight Training System, we also encourage couples to fight in the presence of others of good will to offset verbal or physical inequities.

3. *"Escape hatch."* The "escape hatch" is an intimacy refuge, an activity or territory to be maintained exclusive to the individual and considered taboo to the other family members. These "escape hatches" serve as a reminder that psychological interdependence can be very wearing and requires regular, periodic reprieve from contact. Typically, partners without prior "escape hatch" training are appalled by the outbursts of massive accumulations of the need for independence when they are finally honestly shared. Couples are therefore taught to signal each other and to have for themselves a list of places each can go to or things each can do in order to be alone and recuperate. Intimates are also helped to define for themselves what they will do to escape to safety when tensions become temporarily unbearable. These "escape hatches" are then to be mutually honored.

4. *Recognizing and subverting "thinging."* Many couples originally fall in love with each other's images and react violently when the real person underneath the fantasy tries to break through. These exercises are designed to allow individuals to see each other outside of the stereotyped images they may have of each other. This is done by having couples communicate only via feelings, not intellectualizations. These include openly sharing information about their worst sides and their negative feelings about the other person.

Rituals and the Fair Fight Training System discussed in other chapters are used. They are designed to subvert the kinds of communication blockages and distortions that eventuate in destructive, homicidal behavior. When there are children, the offspring are made an integral part of the fight training and are taught the appropriate exercises. Primary, however, is the necessity for acknowledgment in each person of the existence of aggressive feelings and violent potential toward a spouse or lover. With this acknowledgment and the courage to display openly to one's intimate these feelings along with the loving ones, not only murder prevention, but the development of deeply satisfying relationships can be facilitated.

In some instances fair fight training reveals that two individuals chronically trigger off in each other their worst behaviors and retard rather than promote each other's growth. In these instances a change of partners may even be more promising than working within the existing relationship and the fight training is geared to a realistic exit. It is therefore stressed to individuals in our Fair Fight Training programs that being single or being married can be equally valid lifestyles. It would be unethical and inappropriate to use fair fight training as an artificial booster shot for decaying marital relationships.

## THE EPIDEMIC OF DOMESTIC VIOLENCE

A reported interview with an official of the FBI brought to light the fact that approximately one of every five policemen killed in the line of duty dies trying to break up a family fight. Intervention in spouse fights results in more assaults on policemen than any other kind of violent encounter. In large cities like New York, a patrolman on a beat in a residential neighborhood may spend as much as 40 percent of his time intervening in family squabbles. Therefore, a major portion of the focus in training policemen today is on the psychological aspects of domestic intervention.

The statistics suggest that all forms of domestic violence, from spouse involvement to parent-child or between relatives, have become somewhat epidemic. In at least 25 percent of all reported homicides, the victim is related to the murderer by blood or by marriage. In 1971 alone, more than two thousand Americans killed their mates. This accounted for 12 percent of the total murders committed that year. The likelihood that the murderer will be either male or female is nearly even. That is, husbands are only slightly more likely to kill their wives than vice versa (the percentages in recent years were 54 percent to 46 percent). Male exclusivity in using this kind of lethal violence in a marital relationship is therefore a myth. Though women may be less prone to committing homicide in general, when they do kill, there is a strong likelihood that their husbands will be the victims. Over half of these murders take place on weekends and holidays, when there is more togetherness and an absence of the usual escapes, such as work for the man, household chores or employment for the woman, and school for the children.

Nearly 20 percent of all aggravated assault cases also occur between husband and wife, and these are only the assaults on spouses that are reported. In as much as 90 percent of these incidents, particularly wife beating, charges are never filed or a report even written.

In the reported cases of aggravated assault, the husband is the offender more than three fourths of the time. The matter that precipitates the assault is, the majority of the time, an argument that is relatively trivial in origin.

Child murders and batterings are also on the increase and receiving considerable attention. They have become so great a problem that legislation passed recently in many states requires physicians treating battered children to file written reports. Recent statistics also show that at least two children a week are murdered by their parents in New York City alone. Most of these child victims are between a few days and nine years of age. They are killed in sundry brutal ways, such as being slammed against walls, scalded with boiling water, thrown into incinerators, tossed off roofs or out of windows, suffocated, starved to death, kicked, beaten, strangled, even decapitated.

A recent study of mothers who had killed their babies at birth revealed some interesting psychological data on the personalities of these women. The study found that a majority of them had very passive personalities. That is, they were women who had difficulty making decisions, tended to postpone action, and used childish defenses such as denial ("I'm not really pregnant."). This resulted in their making little to no preparations for the birth of the baby or even considering the possibility of an abortion until it was too late. Infanticide was a desperation act that occurred when they were finally and inescapably hit with the reality of their situations.[3]

There are a surprisingly large number of murders committed by children against a parent or another sibling. In the case of a child murdering a parent, this usually takes the form of a son protecting his mother against a raging or drunken father. Sometimes it has no immediate precipitating cause and may even result from severe repression and overcontrol of the child, who one day suddenly explodes and vents his rage in a murderous act. One recent psychological study suggested that children who kill within the family may be acting as unwitting agents of one of the parents. The parent unconsciously prompts the child to kill and thereby obtains the vicarious satisfaction and benefits of the act without the responsibility. The killer-child rarely premeditates the behavior in these instances; rather, it is usually a spontaneous act in which the stimulating adult inflames the child's latent hostile feelings toward the victim.[4]

It is not surprising that the rate of domestic violence is so high. No one can anger another as much as an intimate who is at one and the same time a source of our greatest pleasures and our deepest frustrations and hurt. What is surprising, however, is that so few know how to deal with these aggressive feelings as they arise, nor how to prevent their escalation and avoid physical assaults of a severe and damaging nature. The myths of family life still revolve around beliefs in "harmonious living," and the emphasis is still on achieving this rather than on learning the processes of conflict resolution. Family fighting is still socially considered to be shameful and something to be hidden, and when violent arguments among intimates do occur, there is a tendency for them to mount toward higher and more destructive levels, frequently culminating in a physical attack.

It is a tragedy of the contemporary domestic scene that naïveté and fantasy still dominate the relationships of marriage and family life. There is a great resistance to accepting, learning to handle, and even cherishing the inherent differences and using conflict for growth. We believe that the greater the denial and lack of awareness of this aspect of intimacy the greater are the chances for violence. Therefore, all violence-prevention work must begin with the fact of the inevitability of aggression and conflict and then finding appropriate ways of expressing and handling this reality.

# CHAPTER 4

# The "Nice" Psychotherapist

---

*"The tygers of wrath are wiser than the horses of instruction"*

WM. BLAKE, The Marriage of Heaven and Hell, *c. 1793*

During a recent dinner break Dr. Goldberg left his office to get some coffee. The street on which the coffee shop is located is heavily populated by psychotherapists—psychologist's as well as psychiatrist's offices. While seated at the counter, the writer got into a conversation with an attractive, articulate lady of about forty seated directly opposite. When he mentioned that he was a psychologist, the woman responded that she had just come from her psychotherapist's office. She then mentioned rather matter-of-factly that she had been in psychotherapy on and off since she was eighteen years of age. First it was a Freudian analyst, then a Jungian; as she became "more aware of her body," she went to a Reichian orgone therapist, and presently she was seeing an existentialist and spending weekends whenever possible at growth centers such as Esalen. Dr. Goldberg thought about that woman for several days. Was she a health-motivated growth seeker or indeed some kind of victim, engaged in an unreal search for a state of being that doesn't exist, meanwhile having her dependency needs exploited?

The authors thought and talked about this person and other

individuals we know who had been in psychotherapy for five to ten years. We began to realize that possibly the traditional emphasis in the training of psychotherapists on the "total" and "unconditional" acceptance and love of the patient may be primarily for the benefit and comfort of the therapist rather than for the well-being of the patient. That is, the totally accepting orientation toward the patient, we feel, is a highly seductive one, which tends to create an unreal euphoria, a "high" similar to a drug experience, which can "hook" a patient into a long-term, dependency-nurturing and basically destructive relationship.

The unreality exists because most therapists tend to suspend or at least greatly inhibit and limit their own aggressive responses toward the patient during the therapy hour. This orientation is a line of least resistance. It is considerably easier, more "rewarding" and comforting, for the therapist to love and be loved by the client than to generate an atmosphere conducive to mobilizing the patient's aggressiveness in which the therapist stands the risk of incurring the patient's anger, resistance, and possible rejection. However, the openly aggressive interaction, we believe, in many instances might facilitate the patient's growth more rapidly and prevent the kinds of dependency that result in very long, drawn-out therapies.

Recent research studies on psychotherapy have suggested that experienced psychiatrists have *more* difficulty than young intern therapists in dealing with anger directed at themselves from patients. One such study even suggested that therapists tend to avoid patients who openly direct hostility toward them. Therefore, patients motivated for therapy are in a sense forced to suppress or redirect their aggressive feelings lest they alienate and lose their therapists.

This study also suggested that therapists tend to reject their patients for the same behavior the patients have been rejected for prior to entering therapy. That is, people come for psychotherapy partially because there are major distortions in their aggressive flow. Many have been nurtured by mothering figures who were incapable of tolerating aggressive behavior and who forced the child to cloak these emotional reactions to an unusual degree, particularly to deny and inhibit their angry feelings. Consequently, instead of being able to express assertive and angry responses openly, they learned to suppress these feelings and now experience depression, anxiety, fear, and guilt as a result.

The individual who is reared in a healthy mothering climate feels secure enough to hate as well as love his mother. He learns to come to terms with these inconsistencies in his feelings, to feel comfortable with the aggressive feelings as well as the affectionate ones. The emotionally troubled person is usually not capable of this emotional flexibility and becomes very anxious in the face of an open display of anger.

In therapy, therefore, patients need to be encouraged to direct their angry feelings openly and directly against their therapist. They can thereby learn that their therapist can survive these outbursts and that the patient will not be rejected in the process. In a therapy atmosphere where the therapist is all-accepting and all-loving, it becomes difficult, if not impossible, for the patients to express these kinds of feelings without at the same time feeling that they are behaving "inappropriately" or neurotically. In turn, the therapist must feel free to share his anger at the patient without feeling that this is a breach of professional conduct. Therefore, patients also must be re-educated in terms of their expectations of what appropriate professional behavior by a psychotherapist is.

## THE THERAPIST AS A SYMBOL

The aggression-avoidance patterns of many therapy orientations cause them to resemble a form of religion. Traditionally, one enters a church or synagogue with "loving," "caring," "understanding," and other "positive" emotions. The priest or rabbi suppresses "negative" emotions within himself and carefully avoids confrontation or conflict with his following lest he alienate them or be considered unspiritual. The reader is asked to compare this orientation with the following description of the role of the analyst from a book entitled *Psychoanalysis and Dasein Analysis* written by noted Swiss psychoanalyst Dr. Medard Boss in the early 1960s:

> Genuine psychotherapeutic eros, in other words, must be an otherwise never practiced selflessness, self-restraint and reverence before the patient's existence and uniqueness. These qualities must not be shaken or perturbed by uncooperative, indifferent or hostile behavior on the part of the patient. *Psychotherapeutic eros must go beyond even Christian humility in its selflessness, its modesty and its triumph over egotism.* . . . A genuinely mature analyst will be able to analyze his patients in the exemplary way in which a certain hermit of the Himalayas cared for the flowers of his small garden. When praised for the extraordinary beauty of that little piece of ground, he simply remarked that he permitted the flowers to unfold into their full blossoming—not for his own sake and aesthetic pleasure, but only for the delight of his God. Patients with whom an analyst is not capable of relating in this way, to some extent at least, should better be sent to another analyst.[*1]

The orientation Dr. Boss demands in his book, we feel, is an extreme of what is emotionally unauthentic and unattainable. The pressure to behave this way forces the psychotherapist to behave as an image, a symbol, rather than as a real person.

Professional psychological publications that have sought to describe the attributes of an effective psychotherapist invariably stress the so-called "positive," "loving" qualities. These include accurate empathy, unconditional positive regard, self-discipline, concreteness, and genuineness. Dr. Carl Rogers, the well-known psychotherapist and creator of his own form of psychotherapy, was one of the original and major proponents of the philosophy that the therapeutic relationship should stress the total and un-

* Authors' italics.

conditional acceptance of the client. Some professionals in the field of psychology have even gone so far as to suggest that anybody, regardless of their educational and professional training, can function effectively as a psychotherapist if he has these positive qualities.

The "good" client preferred by many psychotherapists is also notable for being nonaggressive. An individual who is resistant, confrontive, or freely aggressive with authority figures, who openly and comfortably challenges rather than simply accepts something as true just because it was spoken by a doctor, and who is not comfortable in a compliant role, would not be considered a prime candidate for psychotherapy.

Psychotherapy is a relatively young science, barely seventy-five years old. It has hardly begun to come to grips with the issues and processes of aggression. Psychonanalysis as developed originally by Sigmund Freud relied heavily upon the distant, passive attitude of the analyst. The ideal analytic patient was described as bright, verbal, financially successful, highly dependable, responsible, and nonrebellious. In the analytic process the analyst assumed an extremely authoritarian role and the patient passively took all the cues from him. The psychoanalyst related to the patient in a basically detached and withdrawn style. Every utterance by the analyst was carefully weighed by him beforehand for its potential impact on the patient. Traditionally, analysts perceived anger on the part of their patients toward them as products of a neurotic transference, and their own anger toward the patient as the product of their unresolved problems.

## THE DISCHARGE OF EMOTIONS

Contemporary psychotherapies such as bioenergetics, Rolfing, and the "primal scream" therapy[2] facilitate an intense emotional discharge, often of an aggressive nature. The patients explode with rage. However, the angry and aggressive discharge, particularly in the "primal scream," is experienced regressively.

The patient is shadow boxing with demons of the past. Our general therapeutic approach, however, is designed to facilitate and teach aggressive expression in the service of the present, within here-and-now relationships rather than as a way of vomiting out the past. Patients who have undergone the more regressive therapies claim to experience profound changes within a relatively short period of time. From what is known about the destructive effect of repressed aggression on the body and the emotions, it is not surprising that these dramatic results are being claimed and attained. However, primarily because these are therapies that focus on the discharge and expression of these strong, angry emotions at nonpresent figures of the past, such as "Mommy" and "Daddy," we would predict that the changes or "cures" would be short-lived and that the symptoms would in most instances return after the patient quit therapy. The reason for this is that the aggressive feelings expressed were not done so on an immediate, personal basis between the therapist and the patient as a part of the normal flow of an interpersonal relationship.

Dr. Alexander Lowen, one of the chief living proponents of the psychotheraphy called bioenergetics, makes the profound point, with which the writers fully concur, that "The expression of affection is *not* to be trusted until the repressed negative feelings have been vented. Until this happens the positive expression is in most cases a defense against the underlying negativity. If it is encouraged, that is, if the emphasis is placed upon the giving and receiving of love, the repressed negativity becomes further entrenched and will appear as resentments at the first dissapointment. Further, the muscular tensions that bind an individual cannot be reduced or eliminated without recourse to the more violent forms of expression. After a violent outburst, the road is open for a tender contact."[3]

Lowen facilitates powerfully aggressive outbursts and the discharge of violent, hostile emotions by having the patients pound on foam mattresses, shouting "No!" and "I won't!" repeatedly until they are able to say it with total body believability while screaming and kicking in protest. Lowen states that "It is the rare person who can easily express negative and hostile feelings. These feelings are severely inhibited early in life, with the result that in adulthood they are manifested only indirectly as stubbornness, spite and sarcasm."[4]

The major reservation the writers have regarding these therapies is the indirect way they seem to deal with the expression of aggression. This is reflected in this description by Lowen of a bioenergetic group experience. "In bioenergetic group therapy these feelings of negation and others of hostility are not directed personally at any group members. The subject is asked to express feelings, not act them out. Of course, it can become personal, but even in this case the action is always directed at the bed. One pounds the bed or beats the bed, never another person."[5] The aggressive expression is being directed at absent figures. Consequently, the patient is not learning to experience and constructively express these feelings on a here-and-now, I-thou basis.

In general, the writers feel that contemporary therapies that facilitate the expression of intense, aggressive emotion must ultimately fall short if the aggressive discharge is directed at nonpresent figures of the past, the discharge of aggressive feelings is seen as part of a "treatment" rather than as part of the normal, interpersonal flow, and the therapist personally sets himself apart rather than allowing himself also to be a real target for these outbursts. The patient is again not learning to experience love and aggression toward the same nurturing figure. Rather, he tends to relate to the therapist as a god to be adored and worshiped.

## FIGHT WITH YOUR THERAPIST

Dr. Bach, the originator of marathon therapy, encourages his patients to express their anger freely toward him, and he in turn has always felt free to express his against the patient. In a recent paper he wrote:

> *I will lose my temper,* sometimes blowing up at the whole group or some particular individual in a near-raging manner. People in the group who did not like this display of angry, "irrational" outbursts on my part have told me off about it in various groups. . . . Peggy, my wife, has observed, often with much group support, "George, you sometimes attack untherapeutically. Sometimes you are just plain mean. You especially blast people you like because you expect more than they deliver. When they fall short of your image of them you get rough. You are also very rough on people whom I know you would like to impress and be loved by. When one of those people does not think you are 'up to snuff' in some situation during a marathon, you get furious with him! Let any one of those people whom you are drawn to confront you with an imperfection and you go into a mouth-foaming fulmination! You can't tell me that's therapeutic, cutting people to ribbons, especially since you yourself can't take it. I think all you 'attack therapists' are long on dishing it out and very short on taking it. That goes for you and your colleagues." Then she named several colleague friends practicing attack therapy.
>
> In defense of myself I reply that I have never seen anyone devastated by me or by the group's attack. I insist that my so-called irrational "rage" is *both* a form of caring about my relation to the other person and of catharsis for my own tension. I feel better after spewing some hostility. The spewed-on has the privilege to spew back at me. It is a great experience for anybody to counterinsult me, and I *can* take it. An occasional, rotten, name-calling spree is just my silly way of having a temper tantrum when people I care about do, say, or think opposite from what I had expected of them! When people occasionally see me in such a ridiculous, rage-olic moment, they are thoroughly impressed forevermore that I am nowhere near godlike!
>
> I take on anyone who tries to hide from encountering me and/or the group. I firmly insist on a confrontation with group members who obfuscate their persons! I am allergic

to people who say, "I don't know," when they are asked to tell us how they feel about the group or about me or about themselves. If *you* don't know *your own* feelings, who the hell do you think will ever know them? Stop playing "I am a mystery." Do not obfuscate! I refuse trying to divine you or guess what makes you tick. *You* have to come forth and own up to your feelings free and clear. At least you must try!

Sometimes, when the group like a wolf pack attacks one single member, I may not join the group. They are doing fine without me. But I would *not* protect an individual from group attack because handling oneself alone in relation to total group pressure is a significant growth experience. I do not wish to spoil this experience for anyone by "protecting" him from an attacking group. Often I let the fighting be done by members vis-à-vis each other without getting into the act. Because I sometimes get tired of fighting I sort of recoup in peace by letting others carry on. I will share my "spectator" feelings about it later on.

As the marathon grows and people become more real and authentic, I can afford to relax my militant attitude and give more of my gentle, supporting side. But we must all first relearn how to fight to regain our genuineness. Only after this are we then ready to share love. In the homestretch of a marathon, there is usually no fighting at all because the wrath did go. . . .[6]

## THE Z-PROCESS

In recent years some other therapies have also worked toward achieving aggressive flow within the therapeutic relationship and with considerable success. Dr. Robert Zaslow has used a technique he calls Z-process with autistic and otherwise disturbed children. In working with these children, Dr. Zaslow initially assumes total control over the child by holding it in a cradle position. If the child is too big, assistants are used to help in holding it. According to Zaslow, since the child acts like a baby, he is being held like a baby. Holding the child in this position incites intense, rageful resistances and hostility toward the therapist. The therapy that ensues, too complex to describe here, releases an enormous amount of this rage and forces the child into a confrontation with his feelings and with the therapist and disrupts the child's usual passive-aggressive "sickness" style of relating. As Z-process therapy progresses, the child's responses move from increasing angry arousal to violent rage and eventually to affectionate attachment and appropriate behavior. Zaslow's therapeutic achievement reinforces our notion that genuine affection is facilitated by the release of repressed aggression. Therapists who work with children and use "love" techniques solely, waste enormous amounts of time, as the child is really incapable of responding to and returning such a response prior to a rage expulsion.

Zaslow cogently points out (and the authors share his perception) that "Most therapeutic systems falter precisely because they fail to develop rational and systematic therapeutic techniques for handling resistances and because they are incapable of handling the full expression of aggression, anger and rage."[7] Indeed, it seems that many therapists are afraid of intense, angry explosions on the part of their patients. Before patients can learn to become comfortable with their aggression, therapists will have to become comfortable with their own and that of their patients when they are the targets of these feelings.

Constructive aggressive interchanges between therapist and patient and among the individual members are facilitated and achieved best we feel within the group therapy medium. That is, the fears individuals have of destroying or being destroyed by rage and the loss of control over these feelings are softened and checked by the presence of other group members. Dr. Bach has pioneered in the use of aggressive confrontation techniques with short- and marathon-length groups. Research with approximately two thousand individuals who have gone through these experiences suggests that according to the the feedback from participants, aggressive confrontation encounters were experienced as the most helpful and change-producing aspects of the experiences.[8]

The aggression formats have also been effectively utilized with married couples, singles, families, schools, and in office situations. The remarkable finding of these aggression-oriented group experiences is the recurring phenomenon of genuine warmth, caring, and intimacy that emerges after the constructive aggression interchanges. These group experiences belie the commonly held notion that the free expression of these "negative" emotions drives people apart. Instead, it confirms the views of the psychologists who recently wrote that "life itself without confrontation can become directionless, passive and impotent."[9] The person who remains unchallenged tends to remain locked within himself.

## THE AGGRESSIVE CONFRONTATION APPROACH

The aggressive confrontation approach in groups brings the therapist and patient into more immediate and real contact with themselves and others. In the group they are challenged to break through discrepancies between what they say and what they do. Confrontation, rather than being irresponsible or self-indulgent behavior by the therapist, is the ultimate way a therapist can take responsibility for providing the patient with an authentic relationship. The therapist thus steps down from the godlike posture and allows himself to be a target for the client.

This aggressive confrontation orientation has been particularly effective with drug addicts, a group with whom traditional psychotherapy has been almost totally ineffective. In a dialogue between Mr. Charles E. Diederich, the guiding spirit and founding father of Synanon and Dr. George Bach, the pros and cons of an approach that has been termed "attack therapy" were discussed.[10] The participants engage in intense, aggressive confrontation that often produces remarkable results.

The late Abraham Maslow, after participating in a mara-

thon attack group, commented, "What I have read about Synanon, as well as what I saw last night and this afternoon, suggests that the whole idea of the fragile teacup which might crack
or break, the idea that you mustn't say a loud word to anybody
because it might traumatize him or hurt him, the idea that people cry easily or crack easily or commit suicide or go crazy if
you shout at them—that maybe these ideas are outdated. . . . I
heard from a friend of mine, who is very much interested in
Synanon, about a drug addict who had been through this kind
of thing and who, for the first time in his life, had experienced
real intimacy, real friendship, real respect. This was his first
experience of honesty and directness, and he felt for the first
time in his life that he could be himself and that people wouldn't
kill him for it."[11]

## THE THERAPIST AS INDIRECT AGGRESSOR

Because the traditional role behavior of the psychotherapist
is so heavily embedded in notions about being loving, caring,
warm, and understanding, and because direct expressions of
aggressive feelings are considered taboo, the psychotherapy relationship lends itself to considerable contamination by indirect,
hidden aggression. For one, therapists go to great lengths to
project the attitude that they are not in almost total control of the
relationship, not in a position of almost total power and not authoritarian figures. And yet even a superficial examination of the
relationship readily reveals that the therapist is in fact heavily
in control and calling most of the shots. This is often done, however, in subtle ways. By his nods, his comments, his gestures,
and his expressions of interest, the therapist steers the interaction into any direction he wishes. We feel it is particularly destructive for a therapist to deny the immense power he has
within the therapeutic relationship.

The aggression that is suppressed takes many alternate
forms. The traditionally withdrawn, nonemotional, and guarded

posture of the psychoanalyst can be interpreted as one such form of indirect aggression. The anxious, unsure patient looks to the analyst for some feedback, cues as to what the analyst is thinking. When the analyst remains poker-faced and says nothing, the patient's anxiety is increased. Often the patient will be inclined to read the analyst's mind and to imagine the worst. "He probably thinks I'm crazy and doesn't want to tell me," is a typical patient fantasy.

The therapy relationship is a very loaded one in a power sense, with the power being almost exclusively in the therapist's hands. If the patient senses hostility, boredom, disinterest, or morbid curiosity coming from the analyst or therapist, the latter can deny it and lay it back on the patient. "You're projecting your own feelings," may be a typical response. Few therapists will openly and directly admit to being bored, angry, disinterested, or voyeuristically motivated while their patients are talking. The resistance of the therapist to sharing these aggressive feelings and responses openly is really more for the benefit and comfort of the therapist than the patient. The patient will probably sense the therapist's boredom through the therapist's nonverbal body and facial cues anyway. The therapist's denial of these feelings will only serve to further hamper and abort the patient's attempt at achieving an emotional interpersonal reality.

## THE THERAPIST IS NOT YOUR SOCIAL FRIEND

Though the therapist communicates a totally accepting manner, the patient knows that this "total acceptance" is contingent on the payment of the fee, and yet this contingency is rarely verbalized or acknowledged to be what it really is. Many therapists seek to create the illusion that the relationship is one of genuine intimacy and love. Undoubtedly genuine affection may be present. However, one does not pay friends for their time, nor is a real friendship confined to a specific hour on a given day. In reality, the therapist is not the client's friend, nor is it likely that he ever will be. It is a professional transaction like any other, contingent on payment of the fee and the therapist's schedule, and should be recognized openly as such by the patient. Any intimation of deep friendship is a travesty of that word and a destructive illusion, which may eventually produce a sense of deep betrayal and bitterness on the part of the patient.

Therapists who speak vaguely of the patient's "deep-rooted" problems which, according to them, may take years to work out, are engaging in a form of hidden aggression known as "mystification." That is, rarely do they inform the patient of precisely what these so-called problems are. Nor do they ever make any promises that if the patient in fact continues to come for "years" that the "problems" will be alleviated. The pronouncement merely has the effect of nurturing a profound anxiety and dependency.

The psychotherapeutic relationship is a loaded one in still another way. The therapist typically only takes responsibility for the patient's improvement and progress, not his failures or resistances. That is, if the patient responds well to the therapeutic process, the good results are attributed to the fine skills of the therapist. If, however, the patient is not improving, the responsibility is placed squarely on him. The patient is told he is resisting change or just isn't "ready."

In 1962 the Group Psychotherapy Association of Southern California organized a conference, chaired by Dr. Bach, on the theme of aggression in therapy. Dr. Carl A. Whitaker, an eminent and innovative psychiatrist, and trainer of psychiatric residents, discussed some of the typical ways by which psychiatrists try to conceal their "hidden hostilities," which they feel but are afraid to express openly.

"Typical of some highly trained professional psychoanalysts is to hide their hostility with what I call 'hot' interpretations where the patient doesn't even understand what we're saying. I am not even sure we do sometimes, we just put one and one together and get four and say to the patient now this is how it is.

Boredom is another one of the most subtle ways of hiding hostility, deep bitter hostility."[12]

## THE THERAPIST AS VICTIM

In many ways the therapist is also a victim of the aggression taboos of our society. The therapist who aggressively confronts may be accused of acting unprofessionally. The typical patient expects the doctor to have a professional demeanor characterized by a controlled, even-tempered, soft-spoken attitude, and most patients would flee from a therapist who was open and confrontive with his feelings.

The patient who is upset by a therapist's confrontations may retaliate in various indirect ways. He may play the part of a helpless victim who has been callously attacked. Or he may begin to act sicker or threaten to quit therapy altogether. The ultimate way of indirectly punishing a therapist is for the patient to attempt suicide, thereby hoping to make the therapist feel guilty or tarnish his reputation. Many therapists therefore avoid being open and direct with their patients for fear of these threats. To release themselves from these binds, the psychological and psychiatric professionals must retrain the patients, by beginning to become real people in the therapy room themselves and refusing to collude with the patients by playing out the image they believe the patient expects.

## SEX BETWEEN THERAPIST AND PATIENT

In recent years considerable attention has been paid to the apparently increasing phenomenon of sex between therapist and patient. Almost exclusively this takes place between a male therapist and a female patient and not vice versa. Some authors, such as Dr. Martin Shepard in his book titled *The Love Treatment: Sexual Intimacy Between Patients and Psychotherapists*, maintain that in some instances sexual intimacy can be a therapeutic part of the relationship.[13] Others, however, have labeled this kind of behavior as rank exploitation and the result of unresolved emotional problems on the part of the doctor. Undoubtedly, the meanings of such a physical involvement are many and complex. On one level, however, this behavior can be seen in terms of its hidden aggression aspects.

A recent professional research paper discussing the personality characteristics of the seductive therapist described him as "withdrawn and introspective, studious, passive, shy . . ."[14] Interestingly enough, in a recent book entitled *Women and Madness* by Dr. Phyllis Chesler, a number of women who had had affairs with their therapists were described as follows: ". . . they all blamed themselves for any 'mistreatment' by men . . . and *they were slow to express anger.*"†[15]

It does not require great psychological sophistication to recognize the covert aggressive aspects of the typical therapist-patient sexual relationship. In general it is one of master-slave; total control (the therapist) and total dependence (the patient). It is invariably the therapist who decides if, when, and where the sexual encounter will occur, how it will be performed, and how often and at what point it will be terminated. Should the encounter turn out to be generally unsatisfactory, it is the patient who is more vulnerable and prone to blame herself. If it is a success it will undoubtedly be attributed to the therapeutic powers of the doctor. Furthermore, the patient is not encouraged to assert her needs directly, and her demands are often not paid attention to. Typically, she is too self-conscious to make her feelings known, for every utterance may be placed under analytic scrutiny. For example, should she express resentment over the extreme limits of the relationship, this protest could be thrown back at her as being a manifestation of her problem. Or, in passive-aggressive style, the therapist might not even acknowledge or respond to this feeling.

In general, all feelings she expresses, despite the intimate

† Authors' italics.

nature of the experience, may be treated objectively as "material" to be explored rather than as a legitimate expression of an I-thou feeling. It is truly a no-win situation for the patient. As Dahlberg pointed out, ". . . it's too easy to sleep with a patient. They come for help and must put their faith in us. They have no alternative. If they hold back too much, there won't be any therapeutic alliance and there won't be any therapy. The cards are all in our hands."[16]

Sex between therapist and patient under the guise of "treatment" for frigidity or other sexual disorders is exploitative, phony, and downright hostile. For one, sexual problems are frequently merely symptoms of underlying identity and self-image problems or expressions of indirect aggression and infantile anxieties. When there is a legitimate basis for symptom treatment, such as when sexual problems are largely the result of early repression and trauma, ethical practice would require treatment on the order of the Masters and Johnson model.[17] That is, the therapist should involve a male who is a part of the patient's love life and could provide an available, involved, and more complete relationship or a trained male surrogate.

The psychotherapist who involves himself sexually under the pretense of treatment would also be ethically bound to carry the treatment out to its successful completion in the interest of the patient's needs. This is rarely if ever the way it happens. Instead, the therapist often suddenly abandons the sexual relationship, or, as in the case of a number of Dr. Chesler's women, abandons the patient totally and stops communicating with her in any way. Invariably, this results in a painfully traumatic experience of abandonment and rejection, reinforcing the patient's already impoverished self-image.

For many women, going to bed with their therapist is experienced as a personal triumph. They have broken through, become "special" in the therapist's eyes and feelings, and have made a conquest, which also has acted as a leveler by removing the therapist from his godlike pose. It is also true that many women who have sex with their therapists have sent out seductive signals. In a sense, they can be seen as using their sexuality in the service of aggression. Sexual involvement with the therapist becomes their way of trying to impact, to gain a foothold of power or control in a relationship in which they feel otherwise unable to assert themselves or make demands directly. Such women when seen intensively over a long period of time in therapy may even become difficult for the therapist to resist. Melissa, one of Dr. Chesler's interviewees, was quoted as saying, "I think that he just finally couldn't resist me any more. I think I just put too much pressure on him. . . . I was making moves from the very beginning. . . ."[18]

There are instances when sex between therapist and patient might be justified. However, the writers feel that this is always contingent upon the signals being openly stated and clear. That is, the therapist should take responsibility for acknowledging his sexual desires and for acting them out for his *own* sake, not the patient's. Any pretension of sex for "treatment" we feel is a sheer travesty unless the therapist is equally willing to help all of his patients who are experiencing sexual difficulties in this way—men and women, young and old alike—and to carry this course of treatment out to its successful completion.

## HOW TO CHOOSE AND EVALUATE YOUR PSYCHOTHERAPIST

A part of the obsession with "nice" in our culture is the manner in which patients often describe their "shrinks." A patient recommending a psychotherapist to a friend will often be heard to describe him as follows: "He's really nice. I know you'll love him. He's supersensitive, gentle, and kind."

This old model of the "nice" therapist is also one who encourages you in cathartic, hostile outbursts against absent figures such as cold fathers, mean mothers, unfair employers or teachers, rejecting spouses, and friends who lack understanding.

This "nice" therapist then sides with you against them, acting as your ally. This invariably succeeds in making you, the patient, feel "understood" and temporarily better, but they do not deal effectively with the key issue of how you can express and mobilize aggressive feelings in the present in interchange with the person sitting with you. Your therapist, to be effective, must soon block the endless hostile ramblings about people who are not present by being real enough so that he facilitates aggressive as well as loving interchanges directly with him in the room.

Beware of the therapist who is always "nice." This ever-kindly, ever-loving therapist is an aggression castrater. By his behavior he makes you feel as if you're guilty, disturbed, or in the throes of a "transference reaction" whenever you feel or wish to express angry feelings directly toward him. There must be something wrong with you if you feel so angry toward someone who loves, understands, and accepts you so totally. Consequently, he will probably join you in a trip back into your personal history to trace the neurotic causes for why you're feeling angry toward him.

In evaluating your therapist in this respect there are a number of questions you might ask yourself:

1. Is your therapist willing to mix it up with you? That is, does he give you critique, indicate openly when he's feeling bored or irritated, share his frustrations, and invite you to do likewise?

2. Is your therapist always loving, kind, accepting, and gentle, and does he treat you with kid gloves? If the answer is basically yes, ask him what he does with his aggressive feelings. Ask him if you're so perfect that he never gets angry, bored, or fustrated with you.

3. Does your therapist play a godlike role by remaining aloof and detached and never revealing his own personal feelings? Ask him why he's afraid to allow himself to be a real

person in the room. Beware of the old-fashioned naïve answer that you as a patient are there for an hour, which is to be spent exclusively discussing your feelings. There is another person in the room who is interacting and experiencing feelings. Why is he afraid to reveal them? Therapy at its best is a relationship between two people reaching for a mutual emotional reality.

4. Are you comfortable getting angry at your therapist? What happens when you do? Does it make you feel guilty or "sick"? Does your therapist suggest that these feelings are exclusively a part of *your* problem, or does he share his own negative feelings honestly and give you encouragement to share yours?

In general, our model of the constructive therapist is one who is not afraid to incur the wrath of his clients, feels free to share his own aggressive feelings, and does not always imply that these interactions are a product of "sickness." In summary, we would like to quote again from Dr. Carl Whitaker, who offered the following meaningful prescription for the constructive use of aggression by the psychotherapist.

Let me list for you some of the things I think of as characteristic of a healthy aggressive assertive therapist. The therapist should fight for his own individuality right in the group: He has the right to be a person. One of the real compliments I enjoy is when I take an individual patient who enters a group and then he comes to me after the first group interview and says, "You know, you were mean as hell up there, you didn't pay any attention to me, in the group you acted like I didn't exist, you didn't introduce me, you didn't tell them anything about me, you're a rat." I think of this as a compliment. If I am going to be in the group I'll tell them ahead of time that I am going to be a person in the group. I am not going to be the Pop and they're not going to be my children. This is a round table. I am not going to be the director of that group either. So the therapist is fighting for his own right to be a person in the group. I think of it as a very healthy kind of aggression. One of the other forms of healthy aggression is battling the patient stereotyping the therapist, and they'll do it in the group. They'll stereotype you as being mature in your real life. You know if the therapist says so, it must be true. He must be loving, real loving to all patients and to everybody on the outside and consistent in having an untroubled life of his own. He can't have any personal problems, his dreams must be just healthy dreams. "Wouldn't it be wonderful to be married to a psychiatrist?" My wife says "just have them talk to me.". . .

Why must we involve our aggressive feelings? Can't we just let the patient experience his own? Isn't our love enough? Isn't our closeness, our tenderness and our warmth and our identification with the patient enough? And then again the Bible talks to us. "Open review is better than secret love," or another time, "He that hideth hatred with smiling lips is a fool!!"[19]

CHAPTER 5

# The "Nice" Crazymakers

Crazymaking is a special and insidious form of indirect aggression that has the impact of slowly destroying another person's emotional health. It is indeed a draining and wearing experience to be intimately involved and dependent on a crazymaker! It is comparable on a physical level with being bounced off walls or even of being a ping-pong ball in motion, in a noncontrollable, nonstop situation. Emotionally it is an experience of being alternately seduced and lulled into a feeling of safety and comfort, being loved but where the supports are always in danger of being pulled out from under and the "love" suddenly becomes a raging hate.

The basic and necessary ingredients in a crazymaking relationship include:

1. Emotional dependency and thus vulnerability on the part of one of those involved.
2. An unequal power balance.
3. An intense core of rage and resentment, rarely felt or expressed in any direct ways by the crazymakers. Its indirect impact, however, is so powerful that it constantly contaminates the interpersonal interactions with unresolvable, destructive, and reality-distorting messages.

4.    A socially traditional relationship, which cloaks these crazymaking interactions behind a mask of good intentions, helpfulness, caring, and love.

Crazymaking interactions can occur between parent and child, husband and wife, employer and employee, and among friends. Of course, the most lethal of such interactions are found within the context of the parent-child relationship, because within this relationship the dependency is the most intense, the vulnerability and power imbalance is greatest, and the child is locked into the relationship with no escape. In crazymaking interactions in employment settings the employer who has the power becomes "Daddy," and the employee relates accordingly in a childlike, dependent way.

The parents in the parent-child crazymaking interaction have a large core of consciously unfelt, unexperienced rage and resentment concerning their parental role and responsibilities. Having been heavily conditioned as to what constitutes being a "good" and "loving" parent, these negative feelings are blocked out of consciousness.

## THE CRAZYMAKING MOTHER

The mother in these crazymaking interactions who is faced with constant responsibility, pressured to be loving and to fill the needs of the totally dependent child, feels resentful and frustrated. Mother herself still has large unsatisfied, childlike needs of her own, and on an underlying level feels deprived, frustrated, and enraged. However, these feelings are not consciously experienced because of the mother's strong conscience and strong sense of guilt, which tell her that "good" mothers do not have these kinds of feelings. Only "bad," "destructive" mothers do. Consequently, this core of frustration, conflict, and resentment is never fully expressed or released and continually contaminates her relationship with her child. The mother oscillates back and forth between guilt-motivated "devotion" and "concern" followed suddenly, almost randomly by outbursts of hostility, rage, morbid preoccupation, the "blues," or intense anxiety, which can be precipitated by almost any deed or reaction of the child.

All of her actions are hidden behind the cloak of good mothering intentions. She always believes that what she does she does out of love and for the good of the child. The sudden unpredictability of her reactions, however, has an increasingly confusing, damaging, and disorienting impact on the child. Almost any behavior on the child's part might provoke either a rage response or a warm one. The child becomes emotionally seasick, and eventually out of emotional self-protection learns to detach, withdraw, and escape from emotional closeness from this kind of capricious motherly behavior.

## THE CRAZYMAKING FATHER

Like the crazymaking mother, the crazymaking father is also consciously trying to fulfill the social expectations of his role. However, his behavior too is in constant conflict with his own underlying pleasure needs, his own hunger to be dependent, taken care of, and paid attention to. When he first fathered his child he was trying to please society, his parents, and his wife. He expected to win love, approval, praise, and confirmation of his masculinity. But now that the reality of being a father exists, he feels frustrated because baby is getting all the love and attention and he is largely being ignored. Not only is the child taking the attention and love of his wife away from him, the child is also an obstacle to his own needs to indulge in impulsive, pleasure-oriented behavior. No longer does he feel free to look at and pursue the attractive women he sees daily, to go out for a drink with his friends, to play at sports, or to pursue his own interests. When he tries to he is gnawed at by guilt feelings, which tell him that he is being a bad father and husband, depriving and betraying his responsibilities to his wife and child. Therefore, he forces himself into dutiful husband and fatherly behavior.

He goes through the motions of being attentive, caring, and loving. He stays at home nightly, he diapers baby, comforts mother, all the while feeling increasingly deprived and starved. The hidden resentment seeps through continually to contaminate his interactions with his family. His behavior follows a pattern of hot and cold inconsistencies. One day he is filled with feelings of sentimental closeness. He caresses baby and expresses love for his wife. This is followed by days of unexplained, extreme detachment, preoccupation, and sullen or explosive outbursts of resentment and annoyance. He becomes too busy to look up from his newspaper or mail, to unglue himself from the television. Or he goes into brooding moods or tantrums over minor matters such as a dirty sink, a missing sock, or a slightly late meal.

## THE CRAZYMAKING EMPLOYER

In the work setting the crazymaking behavior of the employer assumes a slightly different form. On the surface, the crazymaking employer enjoys the social approval that his position of power accords him. However, on an underlying level he resents the pressures and responsibilities of his job. Or he tries to play the role of "nice" boss but is repressing his strong power drives and authoritarian nature. Consequently, the office becomes a nightmare of erratic, unpredictable changes in which he is smiling one day and withdrawn the next, a "nice" guy one time and then making outrageous, unmeetable demands at another time. He confuses and upsets his employees with his vagueness about what he expects of them, or treats them as if they were stupid or helpless children.

On a conscious level these crazymakers, in any setting be it home or work, see their motivations as being pure, altruistic, and concerned. Their repressed aggression, however, emerges in several different ways:

1.  There are gross fluctuations and an unpredictability to their reactions. In very short order and for the seemingly pettiest of reasons they oscillate from expressions of concern, caring, tenderness, and love to critical, rejecting, punitive, and even insulting outbursts.

The crazymaking parent will heap affection, gifts, and attention one day and be withdrawn, rejecting, and sullen when the child approaches him or her the next. The crazymaking employer will encourage casualness, friendliness, and openness one day and then rage the next over the fact that not enough work is getting done.

2.  The crazymaker often makes demands for perfection and production that are so unrealistic that the victim invariably winds up feeling inadequate and that nothing he does is ever really good enough. The child's performance is compared negatively with the performance of other children, or the employee is made to feel that he is incompetent, inadequate, and unable to meet the "simple" demands that have been made.

3.  The crazymaker often develops a worrisome, overly protective attitude in which in the name of love and concern he treats his victim as a child incapable of functioning independently. In the process, he thereby prevents the victim from thriving, growing, and becoming independently productive.

This crazymaking way of relating is an emotionally defensive form of blocking that was originally termed by Freud a reaction formation. In this process of reaction formation the consciously unacceptable feelings of aggression are transformed into their opposites. For example, rage becomes gentleness, a death wish toward another is transformed into great concerns over the person's health and safety. This defense allows the crazymaker to preserve an image of himself as being a benevolent, loving person.

This crazymaking defense will produce in parents a destructive overconcern for their child's welfare. They become so involved protecting him and doing things for him that they prevent him from growing up. They become constantly preoccupied with potential dangers such as kidnapers, automobile accidents, the hazards of the weather, molesters, bad social influences, and the amount of food the child eats. The child is learning to see the world as a terrifying place fraught with dangers. In the name of the child's welfare the parents are destroying their child.

One such mother, whose twenty-three-year-old son was hospitalized for schizophrenia, would visit her son at the hospital and bring him enough food, warm clothing, and medicines to practically take care of his whole ward. She would solicitously ask whether he was getting enough rest, remembering to wear his rubbers in the rain, and taking his vitamins. She was relating to him as if he were still an immature nine-year-old.

The crazymaking employer likewise is fearful of delegating responsibility and authority. In the name of helpfulness he prevents his employees from progressing, and they tend to become increasingly dependent, passive, and stagnant.

One such crazymaking employer, the supervisor of a vocational placement agency, would inquire daily about each employee's health, and often remark about the fact that an employee looked weary. Indirectly, he encouraged only the very minimum possible amounts of productivity. He benefited because he could feel increasingly in control and reduce any sense of competition from the more superior employees.

When crazymaking occurs between adults it usually assumes a different form from that of parent and child. However, the impact and effect are still controlling and sadistic (*not* consciously intended that way) and are also cloaked in socially acceptable coverings. In the work setting a crazymaking employer makes a vague or unrealistic demand on his employee and later attacks him for misunderstanding the instructions. A photographer briefing a model about the clothing needed for an assignment they were to work on together informed her on the telephone that he wanted her to "wear some dumb clothes." She asked him what he meant by "dumb clothes," to which he replied rather impatiently, "Oh, you know, *dumb* clothes," and hung up. She interpreted "dumb clothes" to mean silly, campy-type clothing, and showed up for work the following day accordingly. When he saw what she had on he became livid. When he finally cooled down she discovered that by "dumb clothes" he had meant a plain, simple dress.

On other occasions the employer may encourage independent decision-making and shortly thereafter attack the employee for being "impulsive" or "stupid" for having made a decision incorrectly or differently than the employer would have made it. The crazymaking employer in a benevolent mood will promote an atmosphere of casualness, relaxation, and conviviality and be the "nice" guy, only to explode a few days later because of the lack of respect and discipline he believes prevail, and resentment over the fact that the office is becoming a "social club" and his "niceness" is being taken advantage of. The employee in each of these instances is placed in an either-way-you-lose bind. If he conforms to the employer's demands he is attacked, and if he ignores them he will also be attacked.

Between spouses crazymaking is also a common occurrence, particularly when there are vast differences in the amounts of dependency, vulnerability, or fear of rejection or of abandonment that each experiences. The wife who screams that she knows what her husband is *really* thinking, or cries out "Talk to me! Answer me!" while she is in the middle of a raging attack that makes this an impossible request is engaging in crazymaking. So is the husband who fails to make his desires or expectations clearly known and becomes resentful because his wife did not "divine" or automatically recognize that he needed such-and-such chore done at a certain time and in a certain way.

The crazymaking spouse declares great love and involvement one minute and then turns suddenly cold and distant as his or her partner buys the message of love and reaches out for warmth.

## THE SOCIALLY APPROVED IMAGE

At a deeper level the crazymaker may really want to be an absolute dictator or resents responsibilities, for he or she wants to be taken care of, rather than taking care of others. Crazymaking spouses do not really want the limitations of a marriage, and resent relating in an equal way. However, they are living up to a socially approved image. Consequently, they play the role of loving wife or dutiful husband. However, the underlying, repressed core of anger over this continuously seeps through to contaminate these relationships and unsettle the person with whom they are involved.

This then is another critical aspect of these crazymaking involvements, an indirect consequence of the cultural taboo against openly displaying and enjoying one's power or dependency. We have been conditioned to feel shameful about our strivings to be powerful and to control others, or of allowing ourselves to be passive and dependent. Today even parents often feel guilty regarding their positions of power over their children and therefore feel they must try to relate to their children as adults or equals. The ambitious politician is another illustration of this. He knows he must hide his power appetites behind mouthings about public welfare and benevolent concerns. On the other side of the coin, individuals are conditioned to repress their dependency motivation and their wish to be taken care of. Open displays of these feelings are largely tabooed. Many men feel uncomfortable and become embarrassed if they are doted on or taken care of. Many women today also feel they need to constantly prove their independence.

These cultural taboos in the dimensions of power and dependency create crazymaking interactions. The powerful person acting as a crazymaker goes back and forth from giving off verbal messages of equality and humility, to sudden arbitrariness and a pulling of rank. Likewise, the dependent person protests he needs nothing, and then becomes frustrated and resentful because he is not being properly taken care of. The communications in these instances therefore come out in a confused mixture of love, then hatred or rage.

Crazymaking interactions are particularly difficult to recognize because on the face they often appear as the ultimate in socially acceptable behavior. On the surface crazymakers are concerned, responsible, dedicated, fair, etc. They would undoubtedly be described by neighbors, associates, and friends as conscientious and good people. This is the most insidious aspect of crazymaking behavior. It is lethal aggression cloaked in well-intentioned, socially respectable behavior and is therefore almost impossible to recognize and even more difficult to confront and block. The damage is all done through subtle bindings and manipulations in the name of concern, caring, and good intentions.

Crazymaking relationships are particularly difficult to root out or change because victims tend to collude with their crazymakers. Persons can drive themselves crazy through excessive isolation. However, one cannot drive another crazy without the full cooperation of the victim, albeit this cooperation is largely unwitting and unconscious. Even though crazymaking ultimately proves very destructive to its victims, causing extreme detachment, instability, overdependency, chronic anxiety, and even breakdown, the victim's poor self-image and deep feelings of inadequacy tend to cause him to cling to the crazymaking relationship and to view it as a critical, life-sustaining involvement. Such a relationship of hate disguised by love is all the victim feels he is worth. For example, young people in mental hospitals often protest vigorously that their parents were loving and good and had nothing to do with their craziness. Those involved with crazymaking employers frequently reassure themselves about how benevolent and loving the employer really is in spite of the few minor "faults." The victims have learned to be frightened and overwhelmed by the "cruel, evil world" outside, and the crazymaking relationship, destructive as it is, seems safer and more secure than the uncertainties of the "real" world out there. It is comparable to the situation in which recently released prisoners commit still more crimes so that they can be returned to prison where they have experienced at least some safety, security, and recognition, or of mental hospital patients who are greatly improved and then regress into crazy behaviors as the time for their discharge approaches.

A long-term relationship with a crazymaker is an exhausting one, physically and emotionally. As opposed to an aggression-healthy involvement that revitalizes, the crazy-making interaction is one of chronic oscillations, unpredictability, manipulativeness, confusing messages, and bindings. The only way out for the victim may be a total emotional breakdown, physical illness, or a violent outburst. Even in short encounters with crazymakers, one may find oneself wishing to run away, feeling fatigued, reaching for cigarettes or alcohol, becoming headachy or escaping into sleep. These reactions are indications of a subliminal awareness of the poisonous, contaminated communications of the "nice" crazymakers.

PART TWO

# The Not So "Nice" Society

# CHAPTER 6

# The Terrorizable Society

---

This book was born of outrage and anger. These feelings are our response toward a socio-emotional climate in which it has become increasingly dangerous to casually engage in everyday activities or partake of simple pleasures. A walk in the park or through the streets; leaving one's home or apartment empty during a weekend outing or vacation; spending a night making love or sleeping outdoors at the beach; taking an airplane trip; picking up a hitchhiker in a spirit of friendliness; going out alone in the evening; leaving one's belongings momentarily unattended in a public place; wearing one's prized jewelry; and children going trick or treating on Halloween are but a small number of routine personal pleasures that can no longer be enjoyed without carefully premeditated self-protection. The sensible citizen has learned to always be careful and take precautions.

Evidence of a growing distrust and fear of one's environment can be seen everywhere. The Hilliard family, for example, lives in a large apartment in New York City. Their front door has three locks on it plus a chain. In the middle of the door is a peephole. No one enters without first being looked over. A German shepherd trained to attack strangers barks viciously at any unusual sounds. The Hilliards never leave their place without turning the radio and lights on so that others will think that they're really at home. When they decide to go away for a weekend, they give their superintendent extra money to keep a special eye on their apartment. Their two sons, age twelve and fourteen, though long-haired, bearded, and "love oriented," have been taught to never talk to strangers and to always carry at least five dollars on them when they go out in order to pacify potential muggers. Mr. Hilliard and his two sons all take classes in self-defense, not for pleasure or exercise, but for protection.

## IS IT PARANOID TO BE "PARANOID"?

The Hilliards are not atypical. City dwellers everywhere are putting unattractive metal bars in front of their windows and peering out at the world through a front-door peephole. Burglar alarm systems and trained attack watchdogs are being sold at premium prices and in all-time high volumes. Police are encouraging and educating people to mark each of their belongings with a hidden identification mark so that they might get them back from a pawn shop after a burglary. Karate and other martial arts of the Orient have become increasingly popular in the past ten years. These forms of self-defense have gone from relative obscurity in the Western world to becoming household words.

This prevailing "paranoid" climate may in fact not really be paranoid at all. Paranoia, in the psychiatric sense, is a condition characterized by a gross distortion of reality. The fear of others today has a considerable basis in reality. Over one hundred million guns are privately owned in the United States, and over half of American homes have at least one gun. The rate of gun homicides in America is over two hundred times that of most other large countries. For example, in Tokyo, the world's most heavily populated city, there were only three gun homicides in 1970. In that same year, New York City, with only three fourths the population, recorded the killing of over five hundred people by gunfire.

In American cities murder, particularly of one person, has become so commonplace and impersonal an event that it rarely draws our interest or attention unless the victim is a person of renown. Today attention seems to be paid primarily to the mass killings in which a number of people or a whole family are killed.

Mary Warner, a mother of three children and in her late thirties, was referred for psychotherapy. She was a slightly over-weight, attractive woman who looked very much harassed. She described herself as a "nervous wreck." She spoke of a child-hood in which she had always been trusting, confident, and fearlessly independent. Now she said she was becoming increas-ingly "scared of everything," as she put it. "I really don't trust anybody. I'm always checking windows and clinging to my hus-band. I'm afraid to walk our dog in the evenings. Everybody around me seems so cold and inhuman."

If a person living in any major city—Los Angeles, Chicago, St. Louis, New York, Dallas, or any other, were to come to a psychologist or psychiatrist with these kinds of bothersome feel-ings of chronic anxiousness, suspiciousness of others, fear of the environment, and a sense that people might harm them, the re-sponsible psychotherapist would have to be cautious before mak-ing an evaluation. That is, he would first have to clearly deline-ate how much of these feelings were, in fact, normal responses to the traumatic realities of our society, rather than being symp-toms of emotional problems.

Indeed, the "paranoid" attitude toward one's environment may be becoming the normal, reality-oriented one. Openness and trust are increasingly being seen as naïve, childlike, and even self-destructive ways of responding. They result all too often in hurt and disappointment. It is not surprising that cyni-cism, playing it "cool," and being detached and distant have become viable, even admired ways of responding to situations and people. Contrary to the lip service often paid to the value and joys of honesty and open communication, the successful, sophisticated person in our society is usually the one who has learned to play the cards close to his chest, disguising his real feelings and motivations and responding to others with an attitude of guardedness and cautious involvement.

## OUR PURITANICAL, NAÏVE ATTITUDES

A diatribe on the socio-emotional climate of this country is, however, really *not* our purpose in this book. Nor is this state of affairs even our major preoccupation and focus of anger. Rather, our anger is directed at the incredible fact that even the rampant violence and the atmosphere of distrust and alienation in our society have not transformed our puritanical, moralistic, naïve attitudes toward the phenomenon of aggression. Aggression expressed openly on a personal level, such as in the free expression of anger, the frank admission of resentment, and honest confrontation are all still considered behaviors that are at best embarrassing, in poor taste, or impolite. Most typically they are considered rude, inappropriate, unacceptable, and even "crazy."

At parties, social events, or any gathering of people, these aggressive displays will almost certainly result in social ostracization. Only "friendly," "nice," "polite," and "interested" conversation is considered to be appropriate and acceptable. Small wonder that so many people are increasingly finding social gatherings and parties boring, phony, and hard to endure. The important dimension of aggressive human interaction is taboo, making other social interactions routine, predictable, and emotionally barren and unreal. Consequently participants at these affairs invariably numb themselves with alcohol and food.

The kinds of individuals who are popular and well liked in this society, and the phrases commonly used to describe them, are very reflective of the prevailing conscious dislike and dread of personally aggressive openness.

1. "She doesn't have an angry bone in her body."
2. "He wouldn't hurt a fly."
3. "He's gentle as a lamb."
4. "They're a beautiful couple. They never argue or fight."
5. "He's really sweet. He'll do anything for you."
6. "She doesn't have a bad word to say about anyone."

In all of these instances the qualities that are praised and admired are those of nonaggressiveness.

## AGGRESSION OUTLETS

Many of the institutions in our society have assumed the role of providing outlets for repressed aggressive energies. Politicians provide outlets for righteous aggression by targeting "enemies"; entertainment media program violent fantasies on film, in television series, books, and even as part of many teenage rock concerts. Professional sports that can provide the most brutal action seem to become the most popular. Newspapers that focus on body counts in war or traffic accidents or who headline brutal murders guarantee themselves huge sales. This successful exploitation of impersonal and anonymous aggression outlets is possible, we believe, primarily because personal outlets in the course of daily living in our society are taboo. We live in a time of intense and insane social violence on the one hand, and taboos against the expression of even the simplest emotions of personal aggression on the other.

This ethic has created a peculiar double standard that says that its all right to enjoy cruelty and viciousness in anonymous, vicarious ways, but that any personal expressions of face-to-face anger are "bad."

The history of man is replete with mechanisms and attempts to control aggression. People have tried to pray it away, wish it away, or play it away. More recently they have tried to psychoanalyze it away and meditate it away. Others still try to drink or drug it away. *But it does not seem to go away!* All we end up doing is giving it away to social exploitation. The increase of violence and brutality in our society is evidence that the traditional approaches to the channeling of aggression have not been sufficiently successful; the authors feel a new ethic for aggression is needed.

## A DEFINITION OF AGGRESSION

Aggression and its various expressions are a source of great fear. To most people aggressiveness is synonymous with unprovoked, senseless, and hurtful hostility. This horrific definition of the term, which we believe is a distortion of a potentially constructive process, has embedded itself rather firmly in the consciousness of most people.

In this book the term "aggression" will refer to a whole gamut of behaviors. Our definition includes behaviors such as the direct I-thou verbal expressions of anger, resentment, and rage; self-assertion; open, leveling confrontations, the active reaching out to situations and people rather than approaching them passively; conflict expression and exploration; open manifestation of personal power strivings; identity protection; negative self-assertiveness, i.e., learning to say "No" with the same comfort and directness with which one has learned to say "Yes"; and nonhurtful physical expressions. Aggressive energy, as we see it, can add a vital dimension to the process of living. That is, it can, when expressed constructively, intensify the depth and authenticity of personal and interpersonal relationships and experiences.

Tragically, traditional ethics have prevented the open expression and even enjoyment of such personal aggression. The repression of aggression begins with the parental admonitions not to raise one's voice, talk back, argue, yell, or rebel. When aggressive communication is blocked and inhibited in relationships, whether they be transient or intimate, individuals enter into a reality-distorting, dishonest contract with each other. What they are saying in effect is, "You pretend these feelings and impulses don't exist in me and I'll pretend that they don't exist in you." This mutual, largely unconscious hypocrisy then destroys much of the capacity to define or control this large reality in oneself and to recognize it in others. It is the critical beginnings that make individuals and societies "terrorizable"—that is, because of the fear of confrontation and other aggressive encounters, we believe that people severely impair their capacity to discriminate between the real and unreal dangers of our society. Manipulators can hide their intent behind a smile, a flattering comment, or a friendly manner, comfortably certain that they will not be challenged or unmasked. This inability to gauge the aggressive potential in others makes individuals vulnerable to being "shocked" and "surprised" when that "nice," "quiet," "helpful" boy or girl down the street is revealed to be a cold-blooded criminal. Most disturbing and personally harmful is the large element of fragility and tenuousness that the repression of aggression adds to even our closest relationships. People find these relationships suddenly going from intense intimacy to total estrangement. This is a common experience in our society. Father finds himself a noncommunicating stranger to his son. Sister turns on sister. Co-workers who liked each other yesterday, suddenly can't look at each other today, because one of them said something "wrong," and husbands and wives of years' standing suddenly become mortal enemies "because of" a petty crisis.

Aggressive feelings that have been blocked from conscious expression within the normal flow of the relationship suddenly emerge in indirect, intense, and uncontrollable forms. The presumed "harmonious" relationship suddenly turns sour as accumulated, hidden resentments and hostilities come pouring through.

The repression of aggression also produces an atmosphere of alienation, which we believe is really in part a form of insulation against one's own aggressive expression and the aggressive expression of others. Many social scientists have attributed alienation to the pace of technology, the sickness of society, or the competitive nature of capitalism. However, a major overlooked root cause is the fear of and inability to genuinely and constructively encounter and relate to each other as the aggressive beings humans are.

Over the years the authors have noted the existence of three distinct coping styles used to avoid direct aggressive encounters. The most prevalent style is the seeking of one's solace and primary satisfactions from the impersonal, material products of our society. This is done by getting stoned or drunk, watching television for hours on end, plugging oneself into the stereo, or hiding inside one's automobile. The second style of coping and avoiding is one of total cynicism in relation to people. People become objects, things to be used for an immediate gratification and then discarded when their utility has been drained. This is a way of viewing others on the basis of the momentary "services" they can provide. The third style is that of wearing a mask of despair. Human beings are perceived as despicable creatures and life as ugly and depressing. This "giving up" attitude ends in negativism, emotional breakdown, or suicide.

A new understanding and way of perceiving and coping with aggression is needed or an even crueler, more alienated style of being than that which exists today will emerge. First, the destructive aspects of repressing personal aggression must be recognized and a new ethic developed to replace the unreal, humanly impossible ones we have set up as our goals in the past. This new ethic must do more than simply free aggression. It must provide guidelines, techniques, and an orientation and basis for understanding and controlling this phenomenon. Then it must also sensitize and educate individuals to the many hidden and indirect manifestations of aggression people exhibit and are victims of daily. For example, many schizophrenic children have been nurtured by seemingly "ideal" mothers. Research shows that these mothers are totally unaware of their aggressiveness and destructiveness. They are mothers who experience their motives and feelings as being pure and loving. Nowhere in their conscious awareness is the rage and resentment that is destroying the child. An awareness of the many shapes and faces of indirect aggression that inevitably must emerge from all who are a part of this aggression-repressive society is critical as a protection against the kinds of destructive hostilities and perversions of aggression that are rampant today.

## AN AGGRESSION TRAINING PROGRAM

The authors, through their practice of psychotherapy, have developed a theoretical framework along with a concrete aggression training program. This program is designed to serve as a stepping-stone toward the evolution of a realistic ethic of aggression. Our view of aggression on which the ethic discussed in this book is based is that the so-called "beast" of aggression can be tamed and its energies used for the good of the individual and society. We believe that the traditional fears of aggression have been based on a perverted and distorted form of this potentially constructive source of human energy.

The past ten years have already seen the emergence of dramatic new forms of psychotherapy that can produce deeply rooted changes of behavior through the constructive release of aggressive energies. These are changes that could previously not have been brought about. Still more exciting is the discovery that the open sharing of aggressive feelings—anger in particular —can be effectively utilized for individual growth and profound, intimate bonding between people. Individuals in our aggression training programs learning to express these feelings constructively within their family milieu or work settings find themselves rising to exciting levels of personal growth. They have also found that these feelings can be expressed without guilt, without excessive hurt, and with much genuine warmth and humanness.

The interpersonally aggression-repressing society is the terrorizable society. The aggression that is prohibited from surfacing in open, personal ways, we believe, eventually creates a perverse attraction for and indirect or direct encouragement of extremely violent forms of behavior, either in the street, on the battlefields, at home, or vicariously through our entertainment media. The repressed aggressive energy searches for displacement targets in the form of scapegoats, stereotypes, and politically approved enemies. A paranoid climate emerges as the aggression that is blocked within each of us individually is projected onto and seen as existing in others, who then become more fearsome than they really are. Our personal lives and relationships also become vulnerable as we are not able to gauge or control our impact nor accurately read the emotional messages of others.

Traditionally, the two major sources of repression in Western man and the primary sources of emotional and interpersonal problems have been repressed sexuality and repressed aggression. Sexual enlightenment, the undoing of its repression, is now well under way. The remaining psychological frontier is the area of aggression. Attempts at liberation of this energy will undoubtedly meet greater resistance than that experienced by the sexual revolution. Aggression has acquired an aura of pain, while sexuality has an aura of pleasure.

The choice that confronts society, however, is clear. Either people begin to accept the risks involved in recognizing and experiencing the aggression within them and learn to utilize its energy constructively, or they continue to deny its existence and give over the responsibility for finding socially approved and acceptable outlets and enemy targets to others and find themselves increasingly more in a terrorizable and paranoid climate.

# CHAPTER 7

# The "Nice" Killers

---

*"People spend too much time looking at the moon and not
enough making love."*

CHARLES MANSON (quoted in *Life*
magazine, December 19, 1969)

The personalities of many of the most highly publicized mass
murderers of the past decade have typically been described in
very positive terms by those who knew them personally. Some of
the descriptive phrases used by their friends and neighbors were
"all-American boy," "a quiet, peaceful man," "the class favorite," "an exemplary father," "a fine Christian," "well-mannered
and sensitive," and "respectful of elders."

During the preparation for this chapter the authors combed
through numerous reports and interviews with the people who
were acquainted with these mass murderers. It was very rare indeed to find that a friend or family member of the killer indicated
they suspected that a violent act would occur or that they sensed
the person was troubled and that something of this nature was
even a possibility. Instead, they invariably expressed shock and
amazement over the event. Some were convinced that the police
had the wrong man. Others searched for a cause in the killer's
recent life to rationalize that "something had gone wrong," to
prove that "the behavior was totally out of character" and that
the killer was "not himself" at the time that he had committed

the crime. Specifically, it was remarkable how often friends and intimates of the killers made an equation between "quiet" or "polite" behavior and harmlessness. It was as if their notion of what killers and killing was all about had come from the old-time Hollywood movies in which the killers were portrayed as "bad guys"—surly, overtly hostile, foul-mouthed bully types.

The prevalent fixation on this stereotype of violent people and violent behavior may stem from the fact that it is a safe and comfortable one to hold on to. It allows individuals to maintain the reassuring belief that killer personalities are a distinct breed who are different from everybody else and are recognizable because they are obviously hostile, aggressive "mad dogs." Evidence garnered from our study and psychological research suggests that more often than not the exact opposite is true. For example, research psychologist Dr. Edwin I. Megargee, who has studied this kind of behavior intensively, reported that "In case after case the extremely assaultive offender proves to be a rather passive person with no previous history of aggression."[1] He further described these violent individuals as people who have powerful inhibitions against *any* expression of aggression and who rarely ever showed anger no matter how intense the provocation. Instead they buried their resentment beneath rigid controls. Our own evidence suggests that not only were the mass murderers "civilized" in their behavior, they were indeed often the very model of our cherished stereotype of a "nice," "well-socialized" person. They were polite, quiet, sensitive, and outwardly gentle.

It is interesting indeed that the bulk of the population who were personally unfamiliar with the killers and who only knew of them by reading newspapers or watching television reports had the opposite reactions to those people who knew the killers personally. To the former the killers were in fact "mad dogs," horribly infected beasts who had to be put to death or isolated in prison for a lifetime to insure the safety and protection of the public. In the minds of these people the killers automatically became objects of revulsion, symbols to hate, and nonpeople. Neither those who knew the killers personally nor those who didn't could see the killer as a total person. Those who knew them personally bought the outward, superficial image the killer presented. Those who didn't could only see the violence but could not see the humanness and personality characteristics the killer shared in common with other people. For indeed, these killers were only more extreme versions of the prevailing ethic that requires the suppression of aggressive feelings. They were self-controlled and repressed in their expression of these feelings like the rest of us, only more so. Then finally one day the boiling kettle overflowed and destructive behavior occurred. Contrary to popular notion, however, the eruption of violence was not an unpremeditated, impulsive, "out of character" behavior. As Dr. Megargee has indicated and our clinical evidence also shows, these "quiet, retiring" people had a history of being preoccupied with violence in fantasy.

### DUANE POPE: MURDER IN THE BANK

"A representative of the worth and dignity of the American small college and the American small town."

It was the morning of June 4, 1967, when a green Chevrolet pulled up near the Farmers State Bank in Big Springs, Nebraska. The man who stepped out was well dressed in a dark suit, white shirt, and striped tie. The police chief, who didn't recognize this stranger, imagined him to be a bank examiner because he was well dressed and carried a small briefcase.

Duane Pope walked over to the bank president's desk and inquired about a farm loan. When informed that the bank didn't make farm loans, Duane took a gun from his case and calmly pointed it at the banker. The tellers began to empty their cash drawers of $1,598, and dropped the money into Pope's brief-case.

Pope then motioned everyone to lie down on the floor on their stomachs. Then with a .22 Sturm-Ruger gun equipped with a silencer, he shot Andy Kjeldgaard, the seventy-seven-year-old millionaire bank president; Frank Kjeldgaard, his twenty-five-year-old nephew; Mrs. Lois Ann Hothan, a thirty-five-year-old widow with two sons; and Glenn Hendrickson, fifty-nine, a cashier. He shot them each twice, once in the neck and once in the back, to get to the heart. Three died instantly, and Frank Kjeldgaard managed to survive because the bullet narrowly missed his heart. Duane Pope took the money, walked to the door, and politely said "Good morning!" to a wheat farmer coming in. Within thirty-six hours of the shooting, the FBI knew who the killer was. He was a shy, smiling farm boy who had been graduated from McPherson College in Kansas only five days before.

The people from his hometown were incredulous. They all remembered Duane as an amiable, quiet young man who had worked his way through college on a scholarship by sweeping classrooms and hauling trash. He had been cocaptain of the football team in his senior year and "apparently, he had no problems at all." Duane Pope was someone who the college and community looked up to as "a representative of the worth and dignity of the American small college and the American small town."

Duane's cocaptain and roommate for 3½ years said, "They got the wrong Pope. There are lots of Popes in Kansas and they got the wrong one." Nick, his roommate, remembered how he and Duane had been studying one night when a spider started to crawl across the floor. Nick had yelled, "Kill him, Duane, he's coming your way." "Nah," Duane had answered, "I don't want to." "And the damn bug crawled right under him. Duane just didn't like killing nothing. He used to stand in the middle of the dorm and swat flies with his 'M'-club paddle, but he only liked to stun them. He didn't like to kill them."

Duane was the fourth of eight children. If he stood apart in his younger days it was only because he was better behaved than most farm boys. His eighth-grade teacher recalled, "There were some fiery mean ones, reaching to make war on the others. But not Duane Pope. He was one of the best."

His high school yearbook listed him as senior class president and a student council member. He was photographed as the basketball captain with the pretty, formally gowned "Homecoming Queen" on his arm. "You want to know what they thought of Duane in Roxbury?" his former roommate asked. "They looked at him and said, 'I hope my kids are like him.'"

His roommate was the only one who knew that Duane could even feel anger. At college Duane hid frustrations behind his smiling, farm boy mask. He wasn't capable of anything else. His roommate recalled, "He never rebelled against anything or anyone."

Duane was also a moralist in college. He wouldn't sample his roommate's homemade Italian wine that they sneaked onto campus. He would turn to the wall to undress and insisted on wrapping a big towel around himself rather than walk naked in his room.

The night after the murders Duane sat in a Salina nightclub against the bar and bragged to the owner that he was a singer with a rodeo. He then sang "Harvest Moon" and danced with a bargirl. When someone mentioned this later to Sid Smith, his football coach, the coach said, "Duane sing and dance? Lord, no! Don't tell me any more. The more I hear, the more confused I become."

His defense claimed temporary insanity. The U.S. district attorney scoffed at that. "The boy is calm, cool, deliberated, poised. He knew everything that was said and he looked me right in the eye. No, those weren't murders at Big Springs. Those were executions."[2]

## CHARLES WHITMAN: SNIPER ON THE TEXAS TOWER

"A real, all-American boy."

Charles Whitman was an Eagle Scout at age twelve. He had also been an altar boy, a pitcher on the church-school baseball team, and a newsboy with the biggest route in town. A neighbor recalled, "Why, Charlie, he was a nice little boy. And he made a handsome man . . . tall, broad-shouldered, and crewcut."

As he grew older, Charles was a Marine and an architectural engineering student who married the Queen of the Fair at Needville, Texas. He also became a Scoutmaster. The father of one of his charges recalled, "Why, I remember last summer [one year before the killings] when he had to go away, my son cried because Charlie wouldn't be around."

The summer of 1966, Charles Whitman stepped out onto the observation deck of the twenty-seven-story limestone tower at the University of Texas campus at Austin. He had already killed his wife and his mother. He peered through the sights of his .30-caliber semi-automatic carbine and fired. He fired again and again and again. In the end, not including his mother and his wife, there were fourteen more dead and thirty wounded.

When Whitman was brought down from the tower dead, his friends were incredulous. A slight, thoughtful boy named Gary Boyd, who had shared classes with Whitman, described Whitman as "A real, all-American boy," big, strong, handsome, neat, hard-working, pleasant to be around, and interesting to talk with. He had made straight A's the previous fall, and in the spring his average was B. He enjoyed civic work, graciously helped fellow students with their studying, admired his professors, and had no enemies."

Even his psychiatrist at the university, whom Whitman had gone to see at the urging of his wife because he had become violent toward her on several occasions, was reported in *Newsweek* magazine (August 15, 1966) to have said that Whitman seemed to be an "all-American boy." The psychiatrist, who recognized that Whitman was "oozing with hostility" because of some of Whitman's reported fantasies, had not become too concerned when Whitman told him four months prior to the killings that he kept thinking about going up on the tower with a deer rifle and shooting people. According to the doctor, it was a fairly common fantasy among the students on that campus.

Even his father, whom Charles had openly acknowledged to intimates that he hated "with a mortal passion," could not recognize the anger Charles had for him. His father was quoted as saying, "Charlie hate me? Why, I was speaking to him no more than two weeks ago and that boy told me, 'Daddy, I love you.'"

Charles Whitman hid himself behind a sunny face of good nature and warmth. Scores of people were fond of him, and when Charles was brought down from the tower dead, a friend remarked, "That's not the Charlie Whitman I knew. When he got up there he was somebody else."[3]

## MARK JAMES ROBERT ESSEX: TERROR IN NEW ORLEANS

"A nice, quiet boy."

His seventeen-year-old girlfriend, Lydia, remarked, "I'd just say it's not him. He's too nice, sweet, and kind. If I had seen it happen, I wouldn't believe it."

And yet Essex had kept the city terrorized for hours on top of the Howard Johnson Motel. Before his body was finally riddled with bullets, there were at least six dead and nine wounded. Seven among these fifteen were policemen. And Essex was linked to two other police murders that had taken place at the beginning of the year.

Some attributed the killings to his hatred of whites. However, others who were close to him never knew of this anger. His girlfriend said, "He never said nothin' about that. Seemed like he was for everybody. He never said nothin' against the white, or for the colored." A drinking buddy, Henry Day, said Essex "was just a regular dude on the corner. Nothin' political ever came up when we rapped."

Essex, a twenty-three-year-old Navy veteran, was working as a trainee in a federal- and state-financed job training program, learning vending machine repair at the time. The director of the project said, "Essex was probably the best student in the class." Both his instructors and fellow students described him as "a very mild-mannered man." He didn't fraternize much with the other students, however. At lunchtime he would sit by himself, studying his course work.

The residents of his hometown in Emporia, Kansas, described him as "a nice, quiet boy," "the average American kid," "the type of guy who didn't deal with dope or nothing like that," "a good Christian boy," "a boy like all the others."

The Reverend W. A. Chambers had felt that the Navy had caused a change in him but eulogized Essex, saying, "I'm satisfied that Jimmy knew Jesus. He not only talked it, he lived it as long as he was in this church."

Most significant was the comment from his girlfriend. "Sometimes you could be talking to him and he wouldn't listen and would have to ask you again what you'd said. He was so-o-o-o quiet. I used to say, 'James, say something.' He'd just look at me with a smile on his face and say, 'What is there to say?' "[4]

## JUAN CORONA: YUBA CITY MURDERS

"An exemplary father and a fine Christian."

Juan Corona was a taciturn farm labor contractor. His commitment to the Church was obsessive. He said the rosary every night with his family. He went to Mass three times a week and had recently won a trophy for float decoration at the annual Our Lady of Guadalupe parade. Married and the father of four daughters, he was an active member of a group called the Cursilistas, who were trying to revive religion among the Chicanos.

In January 1973 he was convicted of having slaughtered at least twenty-five men. The faces and chests of these itinerant farm workers, whom Corona had recruited from among skid row winos of Yuba City, had been hacked with a heavy, knifelike machete. In his labor camp and his 1971 Chevrolet van, police had found an arsenal consisting of two hunting knives, two butcher knives, a double-bladed ax, a club with bloodstains, pistol shells, and a machete. The killings were not those of a man gone berserk. The laborers had been systematically killed over a two-month period.

The Reverend Joseph Bishop of St. Isidore's Church, who said he had known Juan Corona for six years, called him an "exemplary father and a fine Christian." His wife, Glorida, said, "He was always a good husband. He treated us right, without violence. Such a good husband and father could never have done such a thing." His brother testified, "He reads the Bible and writes all the time."

Juan Corona would go to his brother's bar at night and never drink. "He would just sit silently and look at the rest of us," his brother testified.[5]

## CHARLES "TEX" WATSON: MANSON'S EXECUTIONER

"His mother's 'pride and joy.'"

Charles Watson was convicted as the major killer in the Tate murder case. According to the testimony, he announced himself as "I'm the devil. I'm here to kill," and kill he did. He

shot Steve Parent, eighteen, the friend of the property's care-
taker. He stabbed Sharon Tate while she was screaming, "Please
let me have the baby." He shot Thomas John (Jay) Sebring,
and after ordering Susan Atkins to stab Wojcieck Frykowski,
Watson hit him over the head with a gun butt, shot and stabbed
him, and then kicked the dying Frykowski in the head.

Photographs of the babyfaced Watson taken at his high
school in Farmersville, Texas, reflected an all-American boy,
a big, good-looking kid who starred in football, basketball, and
track. "Tex" got all A's and B's in school. He was a regular
churchgoer at the Methodist Church near his brother's little gro-
cery store and sometimes led services from the pulpit for the
preacher.

At the school he had been "popular all-everything." He was
the sports editor of his high school newspaper. He had been
voted the class favorite. He belonged to the Spanish Club, was
a yell leader, had a part in the senior play, won a prize for
playwriting, was an honor student, and was a member of the
4-H Club, the Future Farmers of America, and the Boy Scouts.

His mother talked of him as her "pride and joy," and related the time in August when he called her and happily told
her how he had met a "Jesus named Manson."[6]

## LEO HELD: PENNSYLVANIA'S KILLER OF SIX

"A quiet, peaceful man, devoted to his family."

It was October 23, 1967, in the town of Lock Haven, Penn-
sylvania. Mr. Leo Held, the father of four children, active in
the Boy Scout movement, terrorized two communities with a
ninety-minute shooting rampage during which he killed six people and wounded six others before he was shot down in a gun
battle in the backyard of his home.

He had reported to work on that Monday morning at the
Hammermill Paper Company. He suddenly opened up with two
revolvers, and his victims "thought he was joking until they saw

him shooting." Even after Held had killed a number of coworkers, including a female member of a car pool he belonged to, he went home and replenished his ammunition by breaking into his neighbor's gun cabinet while he was there. In the process, he killed his twenty-seven-year-old neighbor, Floyd Quiggle, while Quiggle was alseep.

Held's relatives, friends, neighbors, and coworkers were shocked. They could offer no explanation for Held's behavior. His brother-in-law, Harold M. Brungard, a bank executive, described Held as "a quiet, peaceful man, devoted to his family." The Reverend Stephen McKittrick, who had worked actively with Held in the Boy Scout movement, said, "I have no personal evidence other than that he was a level-headed, upright citizen with no more problems than the rest of us. He is a good family man."[7]

## THE LESSONS TO BE LEARNED

There is much to be learned about our culture's attitudes toward aggression, and awareness of violence from these case histories. Indeed, the murderers described are but a small handful of similar personalities written about daily who have "surprised" their families and friends by exploding into violence. In a technologically sophisticated society the common reaction of "shock" that intimates and friends express is an upsetting reflection of a profound naïveté about the nature of aggression in most people. Because society cherishes a fantasy of the aggressionless man and chooses to believe that anger and hostilities don't exist unless they appear in obvious, outward behavior, individuals are bound to be repeatedly surprised, as the intimates of the mass murderers were. People seem to be all too willing to buy external trappings of socialized behavior as reflective of the reality of inner feelings.

Although we are not trying to make an equation between "nice" behavior and violent potential, we wish to destroy the stereotype that causes "nice" behavior to be bought as being emotionally authentic and desirable. Not only is being "nice" no insurance against the triggering of violent behavior, it is perhaps the worst kind of behavior that a society trying to deal with the problems of violence can reinforce. For example, the "nice" killer successfully feeds on the prevailing taboos and anxieties regarding overt and personal expressions of anger and the unreal notion stemming from this, which equates harmlessness with qualities such as "quietness," "politeness," "niceness," and an extremely "sensitive" or "soft-spoken" manner. We believe that all of these manifestations when they exclusively prevail in a person are emotionally unauthentic, a self-protection *against* the expression of anger. When aggressive feelings are expressed openly, they can at least be dealt with. When they are suppressed and hidden behind "nice" exteriors, they cannot. A culture that remains fixated on an "aggression splitting" orientation, which says in effect that some have it and some don't and we better protect ourselves against those who do, is a natural prey for sudden, unexpected, and highly destructive tragedies. The state of California has been terrorized for years by the "Zodiac" killer. He has never been caught, and we predict that many people will be surprised when he is. To have been so successful in escaping attention all of these years he has obviously acquired all the trappings and symbols of "nice" behavior.

## A PROPOSAL FOR PREVENTION

The incidence of sudden, unexpected violence by so-called "nice" people has reached significant proportions. Though we all tend to deny that it can happen *to* us, or even *around* us, indeed it is happening every day, everywhere. The writers lay the blame for this directly on the doorstep of our culture's pathological devotion to the privileges of privacy, and the social ethic that defines it as "nice" and "good neighborly" to never confront, ask questions of, or in any way become aggressively involved with the lives of those around us, unless we are specifically invited to. This excessive respect for privacy is a natural breeding ground for the potentially violent person hiding behind a mask of smiles and polite manners. That is, the potentially violent people are often the withdrawn loners who thrive on anonymity and the knowledge that their real feelings will never be exposed nor their behavior challenged so long as they present a friendly face.

Our basic belief about the nature of aggression in each person is that authentic trust and security cannot be established with another person unless one first knows what a person does with his aggression, specifically his anger, frustrations, and resentments. The ever-sweet, ever-smiling, essentially passive person is particularly one who cannot be genuinely trusted because we believe he is behaving in a humanly unreal way. We feel much safer and more secure with the neighbor who will openly complain about or yell at his neighbor's dog, or even kick the dog when he becomes particularly obnoxious. The chances are lessened that he will quietly and secretly poison the dog at night. Likewise, in the interaction between people, we feel that the person who will openly complain and confront is safer, more real, and more to be trusted than the neighbor who pretends to be accepting of everything.

As a major step toward protecting the community against sudden, unpredictable violence, it is then first necessary to reject the traditional definition of the good neighbor. Typically, in our society this has meant the person who is always friendly, leaves others alone, never gets personal, is polite and smiling, clings to ceremony, and is always predictable in his "nice" way. Our new model of a good neighbor who can make the community safe is one who will share his negative feelings and displeasure openly, who will criticize and confront as well as praise, who will level about what he really feels and will engage others freely in a give-and-take repartee of a negative as well as positive nature.

Indeed, it is the aggression-phobic society, demanding the suppression of negative feelings, that is most vulnerable to the bizarre outbursts of violence that have become a part of our culture. Overcoming this means that people will have to once again be unafraid to become a nation of brother's keepers and reject the prevailing ethic and fanatic belief in privacy, "nice" behavior, and the privilege of noninvolvement.

Society will be far less vulnerable when it has recognized and accepted the normal, natural buildup and need for constructive release of anger and hostility in all people. Rather than admiring the person who has learned to suppress or hide these feelings behind a mask of nonaggressiveness, society will begin to cherish those who risk expression of their aggressive feelings and who seek out ways of doing this constructively.

# CHAPTER 8

# The Hidden Aggressors at Home and at Work

---

The nature of hidden aggression is such that though an overt aggressive encounter is avoided, the end result is a confused, destructive, and unauthentic form of human interaction. In the long run, as these unconscious forms of aggression avoidance continue and compound, relationships become increasingly more difficult to handle, reach an impasse, stagnate or fall apart. The once joyful parts of the relationships become thoroughly contaminated, and whatever spontaneity, pleasure, and genuineness there was in them is severely diminished.

An illustration of the impact of hidden aggression can be seen in the following brief anecdotes. In each instance the hurt that was inflicted by one person on the other was done indirectly and with a seemingly loving or friendly motive. Since neither party was consciously aware of the repressed aggression behind the deed, the situation that evolved was not manageable by the individuals involved. The hidden hostility could only be seen through the ultimately hurtful impact of the consciously well-intentioned words or actions.

1. Rudy Shapiro was told by his doctor that he had to lose thirty pounds or he would be in imminent danger of having

a heart attack. On his birthday, five weeks into a Weight Watchers diet during which he had lost fourteen pounds, his wife Sheila took him for a surprise dinner at their favorite Italian restaurant. Rudy ordered a salad, and Sheila ordered ravioli and a pizza. She managed to finish only a small part of her food and then she said to Rudy, who had been eyeing her ravioli hungrily, "Oh, go ahead dear, why don't you finish it? After all, it is your birthday, and you can always go back on your diet tomorrow. You've been doing so well lately that you really deserve it." Rudy wanted to believe that Sheila was right, and so he ate up the rest of her food. It threw him off his diet, and, it took a good two weeks before he was able to start losing weight again.

2.  Skip and Jean were in bed making love. Skip, who had recently been having problems maintaining an erection, was getting very turned on, and his penis was very hard. His wife Jean was so happy that she blurted out, "Skip, this is so exciting! You're doing terrific, I just hope you can keep that great erection this time!" Whereupon Skip's penis became soft.

3.  Karen Smitty, who was a shy, twenty-four-year-old college graduate, lived at home, never dated, and was employed doing a menial bookkeeping job. The work was far below her intellectual capacities. One evening Karen was reading an article on psychology and casually mentioned to her mother that she felt she could use some psychological help. Upon hearing this, her father looked up from reading his newspaper and in a loving and comforting voice said, "Oh, you really don't need that psychotherapy crap, honey. You're just a late bloomer and you'll do real fine. Besides, it's really hard to find one of those head doctors who's competent and whom you can trust. Julie Nimitz, the daughter of a close friend of mother's, went to one and believe it or not he tried to rape her."

4.  Tom and Ginger were supposed to be leaving for a two-week trout fishing trip the following week. Tom hadn't had a vacation in over a year and eagerly looked forward to it. Gin-

ger, who secretly hated fishing trips, didn't want to spoil Tom's plans. She pretended to be very enthusiastic while she was actually dreading it because she wanted to be a loving wife. Two days before the trip Ginger fell in the kitchen while preparing dinner. She broke her kneecap and the vacation had to be canceled altogether.

5. The owner of a series of apartment houses, a volatile and gruff man, was getting into financial trouble because a high proportion of his tenants were consistently paying their rent late. He instructed his building managers that, effective immediately, eviction notices should be sent out if rent was not paid on time.

The manager of one of the buildings who felt he knew his boss well, thought he would protect him against himself. His reaction was, "I know he doesn't really mean it. He's just in one of his pissed-off-at-the-world moods. If I put that kind of pressure on the tenants now, a bunch of them will just get insulted and leave." So instead he said nothing to the tenants and doctored up the accounts to cover up for the late payers. This continued for eight months until one day the owner's books and tax records were audited and charges were filed against him for the doctored books. A number of tenants were also shocked when they subsequently received eviction notices without prior warning.

6. Michael Rubin had been with a major shoe store chain for eight years. He thought of himself as one of their best and hardest-working salesmen.

When an opening arose for the position of store manager in his location, he was passed up in favor of someone who had been brought in from outside the chain. He complained bitterly to his wife, who, unbeknownst to Mr. Rubin, telephoned the vice president of the company and chewed him and the chain out for being "ungrateful bastards." Shortly thereafter Mr. Rubin received his termination notice.

Rudy's wife, Sheila; Jean; Karen's father; Ginger; the apartment manager; and Mrs. Rubin all believed themselves to be responding out of loving, positive motivations. In each instance, however, the outcome of their "nice," loving behavior was a hurtful one. Rudy was seduced away from his diet. We can assume that on an underlying psychological level, Rudy's diet was a threat to Sheila. Feeding Rudy had always been Sheila's way of proving her love and worth as a wife. Rudy's diet made her feel she had lost an important measure of control over him.

Skip lost his erection when Jean began to wax so ecstatically over it. We can safely conjecture that underneath Jean's "joyful" response was a need to keep Skip impotent. That way she could continue to tell herself that she was a very sexually responsive person and that all of the problems were because of Skip. In addition, Skip's impotency had given her some emotional leverage over him, which was also gratifying to her on an underlying level.

Karen was derailed from getting help for herself after finally coming to the painful realization that something was wrong in her life and that she needed help. Her father, however, on an underlying psychological level apparently needed to keep Karen dependent and controllable, and he was threatened by her desire to change and grow up.

Tom never got to go on his long-anticipated fishing trip. Ginger's resentment about going, which she couldn't express openly because she wanted to be loving, was finally manifested in her self-destructive accident. It forced the trip to be canceled. But now Ginger didn't have to feel that she was responsible for depriving Tom, which might have been the case had she originally indicated that she didn't want to go.

The manager of the apartment building saw himself as being motivated by concern for the owner. In the process of trying to "save the owner from himself," he got him into serious difficulty. On an underlying psychological level, the manager had long been resentful over the owner's authoritarian and arbitrary ways. The manager unconsciously created a situation in which he could feel powerful while indirectly sabotaging his boss. Not only did the owner suffer from the "well-intentioned" act, but it also resulted in the eviction of several tenants who had never been informed or warned of the situation beforehand.

Finally, Mrs. Rubin's righteous indignation and her conscious desire to be a loving, supportive wife precipitated her husband's losing his job. Her gesture of telephoning the vice president suggests that she really saw her husband as someone who was weak and couldn't fight his own battles. By coming to his aid she actually weakened him and placed herself in a stronger position in the relationship. He was now unemployed, and she could be the supporting rock who would stand by him through the bad times.

The aggression in each instance was expressed indirectly and in a socially acceptable way. None of the hidden aggressors would have been faulted by an outside observer. Open, aggressive encounters in each case were successfully avoided. However, because they were avoided, the underlying aggressive motivations will continue to emerge in other forms and have a contaminating, destructive impact on the relationship. With the best of loving intentions Sheila will finally push Rudy prematurely into a heart attack. Skip's impotency, which was reinforced by another failure, will become worse. He will undoubtedly feel increasingly inadequate, agonized, and guilt-ridden over not being able to perform well sexually for his "loving" wife. Karen's father will continue to abort her striving for growth and independence until perhaps she's finally so anxious and withdrawn that she becomes increasingly less functional and has a breakdown. Tom and Ginger will continue to play "ideal couple," thoughtful and understanding with each other until a crisis arises that forces upon them the realization of their total lack of communication and genuine closeness. The owner of the apartment buildings will suffer embarrassment and expense over the incident with the Internal Revenue and will become less trusting of his employees. His evicted tenants will suffer also. Mr. Rubin's wife will now be in a position where she can console her husband and be the strong one while he goes through a crisis that will undoubtedly impair his confidence in himself.

From infancy on, as is explained at length in the chapter entitled "The 'Nice' Mother and the 'Nice' Father," the socialization process for most people reinforces the masking of hostility. In so doing, children are being taught to be hidden aggressors. Since aggressive feelings are not permitted open expression, except under very specific and approved conditions, the children learn to aggress through manipulations, through passive resistance, or in sundry other covert and indirect ways. In the name of social appropriateness and politeness, authentic communication is being sabotaged. By adolescence and then into adulthood the original aggressive feelings and impulses have long been repressed and are finding expression in transformed, indirect, but socially acceptable shapes. The original underlying aggression motivations are lost to the perpetrator and also remain beyond the awareness of his or her target.

## THE MASKS OF HOSTILITY

We have chosen a number of the more prevalent styles or masks of hostility. All of these are unconscious and automatic. Therefore, the hidden aggressor is not aware of the real intentions of his own behavior. The aggression can be recognized because the impact of the behavior on the victim is a hurtful one. Typically, however, the victim is also unaware of the meaning because the hostility is disguised behind the noblest and most loving of intentions.

We feel it is important to clearly define these forms as a first step toward their recognition. In the final analysis, the victim will carry the brunt of demasking the indirect aggression by confronting the hidden aggressor with the hurt he experiences and that is being inflicted in the name of "love." Included along with these descriptions and illustrations are tentative suggestions for self-protection or "insurance" against the hidden aggression. However, we do not underestimate the subtlety of these interactions nor the difficulty in combating them effectively.

## COLLUSION

The father who out of the kindness of his heart gives his twenty-nine-year-old son money to buy liquor and encouragement to live at home is a hidden aggressor. He is colluding with his son's resistance against becoming autonomous and responsible for sustaining himself. In the same vein the employer who brings his obese secretary a box of her favorite chocolates for her birthday is a hidden aggressor. He is colluding with her self-destructive eating habits. The mother who leaves her pocketbook open and full of money in easy accessibility of her drug-addicted daughter is in collusion with her daughter's self-destructive behavior. The "nice" guys on the college faculty personnel committee who routinely stress and praise the teaching skills of a young, nontenured faculty member and do not put pressure on him to publish are in collusion with his laxness and his apparent unawareness that his academic survival will depend on his publications, not his teaching ability. And the secretary of a technical publications division who secretly corrects the gross terminology errors of a fledgling writer with a drinking problem, thereby saving him temporarily from criticism, is also in collusion with his self-destructive behavior.

An extreme example of collusion was reported by a colleague in a case he had worked with while interning in a public mental health clinic. The hidden aggression was so blatant as to be almost unbelievable, and yet the patient was unaware of the hostility that existed behind her behavior. The patient was a forty-three-year-old married woman with a nineteen-year-old daughter. She came to therapy wanting to know how to help her husband, who she said had been acting strangely recently. That is, he had been alternately withdrawn then suddenly violent. It came out during the course of her sessions that her husband had had sexual relations with their daughter when the latter was twelve years old. The daughter had told the mother, who then proceeded to report her husband to the authorities. The father was sentenced to a hospital for the criminally insane for five years. During the time he was in the hospital, the patient, along with her daughter, became avowed nudists and joined a nearby group, which they frequented regularly. When the father was released from the hospital he was encouraged by the mother to join her and the daughter in their nudist activities. The mother was behaving as if nothing had ever happened between him and the daughter.

It is readily apparent, even to an untrained observer, that the woman was unconsciously provoking her husband into further inappropriate behavior and another incident. In addition, the patient herself, who was both frigid and highly moralistic, could use her husband's hangups and emotional problems as a reason to escape from sexual involvement. On the deepest level she did not even want him around, but her moral self-image did not allow her to recognize this fact. Instead, she unconsciously provoked him in the hopes that he would do himself in again instead.

Other forms of collusion are often less deeply rooted or hidden in their manifestations. These more conscious forms commonly take place in the everyday lives of most people and come under the guise of politeness. As an example, the Berlingers, who are white, were invited over by the Crawfords, who were black, and had just bought the house next door. Mrs. Crawford prepared some "soul food" dishes, which she thought the Berlingers would enjoy trying. The Berlingers, who were Jewish, and who ate primarily kosher foods, could barely manage to eat it. However, since they didn't want to offend their new neighbors, they ate with phony gusto and were constantly remarking about how delicious everything was. During dinner the Berlingers, groping for common conversation ground, talked about how they admired Ralph Bunche, Jackie Robinson, and

Martin Luther King. The Crawfords, who wanted to relate as people and not as black symbols, resented this stereotyping but pretended great interest and enthusiasm in return. At the end of the long evening both couples exchanged compliments and said they looked forward eagerly to socializing again. Of course, they never did.

A young, gifted television commercial actress was sent by her agent for an audition that called for eight women to pose as King Henry's wives for an important canned soup commercial. She went to great lengths to prepare for the audition. She outfitted herself in an elegant Victorian dress and bought an expensive wig. The director conducting the auditions recognized immediately that her face was too thin for the part. However, he liked her personally and didn't want to hurt her feelings. So he said to her, "Oh my God! You're perfect! You're beautiful! I love you!"

The model was elated and went home thinking she had gotten the job for sure. When she was never called she felt bitter and betrayed. At a later date when her agent referred her for another audition with the same director, she refused to go.

Had either the Berlingers or the Crawfords risked being impolite, the beginnings of a real relationship could have been made. However, under the seeming motivation of avoiding unpleasantness each behaved in a phony manner, and the possibilities of a genuine relationship were destroyed. It was sabotaged in the name of politeness. Likewise, the commercial director, who didn't want to level with the actress, destroyed the possibilities of any trusting work association with her in the future.

## COLLUSION INSURANCE

In the more deeply rooted forms of collusion the parties involved are usually being gratified, and the collusion becomes difficult to break. The employer who brought his obese secretary candy was doing something each could temporarily feel good about. Therefore it really becomes the responsibility of the recipient or the victim (in this case the secretary) who is being injured in the name of "love" to reject the gift. It may anger the giver but it will also create the beginnings of a genuine interaction.

In the situation between the Crawfords and the Berlingers, a mild confrontation in game form such as saying, "I want to share a reservation I have about this evening and then I'd hope you'll share one in return." The Crawfords might then have said, "The reservation we have is that we feel you see us as black symbols. It makes us feel unreal, and we care enough about having a relationship with you to want you to see us as people." Any such gamelike confrontation will run some risks and cause some anxiety. However, it can also open up a floodgate of stifled feelings and transform stuffy and unreal interactions into vital, dynamic ones.

Had the commercial director simply said, "I like you very much and appreciate the efforts you've gone to. I want to work with you sometime in the future but you're too thin for the part," the lines of communication would have been kept open for an unimpaired future relationship.

## THE "SICKNESS TYRANTS"

Rather than openly asserting themselves and making direct bids for control and power, the "sickness tyrants" use their illnesses and their symptoms to gain these ends indirectly. Typically their message of hidden aggression is: "How can you talk like that to me when I have a headache? You're aggravating me and I'll get sick again." Or, "Do you want to see me in an early grave?"

People do require some accommodations in time of illness. However, the tyrannical invalid who is always either sick, recovering, or on the verge of another illness *uses* these to manipulate, control, and generate guilt in those around him. A former patient of one of the author's said that he was still living with his mother even though he was thirty-two years of age because she had a bad heart, and if he moved out she might have a heart attack and die. The bad heart was being used by his mother as an instrument of control over him.

"Sickness tyrants" never seem to get completely healthy. They need their symptoms as a mode of controlling relationships. Even when they feel good they say it in such a way that it indirectly suggests a dread of the next illness. Usually as children, "sickness tyrants" were extremely repressed in the area of aggression by highly authoritarian parents who prevented them from asserting themselves, displaying anger openly and directly, or talking back. As children they were deprived of any power or sense of control. However, when they became ill, they suddenly found themselves being treated as important, allowed to be powerful, receiving special attention, and being allowed to make demands. Sickness became their safe mode of aggression. As adults this style carried over. They use their illnesses tyrannically to create and generate guilt in others and to gain power and control.

## INSURANCE AGAINST "SICKNESS TYRANTS"

Genuinely sick people are strongly motivated to get better as quickly as possible. The "sickness tyrant" who is chronically wallowing in his symptoms and uses them to make undue demands on others needs to be confronted. There is, to be sure, a socially conditioned anxiety in confronting someone who is sick because of a fear that one will be accused of being heartless or even of being responsible for making him sicker. However, for the mental health of all concerned, the "sickness tyrant" needs to be told that he will not be accommodated forever, and that those around him will not permit their lives to be curtailed or limited by guilt manipulation. Hearing this will undoubtedly make the "sickness tyrant" angry and resentful. However, it will also be an excellent first step toward achieving a state of realistic aggressive interaction.

## THE PASSIVE AGGRESSORS

Particularly those individuals who have been brought up in severely repressive, authoritarian homes in which they were prevented from expressing anger openly will be prone to expressing their aggression in passive ways. There are many varieties of passive aggression, and the following are but a few of the principal ones:

FORGETTING  There are two major forms of forgetting as hidden aggression. In the first and more obvious form of hidden aggression, the aggression affects others. Someone whom you are heavily depending on to do something for you forgets to do it. The chronic forgetter is often an overtly passive, acquiescent person who is unable to assert himself openly by saying, "I don't want to do this." Instead, he passively agrees to everything and then proceeds to forget.

This style of passive aggression has the effect of driving the victim up the wall. After all, what can one say to someone who says, "Gosh, I'm really sorry, it just slipped my mind"? This hidden aggressor is also very selective in his forgetting. He never seems to forget what is important or pleasurable to himself. He only forgets that which is important to someone who is depending on him.

Eventually the chronic forgetter succeeds indirectly in achieving what he was unable to assert openly. That is, people closely involved with him learn not to count on him or ask him to do anything important because they know it might be forgotten. The "forgetter" is thus spared from having to say "No" to requests directly.

Another form is self-destructive forgetting or passive aggression against the self. In this self-inflicted aggression the person forgets something important to himself. "I forgot to call him back for the business appointment," "I forgot my airplane ticket and my wallet," "I forgot where I put the keys to my car," or "I forgot to save the receipts that I needed for tax purposes," are typical examples.

This form of aggression against oneself is directly related to the other kind of forgetting. That is, a person who is unable to assert to himself openly and directly, "I don't want to do such and such," because he doesn't want to feel he is shirking social responsibility, achieves the same result passively by simply forgetting to do it.

To understand the possible hidden meanings of "forgetting" behavior, substitute the words "didn't want to" in place of the word "forgot." This will be helpful to you in interpreting your own forgetting behavior and the forgetting behavior of others.

MISUNDERSTANDING  In this form of passive aggression, aggression is also expressed behind a cloak of great sincerity. "I thought you said you wanted the report a week from Thursday," or "I thought you wanted me to buy a long-sleeved shirt, not a short-sleeved one," or "I could have sworn you *wanted* me to mention to your boss that you were thinking of quitting your job."

The impact of misunderstanding on the victim is often quite hurtful. In employment or socially sensitive situations particularly, misunderstanding can produce very costly and destructive consequences. The misunderstander innocently and naïvely says, "Gee I thought you meant . . ." as the victim tears his hair in frustration and despair.

A well-known psychiatrist in Chicago specializing in hypnosis formed a foundation and conducted periodic training seminars. To coordinate his schedule he hired a full-time office manager. On a day-to-day basis the psychiatrist was a tyrant with his staff and would particularly terrorize his office manager with last-minute rush demands. The office manager was, however, too frightened to express her resentment or to offer any overt resistance.

On one occasion the doctor decided upon very short notice to hold a weekend seminar. He indicated that he wanted 150 announcements to go out that very night. The office manager, who felt she was being unfairly used and pressured, nevertheless proceeded to try to rush out the material. In the process, she "mistakenly" inverted the numbers of the address where the seminar was to be held. Instead of typing 6920, she typed 6029. The problems this would cause him was her way of getting back at her tyrannical boss.

PROCRASTINATION    The stock-in-trade phrase of the procrastinator is, "Don't worry, we'll get to it real soon!" The procrastinator passively aggresses with his exasperating delays and refusal to be pinned down to a fixed date or time. He also induces guilt feelings in his victim with admonitions such as "Don't be so impatient," or "Relax, you'll live longer!"—and then continues to express his hostility by moving at a snail's pace.

Often the procrastinator is one who is expressing his contempt for those who work with him by keeping them waiting or forcing them to repeatedly remind him of the time of a meeting. The hidden aggression behind procrastination is clearly seen by its selective nature. Typically, the procrastinator only keeps certain people waiting and only in certain settings. When he is "turned on" and genuinely involved, he meets the schedule. For example, an unemployed actor took a part-time job in the post office to keep himself going. At the post office he was known as the guy who was always "dragging his ass around." He had to be continually reminded about certain of his duties. However, whenever he was called for a television or movie audition he became "Mr. Prompt" and always arrived earlier than his appointment time.

THE LATECOMERS    This form of passive aggression was formerly viewed as being predominantly a characteristic of women. Being kept waiting by a woman was traditionally considered a normal, acceptable experience. However, individuals who chronically arrive late for meetings, dates, or appointments are indirectly expressing their hostility for the person or persons kept waiting. The prima donna attitude of certain celebrities, consciously or unconsciously wishing to assert their feelings of superiority, often shows itself through late arrivals at meetings and interviews.

In other instances an individual who feels exploited by those he is working with yet feels impotent in terms of changing the situation may also show his resentment by constantly arriving late. This was noted in the interaction among three partners in an advertising firm in Philadelphia. The firm was only a little more than a year old and the partners had initially signed a five-year contract that committed them to an equal, three-way split of the profits. One of the partners felt resentful over the fact that he was responsible for bringing in the bulk of the business. His hidden anger over the situation came through in the fact that he always arrived late for the twice-weekly luncheon meetings. Though his excuses always had a legitimate ring, the chronic lateness was his way of saying, "I'm more important than you, so you'll just have to wait for me."

One other illustration will help to point up how chronic lateness can be a form of passive aggression, a way of indirectly expressing feelings of being exploited. In the mid-1960s the federal government was financing multimillion-dollar poverty projects in ghetto communities across the country. In one major West Coast city a group of psychologists were contracted to service a number of Head Start programs for preschoolers in a large black community.

The psychologists, with only a rare exception, were Caucasian Ph.D.s. They would be assigned to work an eight-hour day once a week at the ghetto site and were paid very handsomely for this. Since they were only at the Head Start agency once a week, they would plan staff conferences and meetings with teachers well in advance. Invariably, the Caucasian psychologists had the frustrating experience of arriving at a 9:00 A.M. meeting to find that a large part of the staff was not present. The absent members would straggle in slowly and often unenthusiastically over the next hour.

The psychologists, who did not wish to further impair the already fragile rapport, were loath to make an issue of it. The lateness of many of the black personnel was their unconscious way of expressing resentment over the intrusion of a Caucasian professional, whom they saw as being there to tell them how to relate to the children of their own community. "How can a white man understand a black person?" was their unspoken message. When, after about two years, most of the Caucasian psychologists were replaced with black mental health workers, the lateness stopped.

Latecomers are also usually creative apologizers who have a wide assortment of excuses ready at hand. These are designed to move the victim off the offensive and onto the defensive. The hidden aggression in this case can be clearly recognized by its impact. Waiting for someone who is late is irritating, frustrating, and humiliating. We assume then that the passive aggressive intent behind being late is to do just that: to irritate, frustrate, and humiliate.

NO CARRYOVER OF LEARNING A recently divorced woman who was talking about her husband remarked, "For eight years I had to tell him each time where my clitoris was." There was no carryover from one experience to the next.

This type of passive aggressor expresses his or her aggression by never anticipating the needs of someone who depends on him or learning from previous experience. Instead, they force the victim to request anew each and every time. Victims of the no-carryover passive aggressors feel frustrated and hurt by this thoughtless behavior. However, they are often manipulated off the defensive by the hidden aggressor, who says something like,

"I can't think of everything all of the time," or "Don't get so uptight. If you want something just tell me!"

The humiliating and provocative aspects of this form of passive aggression are the clearest indications of its undertones of hidden hostility. The husband who puts his wife into the position where she has to remind him daily to put away his clothing or to take out the garbage is expressing his latent resentment.

One client who attended one of our office aggression seminars and who worked in a small shoe repair shop reported that every Friday he would have to remind his employer to pay him his salary. "He made me feel like he was giving me a handout," was the employee's reaction.

## INSURANCE AGAINST PASSIVE AGGRESSORS

Individuals who are closely involved with a child, lover, spouse, friend, employee, or business associate who chronically manifests these passive aggressive behaviors should ask themselves these two questions: (1) Am I overly controlling and dominating this person (the passive aggressor) and therefore making it impossible for him to assert himself directly? In other words, am I preventing him from expressing his anger or resentment directly and thereby forcing him to do so passively? (2) Am I actually more comfortable with passive aggression, even though it's annoying as hell, rather than having this person show his feelings to me openly and directly?

If the reader can answer both of these questions comfortably with "No" and there is a real desire to effect change, the next question should be: In what ways am I allowing this person to get away with this passive aggressive behavior?

There is a common tendency to feel reluctant to confront passive aggressors for fear of being called a nag. After all, the victim rationalizes, they didn't really do it intentionally. Passive aggressors can be very manipulative in their presentation of themselves as innocent and well intentioned. This tends to induce guilt in the victim, who is manipulated away from his offensive position to a defensive one. He may even wind up apologizing for having gotten angry or annoyed.

In dealing with a passive aggressor, one must first avoid being seduced by one's own guilt over getting angry at these behaviors. The important thing is not the benevolent intention of the passive aggressor's behavior but rather its impact. If it hurts, scream in rage and don't feel ashamed of displaying the hurt. Certainly if it happens over and over again, one can assume there is an underlying aggressive motive involved.

The ideal way of dealing with a passive aggressor is to try to surface the hidden hostility and bring the hidden resentment out into the open. If that is not possible, targets of passive aggression must demand some kind of structure that will guarantee them that matters will not be forgotten, delayed, or misunderstood in the future.

To avoid the "misunderstandings" of this form of passive aggressor, have him or her repeat back the instructions or assignment you have given *before* they set out to perform the task. Never take it for granted that they have understood.

To deal with a procrastinator, set a precise, *never* vague deadline and establish a penalty for delays. Be sure to carry out the penalty if the procrastination occurs.

Likewise with latecomers: Make a clearly defined agreement, such as, "If you're more than ten minutes late and you haven't called, I'll leave."

Once a stand has been taken to combat a passive aggressor, failure to carry out one's position is disastrous. That is, passive aggression is an indirect way of expressing hostility. The more the passive aggressor gets away with it, the more likely it is that he will continue doing it.

## THE "RED CROSS NURSE" SYNDROME

With all due respects for the fine work done by the Red Cross organization, we have chosen these colorful words to describe a specific pattern of hidden aggression. We use the term "Red Cross nurse" to describe the person who seeks out, nourishes himself on, and indirectly perpetuates the weakness, helplessness, and vulnerability of other people.

The "Red Cross nurse" enters into and is comfortable in a relationship primarily where the other person is hurting or in trouble. His or her way of helping is a kind of overprotective mothering and doing things for the other person rather than helping the person function for himself. The "Red Cross nurse" also joins the victim in pointing a finger at the cruel outside world rather than helping the person focus on his own responsibility in controlling what happens to him. As often happens, the "Red Cross nurse" will become threatened and resentful when the other person shows signs of becoming independent and strong. At this point he or she no longer feels needed or valuable because "helping" is the only way he or she feels strong and secure.

A striking example of this is often seen in the relationship between alcoholics and their spouses. So long as the alcoholic remains crippled by his habit, the spouse, though masochistically complaining about his or her lot in life, still has a *raison d'être*. The day the alcoholic stops drinking is often the day the relationship begins to fall apart totally.

Likewise we have often noted that many parents of emotionally disturbed children are extremely loving while their child is in the throes of his disturbance. However, once the child is in psychotherapy and begins to behave independently and aggressively, the parents rush to take him out of therapy.

The president of a small printing company had constant employee problems because of his volatile temper and his insulting manner. Employees would suddenly quit without notice because of their deep resentment toward him. He had, however, one loyal "Red Cross nurse" employee who would work fourteen-hour days and weekends when such a crisis occurred and who would support the employer in his practice of always placing the blame on the "ungrateful" employee. By his "helping" behavior, he was making it easy for the employer to continue his destructive style of relating.

## INSURANCE AGAINST THE "RED CROSS NURSE"

It is gratifying to be cared for by someone when one is in need. However, those who find themselves deeply into a relationship with a "Red Cross nurse" are often using this hidden aggressor to avoid facing up to the responsibilities that come with being emotionally and physically healthy. Victims of "Red Cross nursing" are inviting this form of control. The best insurance against it is acceptance of the responsibilities of one's own independence. "Red Cross nurses" get their kicks out of the neediness of their victims. If one is no longer expressing or communicating neediness, the "Red Cross nurse" will often leave or be forced to change and relate in a more directly assertive way based on your strength rather than your weakness.

## MORAL ONE-UPMANSHIP

Behind their holier-than-thou attitude, there exists an unspoken hidden manifestation of a power striving. The moralist's real message is, "I am on a higher plane of consciousness than you."

There are moralists in many areas of life. In politics they may be represented by the pacifists, who see themselves as genuine peace lovers who are in opposition to the "hawks" and the "killers," who lust after war. On the other end of this spectrum, the right-wing moralists who see themselves as the only true supporters of the democratic way of life view all the rest of the population as communist contaminated. In religion, the moralist may be the yoga, Buddhist, or Christ worshiper who sees himself as being on a higher plane of consciousness, enlightened, and with a personal pipeline to God and truth. In other areas of life, the moralist may be the vegetarian who doesn't "kill" to eat or the communalist who feels he has risen above the greediness of the masses and the desire for private ownership.

This is not intended to lump all those seeking more meaningful lifestyles into a group labeled "hidden aggressors." Rather we wish to point out a potential hidden aspect of this behavior that allows the moralist to feel superior and to express his contempt for others behind a mask of spiritualism, righteousness, and higher truth. In the presence of a moralist one may be prone to doubting oneself and one's values and to feel a little less worthy and a little less pure than the moralist. Generating just this kind of impact may be the hidden aggression motive of the moralist.

The underlying hostility of the moralist can be seen in its impact rather than in its intention. For example, many parents have agonized over the loss of their children to the "Jesus freaks" or to some form of cultist religion such as scientology. Inevitably the child's fanatic attempts to convert the family hides an arrogance and contempt that is really designed to express hostility and alienate the parents. The authors interpret moralistic behavior by its impact, which is an indirect way of aggressing by making oneself superior.

A new form of moralist has recently arisen from the "religion" of psychotherapy. This phenomenon originally began with patients who had gone through a Freudian analysis and felt that somehow they were, as a result, more insightful or emotionally healthier than the rest. One divorced man who had undergone psychoanalysis said that it was difficult for him to find a suitable mate because his analysis had made him "psychologically overqualified." In recent years, many fad psychotherapies have produced individuals who claim superiority by being able to feel more deeply or by being more aware or authentic than others. These contentions can best be interpreted by their impact. If the impact is one of setting oneself off and making the other person feel like a lesser being, then we take that to be the real message of hidden aggression that lies behind the psychological "moralists."

## DEFENDING AGAINST THE "MORALIST"

In interaction with a "moralist" there is a temptation to agree with their puristic principles intellectually, while resisting and even feeling resentful of what is being said on an emotional level. The latter feeling is usually accompanied by other feelings of unworthiness for this resentful reaction toward a person who is striving to be so pure. It is suggested that the resentfulness may indeed be a true and healthy reaction to the hidden message of superiority of the "moralist." Accept the feeling, trust it, and express it. Do not be seduced into feeling guilty or less worthy for having this reaction. This is the best defense against the "moralist."

Families who have lost one of their members to a religious cult will be prone to try to seduce him back in pleading, guilt-ridden ways because they are reacting solely to the overt religious messages of their child and the concomitant feelings the messages generate that somehow they have messed up and failed their child. Only a family that can read the real message of hidden aggression can begin to make sense of and react appropriately to the situation.

## THE INTELLECTUALIZERS

At the outset it is necessary to differentiate intelligence from intellectualizing. Intelligence serves to facilitate and improve life. The intellectualizers, however, use their words and ideas to keep others at an emotional distance and to avoid the experiencing of feelings.

The intellectualizers relate primarily by judging, explaining, analyzing, philosophizing, and dissecting. Their impact is cold and mechanical. Individuals involved with intellectualizers find themselves feeling frustrated and frozen out when they try to make emotional contact. The intellectualizer is a hidden aggressor who expresses his hostility by not giving of himself emotionally and thereby frustrating and depriving the other person. The aggression is expressed through detachment and intellectual pontificating. This behavior masks underlying hostility as rationality or understanding.

The preoccupation with techniques in order to solve interpersonal problems is a prime example of this phenomenon of intellectualization as a way of masking hostility and avoiding a direct, aggressive encounter between two people in our society. For example, a couple who is having problems with their sex life will buy books on sex techniques to find out what they're "doing wrong." This avoids a confrontation over the underlying resentments and conflicts that are probably the real source of their problem.

A small chemical products engineering corporation was having communication breakdown problems because of resentments that had built up between their research department and their marketing people. The president decided to deal with this problem by bringing in "experts" to give lectures and conduct courses on psychology and human relations. This was a way of intellectualizing the problems rather than dealing with them head on.

In another instance, a female employee who was constantly at odds with her boss made an appointment to talk with him about their problems. He proceeded to tell her that all their problems were due to her strong latent resentment toward male authority figures. This was his way of avoiding a gut-level exchange of their mutual, personal resentments through intellectualizing the problem and interpreting her behavior psychologically.

## COMBATING THE INTELLECTUALIZER

Because intellectualism is traditionally held in high esteem in our society, there is a tendency to be awed by the "profound" pronouncements, explanations, abstractions, and ruminations, even when the experience of being closely and emotionally involved with an intellectualizer is in reality a boring and frustrating experience. The less brainwashed reactions of children who yawn and become restless in the presence of an intellectualizer represent a spontaneous, authentic response to the intellectualizer's intrinsic lack of emotional vitality. Few adults, however, would feel free or comfortable enough to respond to an intellectualizer by saying, "Your intellectualizations are boring and we're evading the issue of how we really feel about each other. I feel put off by your intellectualizations, and I don't like it."

Combating the intellectualizer means allowing oneself to accept and be comfortable with one's gut reaction to him, which is one of boredom and impatience. Trust the feeling and don't allow yourself to feel less worthy for experiencing resentment over this emotionally empty form of response. Rather than allowing oneself to be seduced into a game of intellectual one-upmanship, it becomes a challenge to provoke the intellectualizer into an emotional interchange. "Cut out the intellectual crap and tell me how you feel" would be an appropriate opener.

## THE NONREWARDER

As employer, spouse, teacher, friend, associate, or lover, the nonrewarder expresses his aggression by never giving positive, rewarding feedback. He or she never says, "That was a job well done," "I really liked that," "Good work," or "That was great!" This will tend to instill feelings of anxiety and insecurity in individuals who are dependent on them. Inevitably the dependent or approval-seeking person is left to feel that they have said or done something that offended or displeased the nonrewarder. Nonrewarding is a way of keeping others at a distance and preventing them from making demands or getting too close. Spouses of nonrewarders often wind up in therapists' offices or on lovers' couches seeking the positive reinforcement they are not getting at home. Friends eventually leave in frustration, and employees of nonrewarders will have to draw on their own sense of worth in order to survive and feel comfortable.

## DEFENDING AGAINST THE NONREWARDER

The nonrewarder is usually not conscious of the rejection of others which he communicates by his detachment. Direct confrontation with a demand for positive or negative criticism and questions such as "How do you feel about what I did?" are therefore necessary in relating to a nonrewarder. This is particularly vital in work situations, where knowing how one is being evaluated is so important to one's sense of security and competency.

## THE DOUBTER

Doubters arouse anxiety and feelings of insecurity in others at critical moments and in the name of concern when their victim is most vulnerable. The spouse who says to her husband, "Did you notice how irritated your boss looked last night during dinner? I wonder if it was something you said?" Or the person who says to his friend, "Maybe you should get a trade instead of going to college like you've planned. I hear college degrees are worthless and graduate schools are impossible to get into." In general, they promote feelings of doubt in others in the name of helpfulness.

After the death of his father, the son joined his mother in carrying on the family's restaurant business. Though there had been many opportunities in the past to expand the business, the mother's fears and doubts had always caused the father to hold off from developing the business to its potential. Consequently, financial survival was always a struggle.

The ambitious son clearly saw the great possibilities that existed and proposed a concrete, workable, and relatively conservative plan for expansion. Her reply was, "You never lived through the depression, so you don't know what it's like. Another depression might be right around the corner. Besides, good help is so hard to find. If we start hiring more people, you only have more people to watch over so that they don't steal from you. You don't want to die of a heart attack before you're thirty-five, do you? I'm just telling you these things for your own good."

Behind the mask of concern and helpfulness, the doubter plants seeds of fear and self-doubt in those around him. His perception of situations and people is consistently negative. Behind his "helpful" counsel is the hidden, hostile wish that you share his cynicism and frustration and that you don't thrive or succeed anymore than he has.

### DEFUSING THE DOUBTER

Doubters have an emotionally poisonous impact. They seek comfort for their own inadequacies and self-doubts by instilling the same in others. They don't want to be surpassed or to see someone close to them become too secure or successful. Theirs is a very negative orientation and needs to be ignored or confronted with anger and a clear statement that their concern is really not helpful at all.

### THE HELPLESS AGGRESSOR

The helpless style of hidden aggression involves the use of weakness, tears, vulnerability, hurt, and fragility as a way of generating guilt, avoiding responsibility, and controlling others. The message communicated is, "You're so capable and I'm so inadequate, you've got to help me." However, once the helpless hidden aggressor has found a victim, he will proceed to drain him with possessiveness, demands, and guilt induction. It is a powerful form of using and manipulation. In the long run, within such a relationship, the helpless aggressors emerge as the powerful persons. Their helpless pose is actually a cover for a tenaciously controlling and engulfing style.

## HELPLESS INSURANCE

Those who need to reassure themselves regarding their strength and worthiness will be the ones who are the most vulnerable to seduction by the helpless aggressor. In other words, individuals with strong self-doubts and a vulnerability to flattery will be attracted to this kind of relationship.

Insurance against helpless aggressors requires a cautious response to anyone who brings out a protective urge or the desire to take over and do things for them. The hidden aggressive style of getting others to take over one's responsibility for functioning is inevitably a seductive, appealing one.

To tap the real strength and rage behind helpless aggression, the following experiment is suggested. In the next encounter when "helpless" is in the midst of playing weak, crying, or looking hurt, say, "I don't believe you. In fact, I really feel you're manipulating me and that you're a hell of a lot stronger than I am." It is predicted that the helpless pose will be quickly transformed into a reaction varying anywhere from a rageful tantrum to a stony silence. The real person behind "helpless" is now being engaged at last.

The styles of masked hostility described in this chapter are but a small handful of an endless variety of indirect and hidden aggression patterns. All are the by-products of suppressing open, direct aggressive interaction and the clinging to a romanticized image of man as being altruistic and peaceful, one who only becomes aggressive when provoked and for righteous reasons. Confronting the hidden aggressor is difficult because he will tend to respond by saying, "I only tried to help," "I didn't really mean it," or "I am not angry." His self-image will not tolerate a perception of himself as an aggressor, let alone a sneaky aggressor.

Hidden aggression can only be effectively recognized, understood, and responded to in terms of its impact on the victim.

It controls, humiliates, punishes, induces guilt or dependency, and in general achieves an aggressive purpose behind a socially acceptable mask.

The short-run effect of hidden aggression is to avoid an aggressive interaction. However, the longer-range price for this pseudopeacefulness is great. Communication is distorted and obscured. Manipulation replaces genuine involvement. The vital potential of human interaction is significantly decreased and replaced by emotional alienation, stagnation, and petty preoccupations. Worst of all, forcing aggression into hidden paths results in a loss of awareness and control over it and consequent vulnerability to its unpredictable, unexpected, and disastrous consequences.

# CHAPTER 9

# Dances Around the Beast

---

Unlike sex, aggression has never lent itself well to avoidance through hiding or by pretending that it didn't exist. Its fruits were too apparent to be ignored. Wars, crimes, the outbreak of feuding and hostilities within and outside of families made the ugly, bothersome "beast" of aggression an undeniable fact. The most that could be done was to deny its existence on a personal level and to point a finger to the outside, placing the blame for its existence elsewhere. To keep it impersonal and channeled as much as possible, numerous socially acceptable outlets, rituals, and vicarious games have been developed throughout the history of man.

All were designed, we believe, to serve basically similar purposes. The major one, of course, was to provide sufficient impersonal outlets so that aggression wouldn't have to be experienced or expressed personally. By creating taboos against its expression on a personal level, it would be possible for each person to maintain an image of himself as altruistic, peaceful, loving, and helpful. At the same time it would allow for the creation and perpetuation of the dichotomy between the "good," "altruistic" *us* and the "hostile," "destructive" *them*. Still to this day, few people are able to pinpoint the source of aggression during a conflict within themselves. Rather, people have become highly adept at locating the origin of aggression in outside forces.

"Dances around the beast" is our phrase for describing the many rituals, games, reaction patterns, and social conventions that have evolved over the history of man to allow him to avoid acknowledging the aggressive realities within himself. In this way he could avoid dealing with this real part of his emotional experience on an immediate, personal level. These "dances" have served to institutionalize personal aggression such that these impulses could be released impersonally and behind a self-righteous, socially legitimate, anonymous mask.

Some are solemn "dances," others are playful, and many are lethal. Regardless of their impact, they all serve this same ultimate function. They allow each of us individually to disown aggression as a reality existing within and between us, helping to maintain the taboos against its personal expression, and facilitating the maintenance of our own altruistic self-image. Some of the most prominent of such "dances" in our culture that will be examined in this chapter include the "spectator dance," the "religious dance," the "police dance," the "sporting dance," the "war dance," the "pacifist dance," and the "scientific research dance."

Periodically these "dances" break down and their deeper, destructive essence temporarily surfaces. Such is often the case during wartime, when it is suddenly discovered that a village or city of innocent, unarmed people including women and children have been senselessly and viciously brutalized by "our side." The aggression that had been legitimized as a part of the self-righteous "war dance" has apparently been indulged in, for no seemingly justifiable purpose. Everyone is "shocked." Or this breakdown may occur as a by-product of the "sporting dance." We are angered and "revulsed," for example, when a boxer is killed during a boxing match.

It then becomes necessary to rationalize these "lapses" in the ritual in order for people to maintain their illusions of righteous, ideologically pure motivations and their lack of personally aggressive motivations. The senseless war killings may then be blamed on battle conditions, morale breakdown, fatigue, or as the result of a temporary lapse. In extreme cases where the sense of guilt is too great, a few soldiers may be pinpointed as being the real culprits, and they are then scapegoated. In the case of the boxer's death, there are usually outcries that the sport be abolished or that reforms be instituted. In each instance the blame has been placed, appropriate noises about change have been made, everybody feels better, and the "dance" continues.

## THE "SPECTATOR DANCE"

"On a March night in 1964 at least 38 neighbors in the Kew Gardens Apartments in New York City watched a young woman named Kitty Genovese being stabbed to death by an assaultive maniac. Although it took him more than half an hour to murder her, brutally and in cold blood, not one of the witnesses ever lifted the telephone to call the police. The victim's cries of terror and her attempts to fight back left no doubt in anyone's mind about what was going on. It was 3:00 A.M. but no one helped."[1]

The Kitty Genovese case was a clear incident in which the "spectator dance" broke down or went too far. Traditionally, the steps to this dance go something like this: A person picks up the morning newspaper, watches television, or listens to the radio and avidly reads about the latest rape, murder, or war statistic. Then the person says to himself something like, "This city is getting scary. There are a lot of crazy people running loose," or "There's a real breakdown in moral fiber," or "When will 'they' ever learn that violence is senseless?" In no case is there an awareness of receiving vicarious pleasure from reading about these killings or crimes.

The "spectator dance" may also take other forms, such as watching television's violent movies or going to violent sporting matches. In the mid-1960s during the Watts riots in the Los

Angeles area, the authors were frankly amazed at the hordes of people who tried to drive into Watts so as to be able to watch the action from close up. In spite of the reports of danger, viewing the violence at close hand was for many people an irresistible attraction.

Nothing guarantees the sale of huge volumes of newspapers more than a gory and shocking murder. Details about the Sharon Tate murder case and the Kennedy assassinations filled newspapers and magazines for months. The public's appetite for the details seemed to be insatiable.

The essence of the "spectator dance" is to provide people with a vicarious outlet while at the same time allowing them to rationalize their fascination and interest as motivated only by curiosity, or for information or educational purposes. Few, if any, ever can or do say to themselves, "I enjoy watching violence" or "I love seeing somebody get killed or beaten. It satisfies a real need."

The Kitty Genovese murder incident was unusual mainly for its detailed documentation of the destructiveness behind the spectator stance. If they were aware of any vicarious excitement or enjoyment in witnessing this cruel scene, and undoubtedly most wouldn't have been, the witnesses would have been loath to own up to it. Instead, they rationalized their paralysis in the face of seeing someone brutalized as the result of being too "frightened," "embarrassed," or simply not wanting to "get involved."

It was absolutely essential for the witnesses to maintain their own altruistic self-images by rationalizing this vicariously pleasurable hostility release with more consciously "understandable," self-comforting, and sympathy-promoting motivations, such as "Maniacs should be dealt with by the police or by a psychiatrist," or "It was none of my business," or "I figured somebody else had already called," or "It was just too horrible and I couldn't think."

In this dance, then, vicarious release is received through observing. The spectator need not even be consciously aware of receiving any pleasure, and, in fact, rarely if ever is. When as in the Genovese case the spectator seems to be caught red-handed, engrossed with the action and doing nothing to stop it, the already mentioned rationalizations have to be created.[2]

## THE "RELIGIOUS DANCE"

"Turn the other cheek. . . ."

Every Sunday millions of people listen to religious preachers on the radio. One such preacher was recently saying, "Do you know what the No. 1 killer of man is?" Then in a voice both urgent and weighty with wisdom, he answered his own question. "Resentment," he said, "is the No. 1 destroyer of human souls."

The preacher was acting as a choreographer for the "religious dance," which is designed to exorcise the devilish demon of aggression. Step 1 of this dance involves labeling a feeling or behavior such as anger or resentment as evil or the work of the devil. The second step involves disowning oneself from these feelings or impulses and "rising above them." In the final step, convinced that these feelings no longer exist within themselves, one sets out to help others become equally as pure. Should the religious person falter and occasionally betray the existence of these taboo feelings within himself, the rationalization process begins. "I was just not myself," "The devil made me do it," "I probably haven't really given myself over fully to Jesus yet."

The theme behind the "religious dance" is that religious or spiritual people are not personally aggressive. Hate, power drives, resentment, and jealousies are unspiritual feelings belonging to the nonreligious. These feelings are kept suppressed by warnings about sin, guilt, and punishment by hellfire. This creates in the religious person a splitting off from this important element of his humanness and in its place creates a "not me" situation. That is, should the feeling or impulse momentarily break out, the person can reassure himself it was "not the real me, but a part of the evil or ungodly me."

Religion, it can be posited, has derived much of its power by providing a process of aggression control through worship of a god who is said to have control over all horrific elements and bad demons. By so doing, it has also assumed the role of gatekeeper over the aggressive impulse. When aggression is acted out, the religious leaders will decide who, in the name of God, its victims will be. It is almost cliché to point out the innumerable wars and killings that have occurred in the name of religion and holiness. The wars in Pakistan and Ireland are only two very recent examples.

Religious leaders have also always seemed to have an uncanny knack for placating and allying themselves with existing aggressive power structures. Though the Pope makes his annual prayer for peace, the Church rarely if ever takes a stand against the warring efforts of a particularly powerful country. Instead, a loose rationalization system always allows it to find appropriate justifications. The Reverend Billy Graham was undoubtedly a better breakfast sermonizer and golf partner to President Nixon than an influence against the wars then going on in Vietnam and bombings that were taking place in other parts of Southeast Asia.

The writers as psychotherapists have seen the effects of traditional conservative religious positions on the process of human communication. In a recent psychotherapy marathon, one highly religious Caucasian male, age twenty-four, repeatedly responded to others in the group who asked him how he felt about them by saying that he loved everybody in the room and had no negative feelings about anyone.

The effect of this young man's proclamations of love for everyone, interestingly enough, was an alienating one rather than one that facilitated trust and intimacy. His "love" for others was not experienced by them as real. In fact, it was experienced as dehumanizing, for he related to everybody in the identical way. Underneath the "love" this young man communicated an arrogance or "put down" attitude that in effect was saying, "I am not bogged down with petty emotions of anger or resentment. I have risen above them."

Radical elements in the Church have begun to have a humanizing impact on it. Many religious leaders have become students of psychology and participants in various self-liberating experiences. Thus, many are beginning to own up to their real feelings and personal aggressiveness. However, so long as religion perpetuates the dichotomous perceptions of people in terms of "good" and "bad," "evil" and "holy," it will remain a powerful force in perpetuating the aggression sickness of our culture.

## THE "POLICE DANCE"

The basis of the "police dance" is the "mad dog" perception of aggression. This produces the myth that says, "If we capture and isolate those 'mad dogs' who have been infected by this aggression 'virus,' the rest of us will be safe."

It has been said that society hates its criminals but loves its crimes. It is one of the striking characteristics of aggression-phobic cultures such as ours that crimes are a source of intense public fascination. Bizarre mass murders assure the media of huge audiences. The book and film *The Godfather,* known mainly for its endless succession of criminal violence and the romanticization of top dog criminals, became one of the most successful commercial films ever made. Over fifty million dollars in gross receipts were received within the first nine months of release.

The "mad dog" choreography also fosters a dehumanizing, alienating, and emotionally unrealistic dichotomy among people. There are the "criminals" and the "law-abiding" citizens, or the "good" guys and the "bad" guys.

Every once in a while a "Watergate" phenomenon occurs, such as that in 1972–73, during which some of the final authorities and symbols of "law and order" in this country were revealed to have engaged in criminal behavior themselves. Nothing is so fascinating and makes for such delicious gossip as when a "good" guy is suddenly revealed to be a "bad" guy. Watergate, for many of the American population, became like a television serial in which the latest developments and intrigues were anxiously awaited. As in all extreme breakdowns of dances designed to maintain the taboos, rationalizations about Watergate abounded. Criminal behavior was interpreted as lapses of judgment, too much zeal, or a trumped-up vendetta by the press.

An inherent danger in this compartmentalized way of viewing people as "good" and "bad," "criminal" and "good citizen," is that sensitivity to the actual aggressive potential of others is lost. We become liable to being suddenly "surprised" by that "nice" kid next door who is suddenly revealed to be a vicious killer. This has become an increasingly common phenomenon in our culture. After a particular bizarre killing or killings, friends and neighbors of the killer, when interviewed, remarked that they "couldn't believe it." "He was so quiet and unassuming," they say, or "They've got to have the *wrong* man." What is the lack within ourselves that causes us to remain insensitive to these kinds of destructive vibrations until a crime has already been committed? The authors feel the cause lies partly in the unrealistic, image-oriented way of dichotomizing people as "aggressive" or "nonaggressive," "criminal" or "law-abiding citizen," "good" guy or "bad" guy and not being aware of the many variations and degrees of aggressive potential in each person.

It may seem a cliché to point out that criminal potential exists in almost everybody. However, in plain fact, from a legal point of view, most people have been guilty of criminal behavior. This may range from white-collar crimes such as stealing materials from the office to smoking marijuana, cheating on income taxes, acting out secret and technically illegal sex practices, or committing traffic offenses when the police are not around to observe. The true crime in our society has become getting caught or being so poor that one cannot afford to hire the finest legal assistance to get one off the hook.

Personal aggression-phobic societies also seem to need their criminals as targets and outlets for righteous wrath for, indeed, they seem to indirectly promote and perpetuate criminal behavior. The prevailing attitude in our society toward the drug problem is one such obvious example. Though some of the most respectable elements of our society have openly acknowledged using marijuana, LSD, and even cocaine, and openly and laughingly smoke pot in their own homes and at parties, those who get caught continue to be labeled criminals. Society is especially venomous in its reaction to dealers. They are viewed as social scum while they are in reality only satisfying an existing demand. Furthermore, by continuing to deny hard-core drug addicts legal access to drugs, they are forced to go underground and enter into criminal lifestyles to support their habit. While the increasing numbers of burglaries and muggings are bemoaned drug addicts are literally pressured into performing these crimes through the refusal to deal with them openly. Furthermore, legal prohibition of abortion until a few years ago made criminals out of distressed, pregnant women, and often well-intentioned, courageous doctors. Prostitution or patronization of prostitutes continues to be a crime in spite of the fact that a very high percentage of men would openly admit to having patronized a prostitute in the course of their lifetime.

All of these point to the fact that on a subconscious level, society may be purposely creating the conditions to produce criminal behavior. In that way it can continue to assure itself of targets for indignation and righteous wrath.

Occasionally, the "police dance" breaks down in a blatant way. It may be discovered, as they did in New York City, for example, that a very high percentage of the police themselves were corrupt. By taking "payoffs" they were guilty of criminal behavior. The "police dance" also breaks down when we read of outrageous police brutality or the impulsive shooting or arrest of innocent people by the police. Sometimes in extreme cases a policeman is prosecuted. Most times these behaviors are simply viewed as "part of the game" and ignored.

At present, the "police dance" is a necessary and oftentimes successful approach to getting the more blatant and vicious criminals off the streets. However, in the long run, criminals need to be seen in part as aggression scapegoats or targets for aggression-phobic parasites who derive stability and gratification from labeling some individuals as criminals and prosecuting them accordingly. Ultimately in an aggression-healthy culture the "police dance" will be recognized for its polarizing and dehumanizing impact—one that makes emotional hypocrites of us all.

## THE "SPORTING DANCE"

We like boxing champions to be vicious animals in the ring and docile gentlemen outside of it. People need to believe that the boxer's behavior in the ring has no valid emotional connection to his behavior or feelings outside of it. Occasionally, as in the case of the late former heavyweight champion, Sonny Liston, who appeared to be as angry in private as he was in the ring, people become very offended by this breach of sport ethics.

Similarly, in football, hockey, or other violent sports, society encourages extreme aggressiveness on the playing field and then demands that these feelings be denied off the field. The "sporting dance" is theoretically designed to allow participants to "blow off steam" and to discharge aggression through the ritual of sports in a way that is impersonal. As an outlet for an energetic, aggressive interchange, the "sporting dance" can be one of the most pleasurable "dances around the beast." As a meaningful way of dealing with conflict and aggression, however, it is sorely lacking.

The competitive orientation of athletics creates a dehumanized, stereotyped way of perceiving the opponent. We "love" our team and we "hate" theirs. The game becomes a war in miniature, and our aggression is directed at the hated "thing," the other players or team to be "killed" or "destroyed." The aggressive discharge is split off from any authentic interpersonal experience. The opponent is a symbol, and the aggressive interchange is impersonal. It is very upsetting to everybody when occasionally it does become personal and one person shows his real anger toward another. Then, if a fight or feud breaks out, it is attributed to getting "carried away," and the participants are punished or penalized. In this way the impersonal nature of the "dance" can be maintained.

Audiences to the "sporting dance" in aggression-phobic societies will demand increasing amounts of viciousness and destructiveness from its athletes. In our society, for example, the commercial popularity of baseball is on the wane. The game is considered too slow and too tame. On the other hand, football and hockey, both with greater aggressive potential, are steadily gaining in popularity. The success of boxing matches is measured in terms proportionate to its brutality.

Watching sports events used to be thought of as a healthy, vicarious aggression outlet for the spectators. However, the obsession with football and basketball games on television has now made it an alienating influence and a form of indirect aggression by the viewer toward the rest of the family. It is his or her way of isolating themselves. That is, father or other family members stay glued to the television and resent the other family members' demands for attention or involvement.

## THE "WAR DANCE"

The "war dance" shares in common with the "police dance" the dichotomization of aggression in terms of the "good" guys and the "bad" guys. The other side is viewed as an evil force: hostile, vicious, and malevolent. "Our side" is invariably viewed as benevolent, peace-loving, and motivated only by the purest of motives, forced into war by the unreasonableness of the other side.

The "war dance," as one of the oldest forms of cultural aggression discharge, has traditionally generated many side benefits for aggression-phobic cultures. The rates of crime and suicide usually go down dramatically during war. Sharing a commonly held enemy seems to have the effect of bringing the people of a nation closer together. This is, in fact, one of the ironic and tragic by-products of war. Nations experience a solidarity and mutual warmth during wartime that they cannot seem to duplicate during peacetime. The commonly shared enemy target is the binding influence. War seems to bring nations together in the same way that tragedy can bring an alienated warring family together.

In addition, the "war dance" has other "positive" side effects. It creates heroes, stimulates economies, gives meaning to the lives of many who are lost and directionless, and provides educational and financial fringe benefits to its participants. However, as a meaningful design for eventual aggression control ("The war to end all wars!") it is a total failure. Participation in war requires the stereotyping and dehumanization of one's enemy. One has to view the enemy as an object or "nonperson" in order to be able to casually and impersonally kill him. Each participant, no matter how brutal his participation, rationalizes his participation with proclamations of righteousness. Each side views the other as the instigator and themselves as the wronged party. The "war dance" thrives on impersonality and distortion. As such it is totally outmoded and useless as a method of preserving peace and safety. Rather, it only intensifies the alienation and dehumanization process already existing among people.

## THE "PACIFIST DANCE"

The "pacifist dance" is a variation on the "religious dance" with its perception of aggression as the "evil" behavior of "bad" guys who haven't yet learned the beauty and meaning of life and love. The pacifist philosophy is one that says aggression only breeds more aggression and that at some point this destructive chain must be interrupted. Pacifists seek to be the influence to do just this.

The notion that aggression breeds more aggression contains within it the underlying belief that aggression can be eliminated altogether. The authors view this as a romantic fantasy, borne as a psychological defense against the feared and hated aggressive impulses within the pacifists themselves. There is not a shred of evidence in support of the belief that aggression can be totally eliminated. Rather, the task is one of acknowledging openly its reality in all of us, eliminating the taboos against its expression in personal ways, and then training or socializing its expression into constructive channels. The pacifist confuses his own passive defenses against aggression with peacefulness.

There is even evidence that pacifism can be ultimately very destructive in its naïveté and unreality. India, long a pacifist nation, has given this philosophy up in the tragic realization of the implications for its future relationships with neighboring countries. In our country the history of the blacks serves as a good lesson in point. The movement toward black liberation gained its greatest momentum after it abandoned the pacifist philosophies of Martin Luther King.

The "pacifist dance" is also a form of disguised aggression. By its "good" guy orientation it automatically creates its opposite. Those who oppose are "evil," "warmongers," or "killers." The pacifists' unspoken message is therefore colored by arrogance. Pacifists have seen the light. *They* have evolved to a higher, more spiritual level of consciousness. They are the truly peace-loving ones. Others are still lost in the dark.

The "pacifist dance" breaks down when conflict and dissension arise within its own ranks. Some pacifists are then viewed by others as not being "pure" enough. Divisions begin to occur and splinter groups develop. The pacifists are at "war" with each other, and this is blamed on the fact that some do not really "understand" the "real meaning" and practice of the philosophy or have not sufficiently evolved. No significant change of perception that would allow the pacifist to acknowledge his own aggression takes place. This awareness is rationalized away under the cover of ideological disputes.

## THE "SCIENTIFIC RESEARCH DANCE"

A more recent approach to the "beast" is the "scientific research dance." In this case the choreographers are the social scientists. Their aim is to learn how to contain the "beast" by accumulating information about it, studying and analyzing it.

A recent issue of a prominent journal of research in the social sciences illustrates some of the limitations to this "dance." The issue was dedicated to an exploration of "prosocial" or so-called "helpful" forms of social behavior such as altruism, sympathy, and charity. The stated reason for this was that too much time had already been spent investigating the negative or antisocial aggressive behaviors. This approach reinforces the perception of two kinds of behavior, the altruistic and the aggressive.

Some social scientists have suggested that aggression might be controlled by the conditioning of verbal behavior. The underlying theory here is that by eliminating the vocabulary of violence and hostility, somehow the emotions accompanying them can also be eliminated. The "scientific research dance" is couched in sophisticated academic parlance but the approach to aggression remains largely traditional.

## DANCING WITH THE BEAST

The "dances around the beast" all have one large element in common. Aggression is viewed as a destructive energy that must be channeled into impersonal ritualistic structures so that people will avoid destroying each other. The "dances" may have been functional at one time. However, they no longer seem to be serving the function of harnessing, containing, or rendering harmless the aggressive "beast." A new way of dealing with aggression is needed, and we propose it to be direct engagement, or "dancing with the beast."

The ingredient for this encounter would first involve recognition of the "beast" in each person. This would lead to a lifting of the taboo against all nonviolent forms of its expression and the use of constructive rituals and techniques to express them with. Destructive elements would be separated out from its constructive elements and the vital, growth-nurturing energies of aggression would be utilized.

# CHAPTER 10

# Like Sex: Suppressed, Repressed, and Tabooed

The repressive attitudes toward sex that prevailed in the Victorian era have remarkable parallels to our attitudes toward the expression of various forms of aggression today.

1. *Then,* sex was considered dirty, bad, and even dangerous, except under clearly defined, socially approved conditions.

*Now,* aggression is considered dirty, bad, and dangerous, except under clearly defined, socially approved conditions.

2. *Then,* free and casual sexual activity was considered improper. A dichotomy existed, for example, between "good" girls and "bad" girls. "Good" girls did not lose their virginity until they married. Only "bad" girls had premarital affairs, or indulged in sexual activity purely for pleasure's sake. Men sought to marry the "good" girls and took advantage of the "bad" girls.

Similarly, "good" boys did not masturbate or even act in sexually aggressive ways. Those who did were considered to be behaving like "animals."

*Now,* "good" people in general do not fight, lose their tempers, or get into arguments. Nor do they say impolite or "unkind" things that might make others uncomfortable or hurt their feelings. Above all, they avoid conflict and open displays of aggressiveness, and they are welcomed into "nice" homes. Only "bad" people lose their tempers readily, give vent casually to angry feelings, or tell people off.

3. *Then,* sexuality was the cause of agonizing conflicts. Women agonized, "Should I or shouldn't I? If I do, he'll think I'm a tramp. If I don't, he might lose interest." Men struggled with issues such as, "Will she think I'm too forward and get insulted if I try to kiss her on the first date?" or "I want to masturbate, but I know it's a wrong thing to do."

*Now,* the expression of aggressive feelings is a source of agonizing conflicts. The following are some typical examples: "Can I tell my employer that I resent the demands he's putting on me? If I do, I might alienate him and get fired. If I don't, I'll hate him and my job and he'll continue to take advantage of me." "I'm bored with their company and I want to leave, but if I tell them I might hurt their feelings. If I don't tell them I'll be climbing the walls soon." "If I tell her 'No' the next time she asks me to do her a favor, she'll get angry. If I say 'Yes,' I'll hate myself for allowing myself to be used."

4. *Then,* many sexual feelings and experiences were a source of embarrassment and were kept secret. For example: "Don't tell anybody that we're having sex." "I hope he doesn't find out that I'm frigid." "I can't let anybody know that I have homosexual fantasies."

*Now,* aggressive experiences and feelings are a source of embarrassment and are kept secret. For example: "Don't tell him I said I was annoyed with the way he's handling things." "I don't want anyone to know I lost my temper over that." "Don't let them know we've been fighting (arguing)."

5. *Then,* men and women were seen as having opposing sexual needs. Men were considered to have strong sexual drives. Women were considered to have little or no sex drive and were also assumed to find sex a distasteful and painful business.

*Now,* only men are considered to have strong aggressive drives. Aggressive women are considered to be behaving in a masculine way. It is generally assumed that women find aggressive behavior distasteful and frightening. Women who do assert themselves, such as the contemporary career woman, tend to be viewed and treated more as men than as women.

6.  *Then,* open and direct expression of one's sexual feelings toward another was a source of discomfort and anxiety and was therefore usually kept to oneself. Individuals felt guilty for harboring "lustful" feelings and feared rejection for expressing them.

*Now,* open and direct expression of angry feelings toward another is a source of anxiety and embarrassment and is therefore kept to oneself. People feel guilty for harboring hateful, jealous, or resentful feelings, and fear rejection for expressing them openly.

7.  *Then,* sexual feelings that came out impulsively under the influence of alcohol or in any other way as a result of getting "carried away" with the moment, produced feelings of guilt and shame afterward.

*Now,* aggressive feelings expressed impulsively, such as the losing of one's temper or making a spontaneously angry or unflattering comment, produce feelings of guilt and shame afterward. ("I made a fool of myself," or "I really lost my cool.")

8.  *Then,* for men unself-conscious sexual abandonment and acting out of one's sexual fantasies were reserved largely for experiences with prostitutes, casual affairs, or involvement with "promiscuous" women but rarely with one's spouse. Men didn't want to "use" or "abuse" their wives in this way, and wives didn't want their husbands to think that they were anything but "ladies."

*Now,* aggressive abandonment and the total acting out of aggressive feelings are reserved for anonymous, impersonal targets such as "enemies" or hated strangers or groups but are seldom displayed toward intimates. The reasoning is, "I care about you, so why should I fight with you?"

9. *Then*, when people did not hide their bodies or were being openly erotic, people averted their eyes and out of embarrassment avoided watching or looking at them directly.

*Now*, when two individuals argue, fight, or have angry outbursts, people become embarrassed and avoid looking at them directly.

10. *Then*, sexuality was the source of widespread ignorance, distortions, and mythology. Some of these myths were: "Masturbation can make you go crazy." "Women don't have strong sexual needs." "Excessive sexual activity will drain your energies."

*Now*, aggression is a source of widespread ignorance, distortions, and mythology. "Anger is destructive." "Quiet, gentle people are harmless people." "Conflicts between people can be permanently resolved if we would only learn to communicate." "Good babies cry less."

11. *Then*, the repression of sexual feelings was the major cause of many psychosomatic symptoms, such as backaches, headaches, cramps, and various other symptoms.

*Now*, the repression of aggressive feelings is one of the causes of many psychosomatic illnesses such as hypertension, arthritic conditions, asthma, and skin eruptions.

12. *Then*, a major cause of many emotional symptoms and mental disorders was the inhibition and repression of sexual feelings. Symptoms such as anxiety, guilt, depression, and hysterical symptoms were interpreted by psychoanalysts to be the result of repressed sexuality. Extreme repression of sexuality was said to produce severe emotional disorders.

*Now*, a major cause of many emotional symptoms and mental disorders is the inhibition, suppression, and repression of aggressive feelings such as anger, rage, and various forms of self-assertion. Symptoms such as anxiety, guilt, depression, etc., may be interpreted as expressions of repressed aggression. Extreme repression of aggression can produce very profound emotional disorders.

Analogies of sexual repression to the repression of aggressive feelings may appear to be inappropriate. Society looks on aggressive expression as fearful, while sexual expression is viewed as pleasurable, necessary, and vital.

In time, however, we believe that aggressive processes will also be recognized for their pleasurable, necessary, and vital aspects, and the present repression of that experience will seem as outmoded and destructive as the repressions that once enveloped the experience of sexuality.

# CHAPTER 11

# The Psychological Hazards of Mismanaged Aggression

Inhibited aggression, as a major source of emotional symptoms, is to today's society what inhibited or repressed sexuality was as a creator of emotional problems during Freud's era. In the time of Sigmund Freud psychoanalysts were first beginning to discover the enormous part that repressed sexuality played in the development of emotional symptoms. Freud personally developed his theory after working with numerous patients in whom this had created hysterical symptoms, such as paralysis, loss of sensory acuity, and other physical problems. These symptoms existed with no apparent physiological basis for them.

It was discovered that many of these hysterical symptoms were an unconscious protection against the expression of some taboo sexual desire such as masturbation, incestuous feelings, promiscuity, exhibitionism, or voyeurism, or simply engaging in premarital or extramarital sex. One patient's "paralyzed arm," for example, was interpreted as his unconscious self-protection against acting out an impulse to masturbate, while another patient's "blindness" was viewed as a protection against acting out voyeuristic impulses. In the more severe forms of mental disorders that Freud worked with, such as paranoia, he found repressed homosexual wishes to be one of the critical underlying causative elements. Freud discovered and formulated his controversial Oedipal complex by studying the case of a small boy's phobic reaction to a horse, a reaction that had no actual basis in reality in the child's experience with horses, and found that this reaction was a displaced fear connected with his repressed incestuous wishes. In general, Freud's analytical emphasis, as is now widely known, was on the enormous impact of sexual repression on the individual's personality development and the development of many kinds of emotional symptoms.

Since Freud's time, sexual liberation has imprinted itself quite heavily on the cultural consciousness. The old mythologies regarding sex are rapidly being destroyed by sex researchers and enlightened sex educators. A dramatic example of this cultural change of consciousness was the widespread popularity of the best-selling book *The Sensuous Woman*. In it, the author recommends masturbation for women to help them reach their sexual potential and to facilitate their day-to-day sexual intimacies.[1] As recently as twenty to thirty years ago one of the prevailing fears about masturbation was that its frequent indulgence was a factor in making people go crazy. We've clearly taken some giant steps forward in liberating our sexual consciousness from these destructive and harmful distortions. Today premarital and extramarital sex, abortions, masturbation, public nudity, and pornography have all become an integral and, to a great extent, accepted part of our cultural consciousness. Consequently, the role of repressed sexuality as a core cause of emotional symptoms has also been diminished greatly.

However, mental illness and widespread emotional problems are still very much with us, though their kinds and causes have been changing. Instead of hysterical symptoms being among the most prevalent, depression, anxiety reactions, and an inability to express feelings have taken its place. All of these emotional problems, we believe, contain large components of repressed aggression. Research studies in many of today's psychiatric and psychological journals have increasingly brought this to light. In fact, many of the innovations in the psychotherapy process today involve ways of facilitating anger and rage release. This goes along with the increasing awareness that these repressed feelings play a major role in the etiology of many damaging emotional symptoms.

## DEPRESSION

The relationship of mismanaged aggression to the eventual development of a deep depression, for example, can be seen in the not atypical interaction between Carl and Ruth, a couple in their early fifties. Throughout their relationship, Carl had felt enormous resentment toward Ruth while at the same time being very dependent on her. He also felt very much controlled and restricted by her and would quietly seethe with frustration and unexpressed rage. For example, when he would mention that he wanted to spend an evening alone with his friend Jack, just talking and having a few drinks, she would become extremely upset. She would scream and threaten until finally he would give in and cancel the date.

At other times, when he was walking along the street with Ruth, he might notice an attractive woman and would momentarily look at her. His wife would see him do this and would immediately accuse him of acting "like an animal" and of ignoring her. Evenings he would often sit bored watching television, too afraid to assert himself to do some of the things he really wanted to do, such as go out to play poker with friends or go to a basketball or hockey game. When Ruth would goad him for watching television and call him a "lump" for not having more active hobbies, he would get so angry inside at the "either way I lose" position he felt himself to be in, he would secretly wish her dead.

Very suddenly Ruth, who was an apparently vigorous woman, became seriously ill with brain cancer. She was operated on but the surgeon was unable to remove the whole tumor.

She subsequently received a series of cobalt treatments and then she became increasingly weak, frightened, and disoriented. Eight months after the operation she died.

Carl went into a deep depression. He kept saying he wished that he would have died instead. He would speak in barely audible tones and would call Ruth his "angel wife," while he reminisced about how loving and caring she had been. According to him, he had been a bastard who was only interested in his own needs and pleasures. Sometimes he would even blame himself for the fact that she had become ill. "I gave her so little to live for while she gave me everything. I drained the life from her," he would say.

Gone were the feelings of resentment, rage, and anger he had felt over being controlled and stifled by his wife while she was alive. In fact, he couldn't even really remember any of the many things she used to say or do that he resented her for so much. Those few he could remember, he would now blame on himself. All he could remember now was her "sweetness" and "kindness."

Months went by, and Carl's depression did not let up. He became increasingly immobile. Outside of going to work, which he barely managed to do, he would mainly just sit around staring into space and making self-accusing remarks. Finally, in desperation he was taken to a psychiatrist by his sister, recommended to them by the family doctor. Upon the psychiatrist's advice, Carl was given a series of twelve electroshock therapy treatments to pull him out of his depression.

When Ruth died, Carl was overcome with guilt regarding all of his aggressive feelings in relation to her. In some magical way he felt that his angry feelings, his resentment, his attempts and desires to assert himself independently and his occasional interest in other women had helped to kill her. He forgot totally the many irritating things she used to say and do.

In our aggression-phobic society it has been traditionally considered to be "wrong" to harbor angry, resentful feelings or independently assertive ones in the marital relationship, but even worse to experience these feelings after a person dies and to acknowledge relief, pleasure, or satisfaction over the death. They would be considered "horrible" and "hostile" if spoken aloud. No wonder so many people go into painful depressions after a death or divorce. They are in part suffocating on their own repressed anger and feelings of guilt!

Carl's reaction, though extreme in many ways, was not atypical of that in others. Depression in both its milder and more severe forms is a rampant phenomenon in our society and is intimately tied in with guilt and the repression of resentment, anger, and rage. People collude with each other to cover up these feelings. For example, friends of Carl never mentioned the incessant complaining and fighting they had seen over the years, Ruth's need to control him, her bitchiness, and the humiliating hassles in which she used to engage him in, in front of friends. Rather, they would try to be "helpful" to Carl by trying to persuade him that he had not been a bastard but had been a loving, sweet husband. They would, however, never challenge his assertion that Ruth had been a perfect woman, his "angel." That would have been considered extremely poor taste. Therefore, there was no way Carl could release all of the repressed aggression. He was left to wallow in his depression by well-intentioned friends who didn't want to upset him. Their kindly suggestions for Carl were that he take weekend trips, drink some wine or liquor, or eat the food they brought him and he would then feel better.

## ANGER HELPS

It is both interesting and revealing that our cultural definition of "helping" someone only involves being supportive, kindly, gentle, and positive. Individuals are not socially conditioned to see anything constructive or helpful in engaging someone in an aggressive interaction by confronting them, getting angry at them, or facilitating the release of their angry feelings by letting them get angry in return.

Paradoxically, the one thing that might really have helped Carl and saved him from having to undergo the electroshock therapy would have been to help him re-experience, express, and accept the frightening but very human feelings of rage he had felt toward Ruth while she was still alive. In terms of what psychotherapists today know about depression, Carl was suffocating on these feelings, feelings that he had too much guilt to accept and express and that were now being turned against himself in the form of self-hate and self-accusations. In his eyes, all the troubles of the marriage he now saw as having been *his* fault. *He* was the bastard, and *he* was the guilty one. While surrounded by "supportive," "loving" friends, Carl was sinking deeper and deeper into himself until there was the real danger of suicide, and so he was given electroshock therapy. Clearly, for Carl, love was not enough.

Typically, as psychotherapists working with depressed individuals, one of the first questions that needs to be asked is, "Who is the depressed person angry at and feeling too guilty about to acknowledge or express it?" In the instances of particularly extreme depressions bordering on suicidal impulses, the important question to be asked by the psychotherapist is, "Who does this person want to kill?" (though the actual impulse is usually out of conscious awareness) or "Who does this person hope to punish by hurting himself?" That is, it is known that profound depressions often cover intense repressed rage and hate.

The writers' work as psychotherapists in cases of depression and bereavement, in particular with widows and widowers, focuses initially on the release of angry feelings. Throughout the mourning rituals of Western culture there is no opportunity to release normal anger against the dead partner. Yet there are many valid reasons for feeling this anger. There is the acute anger for having been left or abandoned by the dead person. There is acute resentment over the fact that it is now too late to work out the conflicts that should have been worked out earlier and too late to have the discussions that should have been had. The depression after death, therefore, is often highly interwoven with rage.

Our program of therapeutic work with these widows and widowers includes first the making of a "museum list" in which they are asked to write in detail all of the things their dead partner had said or done to hurt them or that made them feel resentful at the time, but that they had never been willing or able to confront the partner with. After that, they are asked to confront a surrogate (substitute person) with that list in a full raging voice. In some instances we ask them to pummel a cloth dummy instead with fists, kicks, or a bataca bat while screaming out their feelings of rage at the dead person. From the intensity of the rage that emerges and the feelings of relief and lifting of depression that result afterward, we see the dramatic interrelationship between depression and the repressed anger over "unfinished business" with the dead person.

## RELEASING SELF-HATE

The mild depressions or "blues" that afflict so many in our culture we feel relates intimately to the chronic backing up of aggressive feelings against oneself. For people who are chronically prone to these kinds of feelings we recommend a "self-hate, self-forgiveness" exercise to be done every evening before going to bed. The person is asked to remember all of the things he or she did or didn't do during the day and for which he or she feels angry at himself or herself. After this, the person is asked to scold himself verbally and physically with a mild slap and insults such as "You idiot!" "You stupid fool!" "You goddamn insensitive, self-destructive creep!" This barrage should be continued until the individual feels satiated and begins to feel "This is silly! I'm not that bad!" or "Okay, I've punished myself enough." This then is to be followed with expressions of self-forgiveness, such as stroking one's face and saying in effect, "You're human and you have a right to act in human ways!"

It is characteristic of the socialization process, particularly among the middle class, to punish aggressive expression in children. The child is admonished, "Don't raise your voice to your elders," "Don't talk back," and "Children should be seen and not heard." At times these admonitions become particularly extreme in their inhibiting and emotionally destructive quality. "If you talk back to your mother like that she'll get sick and it will be your fault," "If you talk to your grandmother freshly, she'll go away forever," "If you don't stop fighting with your sister we will give you away," or "We will call the police and have them take you away." At almost every stage in the socialization process aggressive expression is inhibited by threatened punishment, or the instilling of feelings of guilt and shame. When this kind of feedback is particularly repressive and guilt-inducing, it lays the foundation for intense emotional problems.

It is safe to say that people with emotional problems of all kin·ls and severities share in common the inability to manage and express aggressive feelings because they were punished and made to feel guilty about them when they originally experienced and expressed them. Consequently, many individuals, disturbed and normal as well, are not even able to recognize the presence of these feelings within themselves, for they have learned to associate these feelings with one or more of the following disastrous consequences:.

1. *Abandonment.* As a child, the expression of various forms of aggressiveness were met with the threat that the parent would leave or the child would be left behind or given away. "If you raise your voice like that to Mommy again, she will go away and never come back" or "We will give you away to another home and never come to get you."

2. *Excessive punishment.* In these instances aggressive expression is met with the threat of extreme punishment, such as

beatings or deprivation. "Talk back again like that and I'll beat the hell out of you" or "If you contradict your mother again you won't be allowed to go out after school for a month" are variations on the theme of what the child is told.

3. *Doom.* Doom-oriented threats create links in the child's mind between aggressive behavior and horrible consequences to the person they're directed to. These links, of course, are exaggerated and out of proportion. Examples are "If you yell at your mother she'll get very sick and it will be your fault!" or "Do you want Grandpa to get a heart attack because you always have to give him an argument?"

4. *Destruction.* Related to the doom-oriented threats, these threats suggest that the child's aggressive behavior will have severe destructive effects interpersonally. For example: "Because you don't listen, Mommy and Daddy fight all the time. One day we will get divorced because of you" or "If you aren't nice to Grandmother you will hurt her feelings so much she will never come back again!"

5. *Death.* Threats of dying are made by the more disturbed and destructive of aggression-forbidding parents. "Stop your nagging and freshness or mother will kill herself" or "Someday when Mommy and Daddy are dead you'll be sorry that you talked like that."

The authors' own clinical experiences coincide with the observation of other psychologists and psychiatrists who have documented how parents of emotionally disturbed children typically have placed these children in impossible crazymaking binds in regard to the children's aggressive feelings. On the one hand, the parents provoke anger and resentment in the children through insults, blocking the child's attempts at growth, and by meting out excessive punishments. Then they threaten to punish the child for the child's expressions of anger in return. They leave the child no safe or direct outlet for normal feelings. For the sake of his emotional survival, the child finally withdraws and often loses touch with these feelings completely. He has been taught to see these aggressive feelings as being dangerous. To protect himself against them the child learns to block them out totally and deny their existence within himself. Once they are repressed in this way the child, when he becomes an adult, must increasingly isolate himself from intimate human contact to avoid interactions that might precipitate or threaten to force the expression of these feelings that in the individual's mind have developed fearsome proportions and will result in horrible consequences.

## CATATONIC SCHIZOPHRENIA

Translated into adult symptoms of emotional disorders, the repressed aggression can produce anything from migraine headaches to depression or, in extreme cases, the form of psychosis called catatonic schizophrenia. One of its victims was Leonard M., who was an aerospace engineer for one of California's leading aircraft companies. He was known among his coworkers as being highly creative and reliable. Though normally very quiet and soft-spoken, he began to become progressively more withdrawn and reticent. This was in March 1972. On April 12 his wife called the company to report that Leonard was very ill and needed an "operation."

The truth was that Leonard suddenly refused to move altogether. He simply sat, stiff as a statue, and was staring off into space with his eyes closed. He wouldn't feed himself nor allow himself to be fed by others. He had to be taken to a psychiatric hospital where he was diagnosed as "schizophrenic-reaction, catatonic type" upon admission. Leonard continued to sit rigid and unresponsive for several days. When a doctor or nurse moved his hand he would simply leave it in the new position. When they tried to open his mouth to feed him he clenched his jaws tightly together.

After several days of this he suddenly went into a violent, explosive rage and attempted to assault a nearby nurse's aide who was attending to him. Leonard was restrained by three people, and from that day on he began to improve, moving around and taking care of his own needs.

Within several weeks' time, with the help of intensive psychotherapy, he recovered and was able to talk about his illness. He revealed that he had become increasingly withdrawn and immobile because he was feeling very destructive and very guilty about his work, which was connected with defense. The fantasies and self-accusations that he kept to himself intensified until the day when he stopped moving altogether. At that point he believed that one movement of even a finger could trigger an explosion that would destroy the world.

These "world destruction" fantasies are commonly seen in this form of schizophrenia. They represent an extreme example of the distorted sense of one's aggressive power that many people have. Leonard M. had been brought up in a highly intellectualized family atmosphere. His father was a theology professor and his mother a geometry teacher in high school. Each attempt at assertive or aggressive self-expressions on his part was met with extremely harsh, punitive responses and dire warnings. Eventually, Leonard began to spend almost all of his time locked in his room, reading scientific books and working on mathematics problems. He never showed any strong emotions, positive or negative, until his breakdown. His wife later commented that ironically she was glad that the illness happened because Leonard's withdrawn personality was driving her crazy and she was seriously thinking of leaving him because of it.

## THE PREVALENT PSYCHOLOGICAL PROBLEMS

In the process of blocking out the awareness of and denying the existence and expression of aggressive feelings, individuals give up a large proportion of their emotional reality and the reality within their relationships. Many of the most prevalent emotional symptoms in contemporary society are, as already mentioned, the result of this inhibition. The following chart outlines some partial and possible relationships between inhibited aggression and the development of major psychological problems.

| PSYCHOLOGICAL PROBLEMS | POSSIBLE RELATIONSHIP TO REPRESSED AGGRESSION |
|---|---|
| 1. Depression | 1. Aggression directed against the self rather than toward its real, external target or targets in the outside world. Depressed people are in part angry people who are unable to express these feelings. |
| 2. Compulsions (*some*) | 2. Ritualistic, repetitive patterns of behavior that may serve to keep an aggressive feeling encapsulated and under control. For example, the compulsion to check the stove a half dozen times before leaving the house to insure that the gas is off may control an underlying destructive impulse or wish toward one's home and family. The compulsion to keep everything in order, neat and clean, may control the underlying impulse to say, "To hell with it all! I hate doing this!" |
| 3. Obsessions (*some*) | 3. The intellectualization of an aggressive impulse, which severs it from the feeling and protects the person from |

acting it out. For example, a mother obsessively repeats to herself, "I musn't drop my baby," which she fears she will do as she is holding it. The obsession contains and controls the underlying wish to do just that. Another example involves the person who at a party or formal gathering obsessively worries that he will suddenly scream out insulting curse words to the other guests. The obsession controls the underlying impulse to do so.

4. Anxiety (*some forms*)

4. The anxiety arises as the result of an unconscious fear that a frightening aggressive feeling will break through to consciousness and open expression. For example, a bridegroom's extreme anxiety before the wedding may represent a fear of losing control over an underlying desire to walk away from it all. Chronic anxiety can act as an indication of and control over rage against somebody or some situation: a feeling that is, however, too frightening and, therefore, not consciously experienced.

5. Neurasthenia
   (*chronic fatigue*)

5. Energy drained off as a result of repressed aggression (resentment, rage) over one's role. It may be a form of passive aggression, for example in the case of the housewife who is totally out of energy two hours after getting up in the morning. The chronic fatigue disguises her underlying resentment toward her role. The energy returns as soon as she is engaged in doing something she enjoys.

6. Paranoid suspiciousness

6. A reversal of aggressive impulses. The underlying desire to hurt others is transformed through the psychological defense of projection into the suspicion that "others want to hurt me."

7. Paranoid grandiosity
   (*"I am Jesus Christ. I will save the world."*)

7. A defensive, unconscious transformation of an aggressive impulse into its benign opposite. Thus, the underlying feeling of "I hate everybody" is transformed through a defensive process called reaction formation into the opposite feeling of "I want to save everybody."

8. Sexual impotence and frigidity

8. Aggression toward an intimate expressed passively through sexual

nonresponsiveness. It may represent an unconscious desire to punish, humiliate, or withhold satisfaction from one's partner.

9. The fear of "going crazy"

9. In terms of repressed aggression, this symptom may really be a fear that one will lose control and that hidden, terrifying, underlying rage and resentment will burst forward openly.

10. Suicide

10. Suicide is the ultimate form of repressed aggression, redirected from its real target toward oneself instead. The suicidal is a raging, aggressive person unable because of guilt to release these feelings outwardly against their real target. Suicidals frequently have the fantasy that their act will punish a certain person or persons in the environment. "They'll be sorry for the way they treated me when they find out I'm dead" is the unspoken message. The suicidal is locked in by guilt from expressing the rage against his situation or a specific person.

In an aggression-phobic society we are all vulnerable to emotional symptoms resulting from repressed and suppressed aggressive impulses and feelings. Acting them out is, of course, frequently not possible or socially tolerable. However, allowing these feelings into conscious awareness, accepting their reality, learning to control them, and finding suitable outlets for their constructive expression are essential for the development and maintenance of mental health. In the process of blocking out the awareness of these feelings we give up a significant hold on our emotional reality. The extent of this blocking is a factor in determining the potential for this kind and intensity of emotional symptoms.

The concept of "normal" in an aggression-phobic environment becomes a meaningless term. It may be normal to be constantly "nice" in our society because this is considered acceptable, even desirable behavior. This behavior will, however, prove to be interpersonally destructive. Feelings of alienation, depression, chronic anxiety, moodiness, uncontrolled outbursts of anger, and interpersonal manipulation may already be or will soon become statistically normal behavior by the simple fact that much of the population experiences them. However, they may be far removed from our constructive or healthy potential of human interaction.

It has become fashionable in recent years to romanticize madness and interpret it as a higher level of consciousness or a deeper level of reality. While we share the perceptions of psychological theorists such as Ronald Laing and Alan Watts that there are some important realities in insanity and that our society engages in many self-destructive, consciousness-destroying games, we feel that psychotic behavior is in part just another extreme form of repressed aggression. Despite the artfulness and exquisite sensitivities involved in many schizophrenic states, we feel it is misleading and destructive to conceptualize this form of emotional terror as a higher level path to sanity and truth. We believe, instead, that the psychotic is frightened of his strength, his rage, his need to assert and to dominate, and so resorts to complicated, fantasy-oriented devices to control and repress these feelings and impulses. The psychotic, in our framework, is only an extreme victim of the aggression-repressive society.

Achieving this emotional health potential will require the destruction of some deeply rooted myths, preconceptions, and response tendencies that are deeply embedded during the course of the socialization process.

## SIX EMOTIONALLY DESTRUCTIVE ATTITUDES

The following are some typical attitudes toward aggression that we feel have particuarly destructive effects on people.

1. "Getting angry is destructive and wasteful."

This attitude is the bedrock of aggression phobia. To get angry at somebody is said to be destructive to him and to the relationship. The longer and more intensely angry feelings are inhibited, however, the more extreme will be the fantasies regarding their destructiveness. The give-and-take of aggressive interaction must be practiced so that it won't feel overwhelming or be so laden with explosive potential when it is expressed— simply because it has been held in for so long and bursts forth destructively.

Anger, directly and constructively expressed in a spirit of good will, energizes its communicator and grabs the ear and involvement of the person it is directed against. While it may be threatening to the other person, if it is motivated by a desire to communicate a genuine feeling and not to overwhelm, it creates a communication reality. To suppress these feelings is to perpetuate an emotional and potentially explosive unreality. When the dam finally bursts, its power and energy may prove to be unmanageable, and one's worst fears about aggression will be confirmed.

2. "If I tell him (her) how I really feel, he (she) won't be able to take it. He'll (she'll) fall apart!!"

Many of the fears of openly angry, assertive communications

are based on a fantasy regarding the fragility of others. He or she will be extremely hurt, wiped out, or damaged by it.

The fantasy of fragility is usually in the mind of the angry person and does not coincide with the reality of the other person. The fantasy comes because of the underlying awareness of the intensity of one's feelings and the fear of the intensity of their power. The person who communicates helplessness and fragility when anger is directed toward him or her often does so manipulatively and as a controlling device.

To relate to others as if they were fragile and about to fall apart is in the long run to weaken them and to destroy the opportunity for spontaneous, real interaction. In the name of protecting the other you infantilize him or her (prevent him or her from growing up). An honest, clearly expressed aggressive message may be uncomfortable, but will also bring the other person closer to the reality of the relationship and help him or her learn to cope with anger and confrontation and thereby become strengthened in the process.

3.   "If I let go of my aggressive feelings, I might lose control over myself."

Many who hold back aggressive feelings do so because they fear that they will go haywire if they let themselves go. "I might become violent and even kill somebody" is a frequent and typical fantasy.

In general, violence ensues only as a result of long-suppressed hostilities. Those who consciously and obsessively fear they will lose control, rarely if ever do. The fear alone usually demonstrates the presence of such inhibitory controls. Allowing aggressive feelings to emerge regularly allows for the development of a familiarity with them and is perhaps the best preventative against violence.

4.   "It's 'inappropriate' behavior!"

Role inhibitions usually begin with words such as "I shouldn't," "I'm not supposed to," or "It's not right." For example, "Newlyweds shouldn't fight," "Doctors shouldn't lose their tempers," "Children shouldn't be allowed to talk back."

These inhibitions often wind up being the self-destructive price paid for trying to live up to an image that is alien to one's true feelings and real self. Ideally, roles function as facilitators of human interactions, not destroyers of them. When role inhibitions become self-defeating they are best abandoned. For example, for years now schoolteachers have been taught to mask their aggressive feelings and maintain a controlled, even-tempered presence through thick and thin. It is very possible that this unreal way of being is an important factor in the tremendous loss of control, sense of strain, and unhappiness teachers are experiencing in their role today. That is, they are being harmed by unreal role expectations, which are alien to their real feelings.

5.   "If I'm open about these feelings they'll reject me."

It is true that in impersonal relationships and in some settings, such as at work or in transient acquaintanceships, these feelings have to be kept more carefully guarded. With others who are not interested in relating but only in getting a job done or fulfilling a task, one might indeed jeopardize one's position, frighten off a casual acquaintance, or be subject to an unexpectedly powerful counterresponse.

However, close and emotionally involving relationships that require such great amounts of control and guarding may be more destructive to maintain than to abandon. By exposing one's aggressive feelings some people will indeed be driven away, but others will remain. The relationships with the latter will prove to be more satisfying and real, for indeed, to have to feel cautious and prohibited from expressing aggressive feelings within a relationship is already a form of being rejected. The other person is saying, in effect, "I want you as I need you to be, not as you are."

6.   "I'm afraid of what they'll do in return."

Because of extremely punitive experiences in childhood,

some people have learned to anticipate that any aggressive expression will produce horrendous retaliation, such as a physical attack. The original fears stemming from parental threats or responses of hitting or extreme punishment linger and are transferred to present interactions.

Undoubtedly, the openly aggressive person in an aggression-repressive environment assumes some risks for being aggressively real. However, often those risks, when finally taken, turn out to produce breakthroughs that totally restructure a relationship in more constructive ways. The maintenance of one's own mental and emotional health requires and cannot exist without an ever-present awareness, acceptance of, and, if appropriate, expression of aggressive feelings as they appear.

## PART THREE

# How to Live Constructively With Aggression

# CHAPTER 12

# Aggression Rituals

---

*". . . it is only when intense aggressiveness exists between
two individuals that love can arise."*

ANTHONY STORR[1]

The spontaneity that seems to come so naturally to children
who can play with each other, then fight and insult each other
only to make up and be best friends again, all within a short
time span, seems to be lost to adults. Focus for a moment on
the details of a recent social event, the celebration, party, or
gathering for a happy occasion that you attended. If it took
place at someone else's home and proceeded in relatively
typical fashion, you, as well as all other guests, were greeted
at the door with a big smile, a "Hello!" and "How are you?"
You probably returned this with a similarly "jovial" greeting.
Before you even had time to remove your coat and find a spot
in which to get comfortable, you were asked that famous
question, "What'll you have to drink?" Then for the next few
hours it was probably an endless round of boozing, interspersed
with food and cigarettes and accompanied by some polite,
"friendly," but dull and superficial chatter until everyone was
quite stuporous and generally "out of it." At about that time
people began to go groggily to their cars and then home. One
person recently termed such affairs "dip dances." The people

in the room wander from one party dip to another, commenting on its flavor and then going on to the next dip.

While attending one of these social gatherings, if you were responsive to your emotional experiences and feelings you would have probably begun to experience discomfort and irritation and might have said to yourself, "This is boring, what am I doing here?" or "This feels phony and I'm wasting my time." If you tended to mistrust your feelings you might have thought instead, "Is there something wrong with me that I'm not enjoying this as I should be? The other people seem to be enjoying themselves more than I am."

The following day, those people who were so "friendly" and polite and with whom you might have even exchanged phone numbers and made tentative plans to get together with became dim memories, names and faces barely remembered. Why? What was missing? How come these people gathering to have fun didn't?

One major factor that we suggest may be blocking the flow of genuine pleasure and social fun is that the personal and social rituals people presently engage in "for fun" are typically and almost exclusively designed for aggression avoidance and aggression control. The firm handshake, the pat on the back, the big "friendly" smile, and all of the other initial greetings are mechanical behaviors, rituals of reassurance and symbols of "friendliness." In fact, the person who does not willingly or automatically participate in them is looked upon with suspicion and even disdain as being a wet blanket, a party spoiler, or an ill-mannered oddball.

Indeed, where does it go from there for these polite game players? What happens after the initial rituals of friendliness have been engaged in? All too often it goes nowhere. The social interaction that began on this unreal tone also seems to freeze there. Food and drink are then used to fill up the remaining time. Imagine for a moment a party or social gathering in which no food or drink was served. Who would dare to risk it or face the tension and resentful feelings that would quickly build up?

The buildup of closeness, intimacy, or any interpersonal reality demands the sharing of other than "friendly" feelings. The "friendly" feelings are traditionally only ritualistic and impersonal ones. The reality of getting close to someone else means that there will also be an inevitable buildup of personal reservations, doubts, anxieties, and negative value judgments about people we first meet. However, with no socially acceptable ways of communicating these feelings, maintaining polite distance until it is time to go home becomes safer and simpler than taking the risks involved in sharing these aggressive feelings. Consequently, people go home as strangers, shadows to each other, caught in and repeating the superficial "polite" ritualistic social dances. Without anything in their social repertoire to facilitate the sharing of the anxieties, fears, resentments, reservations, and jealousies that occur constantly within initial encounters with others, people are left with the alternative of having to numb their sensibilities with alcohol, food, cigarettes, or drugs.

There are many facets even to the most joyous of social events that will inevitably stimulate resentments and anger in every feelingful individual. The birth of a firstborn baby is a good example. Friends ritualistically give baby showers, and the new father gives out cigars. But where are the rituals that would allow for the expression and release of the inevitable underlying feelings of resentment, frustration, and deprivation that a new baby represents and stimulates? For example, no more long, comfortable nights of sleep, no more undisturbed sex, no more spur-of-the-moment vacations or nights out for dinner and a show, and one more mouth to feed and body to clothe.

When the second- and thirdborn babies come along, the firstborn child is equally expected to be "happy" and is primed for this ahead of time. "Aren't you happy? You're going to have a baby brother or sister!" Parents even become upset if the firstborn openly shows resentment when, in fact, there's no reason why the firstborn should be happy at all. After all, he is being dethroned. Yet, instead of providing rituals by which the firstborn can thoroughly and safely express his natural resentment, parents demand emotional coverup of these feelings and the display of pleasure and love. If these are not forthcoming the child is labeled selfish.

Other such "joyous" experiences also have their share of aspects that are bound to stimulate hostility and other aggressive feelings. The college graduate is "supposed" to feel happy. But in reality, he's giving up the security of school. He is entering an anxiety-evoking change of state and lifestyle. He is losing a structure where goals were clearly defined and where he had acceptable targets for his aggression, namely teachers, exams, and the establishment.

At weddings the guests drink, dance, make veiled sex jokes, and collude in creating unreal expectations for the newlyweds. The wedding couple is informed that they "should" and of course "will be" so happy. The atmosphere demands that the couple keep smiling and act "happy" even though everyone, including them, knows that they are entering into a contract that is a mixed blessing at best. In fact, many honeymoons have become emotional catastrophes because these phony and cruel expectations and fantasies are weaved and can't be lived up to. No way is provided to the newlyweds for a sharing of reservations and resentments over the loss of freedom, sexual anxieties, and the conflicts and pressures that will inevitably arise.

A promotion to a higher-level job, obtaining a new job, or being honored upon retirement are all also treated as happy events. For example, the person who has been promoted to a higher-level job would be committing a serious social *faux pas* if he gloated or patted himself on the back. He must act humble and let others praise him. The resentment of those who were passed up for promotion in favor of him is also not to be openly expressed. Negative aspects of being promoted, such as the greater pressures and stresses, wariness over the jealousies of others, the isolation resulting from the change in relationship with coworkers who may no longer be comfortable lunch or drinking buddies, the sheer trauma of change and the hazards of the "Peter Principle," being promoted from a level of competence to a level of incompetence, are not to be verbalized. These would be considered lack of gratitude or crybaby behavior not befitting a person who has just been put into a position of greater power.

Retirement parties likewise have an emotionally phony flavor to them. They are very much like funerals at which the dead person is suddenly transmuted into a saint. That is, at funerals all of the negative feelings toward the dead person, the resentments, even the feelings of "In some ways I'm glad he's dead," are considered socially taboo. Similarly, at retirement parties the participants wax glowingly about the fabulous retiree and make unrealistic comments about how happy he should be now that he is free of schedules and responsibilities. In return, the retiree sings the praises of the organization. The resentments he may have over being pushed out of the company, the joy that many people may be experiencing now that the old guy is gone and fresh blood can be brought in to replace him must all remain unsaid. No wonder that these events are traditionally so boring to attend. The most important and deeply felt things are considered taboo and never verbalized.

Birthday parties, anniversaries, and Christmas gatherings also all have a large underlay of inherently negative aspects. Statistics show a very high rate of emotional breakdowns, depression, and suicide around Christmastime. These victims of the supposedly happy event may be despairing that they are not feeling happy and jolly as they "should" be and as others "of course" are. They conclude that there's something seriously wrong with them and their lives and therefore, since they're so different and unhappy, what's the sense of going on?

The feeling of "something being wrong" because one doesn't feel what one is "supposed" to feel is probably the most destructive aspect of the absence of rituals that would encourage the expression of aggressive feelings within the context of social experiences. Couples despair because their marriage isn't as happy as other people's supposedly are; parents feel guilty because they're not as happy as they should be over the birth of a child; and so forth. These people then proceed to punish themselves and give themselves messages of self-unworthiness for having feelings that are in reality normal but that people repress or simply hide to perpetuate the myths.

## RITUALS FOR RELEASE OF AGGRESSION

The authors therefore suggest the following rituals as starting points for guiding the release of aggression. We feel that these rituals, or individual variations on them, should become integral, everyday parts of social interactions, taking equal place alongside the rituals of friendliness. These aggression rituals are designed to provide a structure for the expression and exchange of aggressive feelings that inevitably accompany and accumulate within relationships.

The theory of constructive aggression on which ritual expression is based is expressed in the formula:

$$AG_{(c)} = \frac{I.I.}{H.H.}$$

$AG_{(c)}$=Constructive aggression
I.I.=Informative impact
H.H.=Hurtful hostility

This formula states that constructive aggression increases as hurtful hostility is reduced and informative impact is increased. The rituals described in this chapter, therefore, are devices designed to increase informative impact and facilitate the safe release of irrational, free-floating, intense underlying anger that creates destructive aggressive interaction.

These rituals are *not* designed to facilitate specific behavior change. This is left primarily to the "fair fight for change" structure discussed in another chapter and previously described in the book *The Intimate Enemy* by Dr. George Bach and Peter Wyden.

Aggression training sessions in which we have trained individuals in the use of rituals are alternately hilarious, serious, childlike, frightening, and stimulating. The communications are sometimes silly and ludicrous and at other times painfully cruel and distorted. All of them are not only permitted but encouraged. The so-called disordered, inappropriate, and out-of-line communications are both appropriate and constructive within the context of the aggression rituals.

Typically in normal social situations, aggressive interactions are shunned because they seem to have the effect of driving people apart. Within the structured context of the aggression rituals, paradoxically and surprisingly, these aggressive interchanges have the opposite effect of intensifying intimacy and generating trust between the participants rather than producing distance and alienation. This has to be personally experienced or at least observed for one to recognize the speed with which interpersonal cohesion develops in an atmosphere of freely expressed aggression within these structures.

## THE "VESUVIUS"

The "Vesuvius" is a ritual by which individuals can vent their pent-up frustrations, resentments, hurt, hostilities, and rage in a full-throated, screaming outburst. It is only engaged in by permission of those who are involved with the person, and the ritual can be used either in the home or work setting. By agreement it is strictly a one-way explosion of anger, which is listened to quietly but never responded to by the listeners.

The expression of these kinds of feelings, when randomly engaged in, as is usually the case in most people's lives, is almost always destructive in effect. That is, typically when one person explodes in anger he usually does so after using a relatively minor irritation as an excuse for unleashing a torrent of suppressed rage. This invariably precipitates a retaliatory response from the person or persons present. Then a full-scale fight ensues, often with very damaging consequences to the relationship. This ritual acknowledges the inevitability of such feelings in each person and is designed to provide a safe and structured vehicle for its expression.

In the family setting a specific time each day, preferably toward evening, can be set aside for each family member in turn to vent his or her individual buildup of resentment, anger, and frustrations, many of which will have nothing to do with any of the other family members. The listeners provide an attentive, respectful ear but do not respond afterward to any of the feelings expressed. As family members become more comfortable with this technique of allowing each other a few minutes of "rage" time each day, we would encourage them to go more and more out on the limb and express their deepest, most irrational feelings of hostility.

The vocational division of a public social agency in Oregon brings its seven members together in midmorning. Instead of the usual coffee break, each person in turn takes a three-minute turn engaging in a "Vesuvius." On one warm Tuesday morning in August Ms. Gloria Dimus, one of the counselors, stood up and took her turn. "I can't believe this goddamn city," she yelled. "It took me twenty minutes just to get on the freeway this morning. Then I come in here and I've got two appointments scheduled at the same time. That idiot receptionist our lumpy supervisor hired ought to know something by now. She's been here five months. And the fuckin' air conditioning still doesn't work in my office. If something isn't done about that soon I'm going to drag a repairman in here myself and stand there till he finishes. Then I'll present the bill to Mr. Randolph personally."

The members of this unit have found that sharing their frustrating feelings openly is both energizing and also brings them closer together as coworkers.

The "Vesuvius" ritual should be used particularly in conjunction with "happy" events. The prospective bride or groom, the newly promoted husband, the graduated child, or the new mother or father should be encouraged to "Vesuvius" about their anticipated frustrations and all of their negative feelings about the event. Also in times of a crisis such as an illness, death, school examination, or job interviews, the "Vesuvius" should be engaged in.

The "Vesuvius" is prophylactic in design. Many petty, alienating fights, desires to withdraw and maintain distance from an intimate, and individual brooding, moodiness, and depression are the result of suffocated, unexpressed rage. The "Vesuvius" can help to keep the air sufficiently clear so that long-drawn-out battles of silence, or sudden vicious and alienating attacks precipitated by minor irritations are much less likely to occur. This ritual can easily be adapted to a variety of settings where people are in daily contact with each other and where smothered feelings are liable to result in a tense atmosphere.

## THE "VIRGINIA WOOLF"

In Edward Albee's play *Who's Afraid of Virginia Woolf?* the protagonists of the play, a college professor and his wife, were into an almost continuous insult exchange. Their young guests often mistook it for a rational fight over issues. It wasn't. Rather, they were acts of ongoing involvement and love. She attacked him for being unproductive academically. He attacked her for not having children. They maintained their intimacy through this ritual. They gave each other hell so that the other person could fight back rather than turning the rage inwardly against himself.

The "Virginia Woolf" is a free-for-all, no-verbal-holds-barred, below-the-beltline insult exchange between two people. It is held by mutual engagement for a specific predetermined amount of time, such as two minutes. It provides a structured, nonlethal format for clearing the air of the mutual resentments that exist in all relationships but that rarely get aired until they build up to an intense level and result in a destructive, alienating donnybrook.

We have a rule of thumb about the "Virginia Woolf." The reality, intimacy potential, and genuine attachment between any two people, be they brothers, friends, lovers, or whatever, can be gauged by the extent to which they feel free, trusting, and comfortable enough with each other to indulge in a gut-level insult exchange. Relationships that require a "walking on eggshells" type of sensitivity are fragile and tenuous. It requires genuinely deep involvement and a feeling of commitment and security in order to express one's most irrationally angry feelings toward the other.

The basic format for a "Virginia Woolf" between any two people who wish to explore and enhance their intimacy by engaging in this insult exchange includes:

1.  Mutual consent for engagement.

2.  An agreement of absolutely no physical violence.

3.  A commitment to treat the exchange as "off the record," which means it is not to be taken literally, for indeed, the best "Virginia Woolf's" will facilitate the most irrational, cruel, and vicious outbursts.

4.  A specified and predetermined time limit, such as two minutes, which is mutually honored and after which the ritual is terminated.

Specifically, in this ritual each participant, within the agreed-upon time limit, lets loose in a loud, verbally assaultive manner, a torrent of insults against the other person. Both are screaming at the same time. Each participant is encouraged to focus entirely on his own attack and to avoid trying to listen or respond to what the other person is saying. In the ideal "Virginia Woolf," neither participant will have actually heard the other, even though they have been standing face to face and screaming directly into each other's face.

Once the "Virginia Woolf" has been mastered it will have the following characteristics: continuity, the steady stream of abusive and insulting remarks and hyperbole; and gross exaggerations, complete with total body involvement, in the way of facial expressions and gestures emphasizing derisive, sarcastic elements. The beneficial aftereffects are such that the participants report that they feel "cleansed" and much closer to the person they have just insulted. The ritual has also been found to be useful between individuals who have suffered a breach in their communication and find that either they can't talk to each other or when they do they become so excited and irritated that they start yelling at each other. The "Virginia Woolf," even between individuals who feel comfortable in their relationship, helps to keep the emotional signals clear. To reiterate, we feel that it is a sign of the profoundest sense of basic trust and security to feel comfortable enough with another person to engage in this kind of insult exchange.

## THE "HAIRCUT" WITH "DOGHOUSE RELEASE"

The "haircut," whose name was adopted from a Synanon technique, is a ritualized one-way verbal scolding that is accusing in content. The offense that is the basis for the "haircut" can be any irritating, offensive behavior that the person giving the "haircut" feels is causing severe damage to his ability to get close and continue an involvement with the "offender." That is, it is behavior which if left unconfronted will severely impair the quality of the relationship. The purpose of the "haircut," then, is to allow for a catharsis over a hurt, which can then evolve into the "doghouse release," a re-entry ritual that can re-establish the offender into the good graces of the other person.

The content of a "haircut" is limited to a specific behavior that the initiator has found to be particularly noxious and for which the offender accepts responsibility. The breaking of a promise, the betrayal of a trust, forgetting an important event such as an anniversary or birthday, or any such behavior can be an appropriate subject for a "haircut." "Haircuts" are also useful for individuals who only know each other casually or under very limited circumstances but who wish to keep the relationship free of secret buildups of anger by openly sharing their irritations with each other.

As in all rituals, the "haircut" requires mutual engagement. The initiator asks the offender for permission to give him a "haircut," after informing him briefly of the content. If the offender acknowledges the possible reality of the offense, he agrees to accept this one-way scolding. A time limit, such as one minute, is established.

The offender then sits and listens *in silence* to the complaint for the allotted period of time. He may, after the "haircut" has been given, request clarification. However, he cannot respond to, answer, or in any way counter the "haircut" or defend himself either during or after this ritual.

Presuming that the offender recognizes and assumes responsibility for the offense, he may then request a "doghouse release." This is a specific penance, which is determined by the initiator and which the offender agrees to perform in order to get back into the initiator's good graces. The initiator, once accepting such a penance, commits himself to a total forgiving and forgetting.

In some instances, the person receiving the "haircut" may not acknowledge responsibility, or may not wish to request a "doghouse release" in order to re-establish himself in the good graces of the initiator. In these instances, he may simply reject the "haircut" and the ritual is ended.

Susan James and Michael Journey had recently opened up a mail order pet supply company, which they operated from the garage of Susan's home. For four weeks Michael had been promising to install a lighting fixture but had failed to do so. Susan's frustrations over this built to the point where she found herself neglecting certain responsibilities in order to spite Michael, though they were both suffering the consequences.

On the Monday morning of the fifth week Susan asked Michael for permission to give him a "haircut." He agreed, and a two-minute time limit was established. Susan began: "For the past month you've been promising to put in some decent lighting. I feel like a nagging shrew having to remind you every day. I also feel that your ignoring me is a way of saying 'Screw you!' and I'm losing my incentive for working. I resent it, and I'm pissed off as hell at you about it."

Michael listened to Susan, and the impact of what she was saying finally dawned on him. He accepted the "haircut" and requested a "doghouse release" to re-establish himself in her good graces. The "doghouse release" that Michael agreed to involved his completing the lighting work by the following evening and writing a formal note of apology to Susan for his neglect, which was to be pinned to the wall for two weeks.

## THE BATACA FIGHT

A bataca fight is a ritual for releasing anger physically by using bataca bats. These bats are cloth-covered and filled with a soft, resilient material. This allows the fighters to swing at each other with total abandon. The pain is only slightly greater than that suffered in a pillow fight.

The bataca fight, like all the other rituals, is engaged in with mutual consent. When there are significant strength disparities as between a parent and a child, or between a large male and a smaller male or female, the participants must negotiate handicaps or "arms limitations" that will balance out the physical inequities. For example, a parent fighting with a small child may have to fight in kneeling position or on one foot, while holding the bat with only three fingers, in order to equalize the strength.

Physical handicapping to equalize strength should be done carefully and in such a way that once the handicaps are set both participants are free to hit each other with total abandon. Participants must be careful to avoid collusion in their handicapping, such as, for example, the "nice" guy daddy or husband who handicaps himself so much that he is totally unable to fight effectively.

Other limitations are also set. For example, the fighters will want to agree on certain parts of the body that are not to be hit, such as the face or the genital area. A safety zone should also be established to which a tired or overwhelmed participant can retreat for a time out.

A time limit is agreed upon. Most participants find that one to two minutes is enough. Once the fight starts, the fighters engage each other by hitting with the bats. If the participants agree on it beforehand, an insult exchange may accompany the hitting. It is not uncommon to find that individuals who under ordinary circumstances feel too inhibited to engage in an insult exchange ("Virginia Woolf") find that they are suddenly able to do so while fighting with the bats.

Bataca fighting is designed to give individuals a safe, physical outlet for anger release, particularly when words fail them and tension exists. It is both a playful and yet satisfying ritual and fills a gap for many people for whom physical aggression is either totally taboo or frightening.

## BATACA LASHING

A "bataca lashing" is the physical equivalent of a "haircut." It is a mutually agreed-upon spanking in which the offender allows the offended person to physically release his feelings of hostility over a wrongdoing that has hurt or severely impaired the trust of the offended party. The offender who acknowledges the pain he has inflicted and wants to get back into the good graces of the offended party either requests or agrees to the "bataca lashing."

The participants first negotiate specific limitations for this ritual, after the permission for it has been requested and granted. The beating can be limited to short intervals, such as fifteen seconds. If the beating has not been enough to relieve the anger of the offended person, further time periods can be arranged for by negotiation.

The partner who is to receive the lashing is expected to stand still and erect so that the partner can hit cleanly and safely. The offended person giving the lashing is encouraged to express his anger verbally by shouting insults and phrases of condemnation with each stroke.

Randy Arnold, divorced and with two children, had promised to take his son Randy, Jr., to Disneyland on his son's birthday. Mr. Arnold, who had recently become intensely involved with a woman, forgot completely about the date. The next time he came over to take out the children, his son locked himself in his room and refused to come out to see his father. After considerable coaxing the father finally got Randy, Jr., to open up his door. The father handed him a bataca bat and requested a spanking. After a few minutes of self-conscious discomfort Randy, Jr., began hitting his father on the behind lightly. However, within a few seconds' time he was hitting him and screaming in full rage, "I hate you! I hate you!" After about two minutes of this explosive screaming Randy suddenly calmed down and fell into his father's arms in tears. They were now friends again.

The "bataca lashing" is sometimes used after a death or divorce in which one partner is no longer physically available but where there is "unfinished business" in the form of residual anger. A cloth dummy or bean sack is used for a beating up in effigy.

## THE "SLAVE MARKET"

In this ritual the participants have the opportunity of experiencing themselves within their relationship in total dominance and then total submission. They take turns in assuming the roles of "master" and then "slave," or vice versa. This ritual is designed to break the usual rigid power interactions that exist within a relationship, particularly where one person tends constantly to assume the active or dominant role and the other person assumes the passive or submissive one.

Prior to formal engagement a time limit is set, usually three to five minutes, and a decision is made as to who will assume which role first. The person who assumes the role of "slave" then establishes certain limitations by specifically indicating what he does not want to be asked to do (i.e., "I don't want to have to sing or crawl on the floor."). Once the ritual has begun, however, the "slave" is committed to performing immediately and fully whatever is commanded of him so long as the limitations are being respected.

Those who assume the role of "master" creatively will use this ritual as a vehicle to get the "slave" to do things they would ordinarily never do but the "master" would like to see them do. For example, a compulsively proper, soft-spoken person might be asked to yell out obscenities, or a passive person might be asked to behave in a very aggressive way.

This ritual can be usefully applied in any setting in which there are power disparities between the people involved. These include office, school, or home, among others. The ritual facilitates the experiencing of oneself in an atypical aggressive interaction with the other person. Furthermore, the ritual provides an opportunity for experiencing oneself outside of the traditional cultural stereotypes. For example, in male-female relationships men often feel pressured to be dominant while females feel compelled to behave submissively. This ritual forces each person to relate in a different aggressive posture than they are accustomed to and to experience their reaction to themselves under these conditions. It is surprising how many men, for example, discover that they genuinely enjoy being in the role of "slave," being passive and submissive, a role they may have consciously resisted all of their lives.

## "ATTRACTION-RESERVATION"

In this ritual the participants are asked to share openly their reaction to an aspect of the other person that they find attractive and one that creates a "turnoff," or a tendency to withdraw from contact. These may be relatively superficial, such as a reaction to physical appearance, idiosyncratic gestures, a tendency to frown and look angry or to be very attention-seeking ("show off"). We suggest that this ritual be used in the early stages of any relationship and then remain continually in use as the relationship intensifies.

Sharing a "turnoff" or "reservation" as well as an "attraction" is a basic part of keeping a relationship aggressively current. The normal aggression-phobic tendency is to avoid seeing what one doesn't like about another person or simply hiding the information to be polite. This really prevents the relationship from getting off on a realistic footing. At times the lack of sharing reservations may even prevent a relationship from getting started at all.

A friend of one of the writers, who owns a local chicken take-out franchise, employs as many as five teenagers at any given time. He mentioned that things would be going fine for several weeks and then suddenly there'd be great animosity and somebody would quit. It was always a hassle finding somebody new to replace the person who'd left.

Having taken two of our office aggression seminars, he began to encourage his new employees to engage the older ones in the "attraction-reservation" ritual. The following dialogue occurred between eighteen-year-old Bill, already employed for seven months, and seventeen-year-old Clifford, who had just been hired.

Bill:  The thing that turns me on about you is the fact

that you ask a lot of questions. It makes me feel that you really want to learn. I really like that. My major reservation is that you use too much "hip" language. Every other word is "far out!," "heavy!," or "dig." It makes me feel like you're afraid to be yourself and trying too hard to be "Mr. Cool."

CLIFFORD:    What attracts me most about you is that you talk straight. No bullshit. You really seem to say what you mean. That makes me feel that at least I'll always know where I stand with you. My major reservation is that you're so cold and aloof. You seem to take everything so goddamn seriously and you seem to have no sense of humor. That makes me feel I have to be very careful and uptight around you or you'll take something I don't really mean the wrong way.

## SELF-REPROACH

This is a solitary aggression ritual that we suggest be done alone in the evening. The individual is asked to stand with his eyes closed and then to return in memory to the moment of awakening in the morning. Then he is asked to find the thing or things that he did since that he feels angry at himself about, matters that make him feel ashamed or where he feels he really goofed! For example, taking two drinks more than he knows he should have, smiling and pretending to be friendly toward someone he really dislikes, allowing himself to be sweet-talked into a responsibility he didn't want or was unable to say "No" to, forgetting to put money in the parking meter and getting a ticket, etc.

After the person has uncovered all of these disliked behaviors, he is asked to scold himself verbally and with mild physical punishment, such as a slap on the face, while shouting self-insults such as "Dumb, dumb!"; "Idiot!" When he arrives at the point where he no longer feels angry at himself and continuing this ritual feels silly, he should stop.

At this point the person is ready to forgive himself. Eyes

should be opened and an imaginary mirror created out of cupped hands. The individual should kiss the imagined image reflected in his hands and forgive himself by saying something like, "You're only human. You have a perfect right to mess things up!"

This ritual is designed to offset the tendency to build up a backlog of self-hating memories and thoughts that may ultimately play a part in the experience of becoming depressed.

## "PERSISTENCE-RESISTANCE"

The "persistence-resistance" ritual is designed to surface all of the pro and con reasons to a request before an answer of "Yes" or "No" is given. Two very common aspects of difficulty for most people in the area of aggressive expression are learning to assert oneself in the face of an initial rejection and learning to say "No" without feeling guilty when one does not feel like agreeing to a request.

The purpose of this ritual then is twofold. On the one hand, it facilitates practice in self-assertion. On the other it facilitates practice in overcoming and controlling the phony accommodating tendencies in one's personality. The latter is that part of one that is eager to please, to give in, and to say "Yes" even when one is feeling reluctant to do so.

Again, upon mutual agreement the person in the persistence role makes a request. The person of whom the request is being made is asked to automatically say "No" and to defend his resistance with an appropriate reason. The ritual is now in motion. The persister is asked to find as many creative and different reasons as he can to convince the resister to say "Yes." In turn, the resister is asked to express all of his possible reservations, all of the potential reasons why he would be better off saying "No." These should not be forced or phony. Only those reasons that are genuinely felt and believed should be given.

The ritual ends at the point where either the persister gives up and says, "I can see that you really don't want to and I don't want to continue trying because I've lost interest," or the resister says, "You've convinced me. I'll do it." Participants may agree on a cutoff point beforehand, such as seven persistences, after which, if the resister has not acquiesced, the ritual is ended.

As general practice at home, in the office, or between friends or lovers, we feel that engaging in this ritual can be a socially acceptable way of truly and deeply exploring demands and requests meaningfully in order to counteract the tendencies toward phony accommodation, being prematurely pressured into something distasteful, or overcoming the feeling of rejection when one receives a "No" with little or no meaningful exploration as to why. It is also a meaningful aggressive experience for many people just to learn to say "No" and stand behind it or to learn to assert oneself in the face of someone else's "No" and not interpret this as a personal rejection or an excuse for withdrawing.

The following spontaneous "persistence-resistance" exchange took place between a veteran theatrical agent and a young actress who was trying to convince the agent that he should take her on as a client.

SHE:   Mr. G., I would like you to represent me.

HE:   I don't think I can give you the kind of attention and time it requires to build a career for someone.

SHE:   I really feel I have a unique flair for comedy that's pretty rare today.

HE:   They're not making those kinds of films much anymore, and situation comedies on television are dying.

SHE:   I've also done heavy drama and the classics. I've gotten nothing but fine reviews in every summer stock and theater piece I've ever done.

HE:   Good reviews are important, but there are a helluva lot of fine actresses running around this town with a portfolio full of good reviews.

SHE:   I really wouldn't be a drain on your time. I'll do

most of the hustling, and all you have to do is send me out on the auditions that I'll find out about myself.

HE:    I like that, but I've got sixteen clients right now and I don't want to overload myself.

SHE:    How about a two-month trial period? If you don't get good feedback on me I'll go away quietly.

HE:    Well, I don't know really. Call me next Monday.

SHE:    I think I ought to tell you I know I'm going to be successful with or without you. But I'd rather do it with you.

HE:    I think you do have the drive it'll take. I really like that about you. I'll make a three-months' trial arrangement with you.

### "HURT MUSEUMS"

This ritual is designed to surface secret resentments and hurt experiences that have not been previously shared. In most relationships these feelings are accumulated and stored until at some point there is a straw that breaks the camel's back, and a large rift in the relationship develops. At this point the stored-up negative feelings may be so overwhelming that the reconstruction of good will becomes impossible.

If the participants have a current ongoing relationship, the list should focus on the hurts that they feel the partner has inflicted on them, particularly those that have never been previously shared. If the participants are in the early stages of a relationship, such as a new employee with his employer or other employees, or in a new love relationship, the list can be made up of instances where the participant was hurt by another employer or member of the opposite sex in a past relationship and is still carrying the memory of that hurt and fear of its repetition into the present. Communicating this information in a ritual makes it less likely that the new relationship will be contaminated by past experiences.

This ritual is engaged in by mutual agreement. Each person

writes down a list of past hurts in whatever order they occur to him or her. There is no time limit to the list-reading, though one person may call a time out if he or she feels overloaded. The listening partner remains totally silent, never answering or defending as the list is being read. When one participant has finished, the other begins to read his or her list. There is never a discussion of any item on either list until the ritual has been completed by both parties.

After both participants in an ongoing relationship have read their lists, there are a number of options for dealing with the items presented.

1.   Bury certain list items by agreeing that their memory will henceforth be consigned to oblivion.

2.   Barter some items, which means trading them off. "I'll agree to forget about the time you insulted me in front of a client if you'll forget about the time I stayed away all night and never called you."

3.   Agree that some items are legitimate fight issues that need to be dealt with in a fair fight format because they contain possibilities for constructive changes. (See chapter entitled "Office Fights for Change" for details of the fair fight format.)

4.   Enshrine some items permanently in the "Hurt Museum" simply because it is enjoyable to remind the other person of them.

### "BELTLINE SHARING"

In this ritual each participant writes a list of his or her "beltlines" and exchanges them with his or her partner. "Beltlines" are whatever sensitive areas, behaviors, criticisms, or responses one finds emotionally devastating. These "beltlines" are idiosyncratic in nature. What is minor to one person may be very painful to another. For example, some people enjoy being touched while they're spoken to. Others recoil in revulsion and withdraw from further contact. Discussions carried on in a loud voice may be abhorrent to some while not affecting others negatively at all. "Beltlines" that involve personally sensitive areas may include comments about one's weight, job failures, previous traumatic relationships, or remarks about one's emotional stability.

Jerry Bradford who attended our fight training group for married couples along with his wife, from whom he was separated at the time, read her the following list of "beltlines"— things she did and comments that she would make that hurt him very deeply or caused him to become red with rage:

1.   Whenever you tell me that I've only been a success at my work because I'm an ass-kisser.

2.   When I pick up my guitar to play and you grimace or walk out of the room.

3.   Whenever you bring up that business about my first wife having run off with another guy and that I should be grateful because you haven't done the same thing.

4.   When you tell me that I don't have to work as hard as I do and then you go out and spend hundreds of dollars on plants and clothing and keep the big bills coming in.

5.   When I start talking about my work in front of other people and you look like you're ready to fall asleep with boredom.

Though some of these "beltline" reactions may be considered neurotic, until they are worked out in psychotherapy or in some other way, it is important that people involved with each other become sensitive to and respectful of each other's "beltlines" if a relationship of trust and closeness is to be built.

## "INSULT CLUBS"

We all have certain stereotyped notions about people that we attach to their sex, color, profession, religion, appearance, etc. For example, seeing women as being manipulative, hysterical, materialistic; seeing Mexican-Americans as being procrastinators or irresponsible; seeing engineers as being unemotional and computerlike; and seeing Jews as being conniving and materialistically ruthless are some.

Most people like to think of themselves as not harboring such stereotyped perceptions. Our experience suggests that such people are a rare minority, if in fact they exist at all. This ritual, performed in groups, is designed to surface these stereotypes in the early stages of involvement between any mutually hostile groups desirous of working or communicating with each other meaningfully.

Young people harbor many stereotypes about older people, as do blacks of whites, males of females, students of faculty, employers of employees, and vice versa. Particularly in work settings, where such groups need to be able to communicate meaningfully, we feel that the traditional rituals of politeness and extreme concern with protocol are wasteful, phony, and ineffective. Inevitably the barriers remain despite the great efforts expended to bridge them. We have found that an open and total sharing of the deepest suspicions and resentments utilizing this ritual, can facilitate genuine communication based on a mutual reality. Individuals in these groups can speak the "unspeakable" thoughts and feelings that each knows exist but pretend don't, and proceed from there.

In this ritual, upon mutual agreement, each group huddles and gathers an arsenal of their most primitive, irrational, and unspeakable stereotypes of the other group. Groups should allow all of their negative feelings to emerge. This ritual, which is best done in the presence of a referee, is engaged in in turns. A member of one group stands up and while facing the other group sitting down a few feet away, lashes out in a verbal assault for an agreed-upon amount of time, such as one minute. After this he must remain standing while he listens to the response of the group he has just attacked, also for one minute or an agreed-upon amount of time. Then one member from the other group stands up and takes a turn. Eventually each person in both groups is given a chance to vent these feelings. The ritual ends only after everyone has taken a turn.

This is a group version of a "Virginia Woolf" except that both sides do not insult at the same time, as they do in the "Virginia Woolf." The merit of an insult exchange done in a group is that speaking the "unspeakable" when done in this form can even be fun, while if done on an individual basis would be too threatening and anxiety-provoking. It is remarkable to see the "ice melt" after such an insult exchange and to observe distant, distrustful, and hostile groups begin to become more comfortable with each other.

## ADAPT YOUR OWN RITUALS

The rituals described in this chapter are viewed by the authors mainly as transitional structures, bridging devices, and temporary supports, much like balancers on a bicycle. It is anticipated that the reader will be saying to himself that the rituals are contrived. We would agree. They are contrived in much the same way as learning to relieve oneself on a toilet is contrived when compared with the freedom and spontaneity of defecating or urinating wherever or whenever one pleases. In our culture today personal aggression is unsocialized, and we do tend to release these feelings in "dirty," repulsive, and destructive ways, any time and any place, because there are no rituals or formats by which to release them in structured, nonhurtful, and playful ways. People have little or no control over angry or resentful feelings when they well up because their expression has always been suppressed or denied.

As individuals utilize and become comfortable with these transitional devices, they may wish to abandon them and develop their own structures for nonhurtful aggressive expression and release. These formal structures can then be adapted to individual needs. We view these rituals essentially as "permisson givers," which say to people that it is all right to have and express aggressive feelings, and here's a way to do it in a safe, constructive way. It is our hope that eventually the development of rituals to release personal aggression will become an art and/or a science and that creative, inspired individuals everywhere will be stimulated to develop new and increasingly effective and relevant ones.

# CHAPTER 13

# The Aggressive Body

---

Mr. Milton Wright, who had a history of skin disorders, was sitting in his psychologist's waiting room. He had fought traffic in order to get to his appointment on time because his psychologist, Dr. Braun, would make an issue out of it when he arrived late and interpret it as being his "resistance" against the therapy. This particular day he had managed to get to his appointment five minutes early and had already been kept waiting for over twenty minutes. He was feeling restless and resentful and was even beginning to think, "To hell with him, if he doesn't come out soon I'll just leave," when Dr. Braun came into the waiting room. Mr. Wright immediately began to smile—but he also got a sudden and violent itching attack. Noticing this, his psychologist asked him what he had felt about having been kept waiting and what he was feeling right now. Mr. Wright could only answer, "Nothing really, except that I was glad to see you." In this response he was actually being consciously honest. His fear of getting directly angry at his doctor and possibly being rejected for it, as he imagined might happen, caused these feelings to be immediately repressed when the doctor appeared. Dr. Braun pressed him further about the possibility of his having been angry, and Mr. Wright shouted, *"Damn it! I know what I feel like when I'm angry, and I wasn't angry!"*

When they began to explore the intense itching during the session and with Dr. Braun's supportive comments about how it was okay to have been resentful, Mr. Wright started remembering and experiencing the anger and finally was able to express the feeling that the doctor was "shitting on him," as he put it. When he was finally able to look at the doctor and say, *"You* pissed *me* off," the itching subsided. Until then, those angry feelings were being directed against his own body rather than at its real target.

## THE CAUSES OF PSYCHOSOMATIC DISEASES

A recent issue of the prestigious research journal on psychosomatic illness, the *Journal of Psychosomatic Research,* was devoted to the relationship of repressed aggression to psychosomatic illness. One researcher, discussing in a summary way the role of repressed aggression in the development of psychosomatic diseases, arrived at the following conclusion: "It is a hard clinical fact that psychosomatic syndromes do not arise when activated aggression has not been suppressed or repressed beyond a certain degree."[1] In other words, he was saying that psychosomatic diseases have repressed aggression at least as a partial cause at their root. The psychosomatic illness serves the function of warding off this aggressive impulse. It arises because the person is not able to express these feelings directly. The psychosomatic illness may also provide him with the attention and control the person couldn't otherwise get. At other times the illness develops because the aggressiveness or "fighting back" reaction needed to resist the illness is absent. In general, many psychosomatic symptoms are created when the aggressive impulse is warded off and the energy from it is being discharged into a pathway of bodily functions rather than through open emotional responsiveness.

The constructively aggressive individual reads the signals for self-preservation that the body sends out during the body crisis we term sickness. He assumes assertive responsibility for removing causes that bring on bodily distress rather than passively ingesting pills to disguise the presence of the discomfort. This may involve increased exercise to tone up the body and build greater resistances. Or it may mean eating only when he feels hunger rather than passively acquiescing to the schedules and rhythms of eating set forth by others, and by resisting the social pressures at parties or dinner to stupefy himself with food and drink that his body does not require. Most importantly, however, he learns to recognize the needs of his own physiology and asserts himself in accord with his own bodily rhythms and needs rather than passively accepting those rhythms that have been externally imposed. On an emotional level this means dealing with the conflicts and crises in his life directly and assertively rather than allowing the effects of repressed aggression to impair him physiologically.

For indeed, the physiological price of the repression of one's "aggressive body," failing to read its signals, is incredibly high. Scientific research is pointing to its role in many of the major illnesses, from arthritis to sclerosis and from hypertension to cancer. Aggressive impulses and feelings, when expressed in normal and healthy ways, serve a powerful self-preservative function. However, they turn their energy against the body when they are not provided open, expressive outlets. When aggressive feelings are openly and directly expressed, they energize and excite the body's muscular system. The sympathetic adrenal system is mobilized and releases an enormous flow of energy. The muscles designed for active expression become charged with power unknown to them at other times. In the aggression-repressed person the conscious awareness and discharge of this response are blocked. As a result, the individual remains in a state of more or less permanent underlying aggressiveness, which will make him constantly "high-strung," "tense," "ready to explode," and "short." The feelings and impulses that are not given adequate discharge by open expression are retained within the physiology and short-circuited internally to produce the bodily changes that are the foundations for psychosomatic diseases.

## THE ASTHMATIC: A HIDDEN PROTESTER

Jonathan Reynolds was twenty-four years old and single. He rarely dated. His mother, with whom he was living, was a very domineering and old-fashioned lady. Jonathan had to dress neatly for all meals, was not allowed to raise his voice in the house, and had to tell her about every letter and phone call he received. She constantly hovered over him.

Periodically, Jonathan would make attempts at behaving more independently or rebelliously. His mother would ask him who he was on the phone with, and he would respond with an angry, "It's private." Occasionally he would even look through the classified ads for rentals thinking he might move out. However, pretty soon he would start to feel guilty and have an asthmatic attack, just as he had since he was a child. At these times of illness he would turn to his mother, who would be very loving and concerned. She would use his asthmatic attack as an opportunity to reinforce the idea that Jonathan really needed her and couldn't survive without her. Jonathan would soon become docile and grateful.

The asthmatic attacks were at once a cry to be taken care of and a fear of the aggressiveness involved in rejecting his mother's control and asserting himself independently, which he was afraid to do. He and his mother were in collusion on this. His mother preferred his illnesses to his aggressiveness and reinforced the illnesses heavily. Jonathan was frightened of his aggressiveness and readily regressed back into the baby role, wheezing, coughing, choking, and crying for mother's help instead of acting assertively.

In another case, Mary Cole, twenty-four years old when

she came for help, began to have her asthmatic attacks two years earlier. This was only shortly after she had discovered that her husband Mickey had been having sexual relations with other women. She was enraged inside of herself but unable to express it because she was afraid of him.

At about the same time her husband, who was a stock car racing fanatic, was involved in a bad accident. During his convalescence at home he became very demanding on Mary and insisted on being catered to by her. Mary resented this enormously and felt like saying, "Get one of your girlfriends to take care of you!" But she felt too guilty and fearful to say it at that time. She began having asthmatic attacks. The clinic at the hospital referred her to the psychiatric division. As she began to talk about what was going on in her life and could express some of the bottled-up rage at her husband's behavior openly, the asthmatic attacks subsided.

The asthmatic personality is described in psychosomatic literature as dependent, overly conscientious, and afraid of open expression of anger and confrontation toward those he needs. Inhibited in the area of self-assertiveness and unable to discharge anger and rage, the asthmatic reaction becomes an indirect reaction to their world, which they experience as hostile, but feel impotent in terms of impacting on and changing.

Unexpressed rage within a close dependency relationship seems to be a key psychological factor in the personal makeup of the asthmatic. The asthmatic attacks often cease when the person is able to gain enough inner security and strength to express the rage directly and to function independently.

## THE "HEADACHE PERSONALITY"

It is estimated that at least fifteen million Americans suffer from recurrent tension headaches. Migraine sufferers have been described as perfectionistic, driven, and overcontrolled. They remain outwardly calm and polite while hiding their anger and rage inside of themselves. The following is a case illustration of this pattern.

A thirty-nine-year-old single woman worked as an executive for a major advertising firm in Chicago. She'd worked her way up slowly through fifteen years of hard work and felt proud of her ability to make it in a man's world. In the process she had denied herself a social life. She had only been seriously involved with a man once, and at the verge of getting married had decided against it.

Six months before her first migraine attack she met a man in his early sixties who was a lawyer on the verge of retirement. He represented stability to her, and she could feel confident he didn't want her for her money. On an impulse she decided to accept his marriage proposal. However, she got more than she bargained for, and soon began feeling imposed upon. He wanted his dinner each evening and also wanted her to cut down on her work schedule. She began to feel that the marriage had been a mistake. She realized that she had married in a panic, out of fear that it might be getting too late. However, she accepted this as her lot but was getting frequent headaches at work.

Her family doctor after a long discussion suggested a trial separation. She agreed and took her own apartment. After two weeks of living alone the migraines ceased. On and off she would return to her husband for a few days, but each time the result was the same. The headaches returned. She was referred for psychotherapy and during her sessions was surprised to discover how often in her fantasies and dreams she pictured her husband dead, and at times she herself was the killer.

Migraine sufferers in psychotherapy often reveal intensely hostile fantasies toward intimates such as spouses and siblings in which they see themselves chopping their heads open with an ax. These fantasies are in stark contrast to an outward personality that is highly socialized, controlled, and perfectionistic. Only when their general uptightness loosens up do they stand a chance of overcoming these headaches without the use of drugs.

## THE HYPERTENSIVE PERSON

An estimated number of ten to twenty-five million Americans have chronically high blood pressure. This serious disorder can damage blood vessels, the kidney, and the heart, and make the individual vulnerable to strokes.

Again, as in the "headache personality," in the hypertensive person there is a wide gap between internal emotional experience and the external face the world sees. The hypertensive is often described as outwardly calm, friendly, and well adjusted. They are commonly known as loyal, hard workers, and beasts of burden who always take on more than their share of responsibility. The only giveaway to the buildup of their inner resentment and feelings that "Everything is always left up to me!" are occasional sudden outbursts of temper. Otherwise, they are known for their outward calm. It is not unusual to see them remain loyally on the same job for years even though they are being underpaid and overworked. When they are finally promoted to higher positions of power their hypertensive condition often becomes more severe because they have great trouble with their aggression in terms of asserting themselves and giving orders.

Kathy McPhee, thirty-one, was the head of her own thriving travel agency in a small eastern city. She had a knack for making people love her immediately. She was always cheerful and available to help in any last-minute travel crises. However, no one really got close to Kathy. Though quite attractive, she lived alone, never dated except for attending an occasional community function with a client, and had no close friends.

Though she consistently grossed over four thousand dollars a month, she continued to work twelve-hour days. She felt under constant pressure to keep up with the latest travel developments and to stay ahead of her competitors. Twice in the previous year she had hired an assistant and each time had let the assistant go. They didn't meet her high standards of perfection. At the time that her doctor had discovered her tendency to extremely high blood pressure she had just hired a new assistant but continued to feel, "It's all up to me. I still have to worry about everything." Her doctor, who was her only confidant and knew of the frustration, rage, and pressures within her, referred her for psychotherapy.

Underneath the surface friendliness and extreme conscientiousness of the hypertensive personality a constant buildup of resentment is occurring. This breaks through occasionally in the form of an outburst over some petty issue. In Kathy's case, her assistants would be the target of this rage if they happened to do something that displeased her, such as making a personal phone call during office hours.

In psychotherapy, the outwardly cheerful, "friendly" hypertensive reveals intensely hostile fantasies. They often admit to wishing that people who were close to them would go away or drop dead. There is a tremendous sense of bitterness toward family and intimates whom they see as cold, demanding, and responsible for laying all the burdens on them. The hypertensive, however, hides his needs and anger behind a front of hard work, "friendliness," and selflessness.

## THE ARTHRITIC

Recent studies of arthritis have concluded on the basis of considerable evidence that people with rheumatoid arthritis have as a major cause of their illness strong conflicts over their anger and its expression. Patients studied are frequently described in research literature as having had mothers who were highly authoritarian, unreasonable, and overly severe in their discipline. The patient's reactions to this arbitrary authority were always covert. Overt resistance and open expressions of resentment rarely if ever occurred. They were afraid to assert themselves in this way.

Arthritics are also frequently described in research studies as individuals who are introverted and overly sensitive to anger in others. While they themselves are far less willing to express their own anger than others, they also have a strong personal aversion to other people who are strongly or directly aggressive. Some arthritics contain their aggression by exercising great control over themselves and benevolent tyranny over others. Loss of the person they dominate tends to set off the attack of arthritis. Others strike a masochistic pose and are known as "long sufferers." Their style is a self-sacrificing and aggressively inhibited one.

One such example was Michael Bond. He was a soft-spoken, hard-working hardware supply salesman. He had four children and got all his pleasure doing things for others. After a hard day's work he'd help the kids with homework and his wife with the household chores. On weekends he coached Little League and worked for the church. The arthritis in his fingers began in his midthirties. Though the pain was at times very severe, rarely did it cause him to give up his activities.

Some specialists in psychosomatic medicine interpret the gnarled posture of an arthritic's joints as symbolic of the chronically inhibited aggression and as a self-punishing, self-inhibiting defense. The underlying repressed aggression, which seeks discharge through the muscles, results in a simultaneous increase in the tonus of the antagonist muscles. Over a long period of time this traumatizes the joints and is believed to be a factor in creating the gnarled postures and pains of arthritis.

## HIDDEN AGGRESSION AND CANCER

Cancer has been the subject of extensive research during the past ten years. Victims of cancer were described in one study as "inhibited individuals, with *repressed anger*, hatred, and jealousy."[2] Another study found that women who had cancer "were found to have no techniques for discharging aggression directly.

They denied these feelings in themselves."[3] While we are not implying that repressed aggression is the sole cause of this complex and terrifying disease, we feel that these findings are nevertheless noteworthy.

More startling is a recent study by Kathleen Stravraky, who compared a group of patients who deteriorated rapidly after their diagnosis of cancer to a group who had lived longer than predicted. Of the 204 patients studied, those in whom the cancer progressed rapidly to termination were those whose personalities were described as highly defensive, with strong predispositions to be depressive and inhibited in hostile expression. Those with the favorable outcomes, who had lived for a significantly longer time, were able to become more frequently hostile than the cancer patients who survived only an average length of time. This capacity for open hostile expressiveness was seen as a key factor contributing to a favorable prognosis.[4]

Recently in an autobiographical writing a female cancer sufferer described the course of her disease. She made some remarkable observations about her interactions with people during her illness. She described particularly how she and most other cancer patients she knew were prevented by friends and intimates from expressing their plight directly. Friends were empathetic to expressions of sadness and helplessness but became uncomfortable when the patient gave vent to anger and resentment. Sensing their visitors' discomfort, the cancer patients tended to hide their anger and tried to fill silences with happy, cheery talk. This left them feeling more alienated and hopeless than before the visit.[5]

## COLLUSION DURING ILLNESS

The reader might reflect on the collusion to abort aggressive displays that goes on between sick people and their intimates. The very sympathy of others may be repressing the vigorous, aggressive response that results in quick recovery. A dramatic and pathetic example of this collusion was noted recently by the writers. It involved a twelve-year-old boy named William, who was brought in supposedly for the purposes of an educational evaluation. He had been doing poorly in school. However, during the interview he readily began talking about his seizures. At one point during the session he had one. His left arm extended, his right arm flexed, and his eyes and head turned to the right. This continued for about thirty seconds. Immediately afterward he was dazed and confused but aware that he had had a seizure and sought sympathy from the examiner.

In the discussion that followed it became evident that these convulsions, though often real, were also attention-getting devices. That is, sometimes his seizures were caused by abnormal brain wave components, but at other times they weren't.

William continued to come for a few more therapy sessions and began to make improvements. His seizures were occurring less frequently. His parents at this point, surprisingly enough, became openly hostile to the therapist. When they came to pick William up, the therapist met with them privately, and it came out that the parents had been increasingly hateful to each other and close to ending their marriage when William began to have his seizures. William's illness brought them closer together and had had a quieting effect on their relationship. However, now that William was starting to improve, the parents were beginning to turn their hostility on each other again. They finally admitted that they really needed William to remain ill.

Many interpersonal interactions in our culture bear a resemblance to this insidious one we have just described. When those close to us complain of unhappiness or illness, we respond favorably and sympathetically. When they respond assertively or express strength and independence through their ability to confront and express anger, they are rejected. With married couples such an interaction often takes the following form. When one spouse looks hurt, tearful, or frightened, it generates a loving response from the other. When the same spouse asserts himself or herself angrily or independently, the reception is harsh or cold.

## THE HIDDEN USES OF ILLNESS

In an aggression-phobic environment such as ours the experience of being sick can assume many symbolic and covert meanings. In such a culture, sick people are given special sanction, the power to control and demand from others and with no reciprocal expectations.

From early childhood on, many children learn, in subtle and not so subtle ways, that while they are normally powerless in their capacity to impact on their parents and may even be largely ignored, when they become sick something magical happens. They receive attention and affection and are given the license to demand and control the family, something they do not ordinarily have when they are healthy. This seed planted bears its fruit in adulthood. For some adults, for example, chronic illness becomes an indirect way of exerting power, asserting themselves and manipulating others. Unable to gain this power openly through self-assertion during health, they become "sickness tyrants." They expect to be catered to. Those who resist are made to feel guilty, rejecting, heartless, and cruel.

Illness can also control underlying aggression, as was previously pointed out in the case of William by bringing dissident, unhappy families together in the common cause of "helping" a family member who is sick. The sick one, however, soon becomes a permanent necessity used to maintain the family's peace and harmony. The tragic irony in all of this is that physical sickness is being experienced with less anxiety and is seen as more preferable than open expressions of aggression.

People are also more prone to becoming ill in times when they are depressed and their aggressive drives are diminished or lacking. The diminished mobilization of aggression is accompanied by greater vulnerability to illness through lowered resistance to infection and the lowering of physiological defense processes that affect the immunizing responses and endocrine functioning. Coughs, colds, or viruses often seem to come on when there is frustration in a life situation, with a blocking of the aggressive energies needed for a constructive solution.

The full mobilization of aggression is also required for the recovery from illness. We speak of sick people "putting up a good fight" to get better, and we observe others who don't seem to have a "will toward health." Individuals who continue to maintain an aggressiveness or fight toward recovery are known to stand a much better chance of surviving severe illnesses, recovering from operations, and overcoming the residual physical disabilities. Right to the point of resisting death and maintaining life for as long as possible, the open aggressive drive is required. One often hears people bemoaning the fact that so many "nice" people seem to die young while the "bastards" live long lives. The availability of aggressive energy may be an important factor in this folk truth.

## THE QUESTIONS ONE SHOULD ASK

At the onset of any symptoms or illness, but particularly those that are known to have important psychosomatic aspects, the victims would do well to ask themselves the following: First, has there recently been an important negative or depressing change in my life situation or in my relationship to my spouse, family, employer, friends, or in any other significant relationship? Second, are there recent matters that are or might be causing me frustration, anger, or trauma and where I feel immobilized in terms of trying to do anything about it? Third, has any recent experience or conflict activated my aggressive or flight impulses while I was blocked from being able to express or discharge my feelings? For example, did somebody reject, threaten, hurt, injure, or abandon me while I remained unable to release the feelings this brought out in me? Fourth, if my answer to the previous question is "Yes," what is preventing me from discharging the anger, aggressiveness, protest, hostility, or jealousy feelings in a satisfying and effective way? What am I afraid might happen if I expressed these feelings directly? Fifth, assuming I have a block against expressing these feelings, how can I overcome it so that I can become constructively and creatively aggressive on behalf of my health and my life?

## THE AGGRESSIVE LANGUAGE OF THE BODY

The result of social conditioning is such that most of us are no longer in touch with our body's messages; nor are we able to interpret and appropriately respond to its cries of anger at physical abuse or emotional discomfort and distress. We have learned instead to "fight against" the symptom, to try to diminish or overcome it. A blatant though extremely common example of this is the use of antacids to overcome distress after we've overeaten so that one might be able to continue to eat some more. Some enterprising chemical researcher will one day discover the perfect hangover cure that will allow people to get totally drunk, regularly, with the complete assurance that they can muffle the body's signals of distress and protest the following day. In general, the prevailing tendency in our society is to respond to signals of body outrage and resistance against self-destructive behaviors such as overeating, boozing, or smoking, or signals of distress such as nausea, diarrhea, cramps, or bloating by ingesting a chemical substance to muffle or overcome the symptom rather than listening to and learning to interpret these meaningful forms of body language in an assertive way. The symptoms are stifled with a pill, an injection, or other medicinal substance designed to mask the pain and "kill" the signal.

Contemporary forms of psychotherapy such as Gestalt and bioenergetics have placed increasing emphasis on teaching individuals how to listen to and interpret their body's messages. This is viewed as an excellent pathway to growth and therapeutic change. For example, rather than trying to overcome or ignore a feeling of body tightness, restlessness, or anxiety, or a specific symptom such as a headache or impulse to vomit, these therapists try to put people in touch with the message contained within these reactions. During the course of a Gestalt therapy session the therapist might ask the client to give a voice to a bodily reaction by saying, for example, "What is that tightness in your chest saying?" The underlying theoretical point of view is that these bodily reactions are part of the total emotional response and can often provide a more truthful, uncontaminated insight into what a person is experiencing than mere verbalizations and intellectualizations.

An illustration of this process and its significance occurred recently to Dr. Goldberg while he was in the process of looking for a new office. In the rush to find suitable office space, before the lease in the other office expired, he frequently found himself trying to talk himself into liking an office that was obviously unattractive and poorly suited for his needs. Invariably, his body signals, which he would have preferred to ignore, were telling him the truth of his feelings and screaming out "No." That is, a dull headache would appear or there would be butterflies in the stomach or a feeling of extreme discomfort and restlessness. Once while going to an office he had previously looked at and was now seriously considering for rental, the author discovered that he had driven several blocks beyond the address. Another time he lingered over coffee rather than go to an appointment to discuss the final rental terms. In all of these instances the body's messages were clearly saying "No." While intellectually the author was trying to talk himself into certain offices and telling himself the offices were really great, the body signals were signaling resistance against them. When the right office was finally stumbled upon, the body felt light as air, relaxed and comfortable, and there was no impulse to get some coffee or have a cigarette to "think about it" and numb the body's signals.

There are a wide variety of body signals that people receive constantly, messages trying to get through. Mostly, they tend to ignore them or become embarrassed by them. However, there is often something meaningful and truthful being expressed by the body through these signals, and the responses deserve to at least be listened to and consulted. In an overly intellectualized culture such as ours, the body may prove in fact to be the best way back to discovering the truth of our repressed aggressive responses and impulses.

A note of caution, however! Sometimes a body response is *just* a body response. That is, sometimes a yawn is really only an expression of fatigue. At other times, however, it may be a reflection of repressed aggression. The following are only suggested interpretations and not the only possible meanings of various physical responses that may be signaling repressed aggression.

## YAWNING

As socialized members of this culture, people have been taught not to yawn in someone's face, to suppress it if they feel it coming, and to apologize for it if it accidentally breaks through. It is considered rude behavior. Though people tend to interpret a yawn as a sign of fatigue, very often it is an unconscious response to a conversation, interaction, or experience that is lifeless, meaningless, or in plain terms boring. However, because this is something people would rarely risk saying to someone openly, because they wouldn't want to "hurt their feelings," the true response is expressed physiologically rather than directly. The embarrassment upon yawning is over having been revealed for what one is truly feeling.

In the name of politeness and good social graces, employees, whether they be faculty members of college departments, workers in a government or private social agency, employees of the same division in a large private corporation, or board members of a foundation, all work hard to stifle their yawns when attending their respective meetings. The impulse to yawn may be their body's way of saying, "This is boring," "We're not getting anywhere," "Why doesn't he shut up already," "Christ, I wish I were someplace else," "We've gone over this a hundred times in the past," or "We're really beating a dead horse."

In a society that did not suppress aggressive confrontation people would not fear saying directly to another person, "You're boring me." This can be a simple, good-willed message that says, "I feel that we can interact in a more vital way!"

A yawn that is hidden behind an interested façade is a form of collusion that prevents a relationship or situation from moving into a more vital path. It is a disservice to the other person. The person you avoid yawning in front of may also be the person you later avoid getting together with again altogether.

## FARTING

Farting, like yawning, is considered socially rude behavior, only more so. Often the message behind a fart is one of disinterest in the other or even an expression of contempt. While the fart may simply be a symptom of internal gas, it may at other times also be an indicator of a repressed aggressive feeling. People rarely fart when they are happily involved, interested, and "turned on." Folk language has always viewed a "fart in the face" as an expression of total disdain. A child who farts while he's sitting with his parents, a husband who farts while in bed with his wife, a woman who farts while attending church or a PTA meeting, might question whether they are not in fact expressing their feelings of resentment toward the experience or person they are involved in.

Recently, a very gifted European tailor was referred for psychotherapy by his physician. He was on the verge of giving up his profession because of an embarrassing tendency to fart whenever he bent over to measure the pants leg of his male clients. During the course of his therapy it was discovered that the farting took place specifically when he touched the foot area. It turned out that the farting was an expression of his resentment over touching the dirty shoes of his clients. When the tailor realized this, he employed a full-time shoeshine man to clean every customer's shoes before the fitting. His farting problem was solved.

Figuratively speaking, farts should be listened to. They are often very meaningful messages to oneself as well as to others. Ask yourself if you have a tendency to fart only in front of certain people or in certain places. If the answer is "Yes," there's a good chance that the fart contains a message of repressed aggression. If nothing else, do not flee in embarrassment. Rather, accept the possibility that you are holding back negative feelings that are covering your true emotional responses and see if there isn't a direct and constructive way of giving off the same message instead.

## ITCHING

In a case described earlier in this chapter, a man felt anger at his doctor, but was afraid of consciously acknowledging the existence of this feeling, and suddenly developed a violent itch when the doctor appeared. Psychological literature and research have consistently noted that chronic itching is a way of turning one's rage or resentment against the self in a self-punishing way because of a fear or inability to release or express this feeling overtly.

Tom Howard, the head of an assembly division of an appliance manufacturing plant, summoned the floor manager, Steve Stokes, into his office. He asked him for a detailed plan as to how his group would recover from a late schedule resulting from having had to call back thirty thousand broilers and blenders that had a faulty part in them, which had made them unsafe because they were prone to starting on fire. Steve knew he had a personnel problem with a group of rebellious, bored workers but hesitated to mention it for fear he might be accused of being a poor manager. His hands began to sweat, and there was a strong itching sensation on his forearm as he repressed his intense anger over the bind he felt caught in. After a fifteen-minute lecture by Howard on declining profits and rising costs, which he listened to patiently, Stokes suddenly exploded, screaming, "Goddamn it. I'm doing the best I fuckin' can." The itching on his forearm stopped.

Itching that suddenly appears without a good physiological reason (for example, an insect bite) should be considered as a possible sign of repressed anger or rage. Ask yourself if you have recently or are presently feeling hurt or mistreated by something that someone close to you is doing and whether in fact you would be frightened to show that person your anger openly. If the answer is "Yes," it is quite likely that you are turning these feelings against yourself.

## AVOIDANCE OF EYE CONTACT

There are certain people with whom you may find it impossible or extremely difficult to sustain eye-to-eye contact. It feels much more comfortable to avoid their gaze.

This reaction is very meaningful. Its potential meanings are many, but in terms of its hidden aggression aspect it may be saying, "I don't trust him, I sense anger, hostility, or manipulativeness that he isn't showing directly," or "I resent this person but I am afraid to experience or express this feeling."

It is not accidental that with certain people you may instinctively avert their gaze. Courses in public relations that teach people how to be successful in business often stress making eye contact. Such eye contact is phony and manipulative. A possible way to gauge the sincerity of eye contact is to sense in yourself whether you feel comfortable in returning this eye contact. The strong desire not to should be respected and listened to, for it may be a signal to yourself that the other person's eye contact is experienced as phony or manipulative.

Of course, we have simplified the many intricate meanings

of eye contact. However, part of its meanings do lie in the area of aggression and its repression, and this should be recognized.

## BLUSHING

This response is frequently associated with shyness and embarrassment. Someone asks a personal question and you blush, or someone walks in on you doing something you consider private and you redden. The blushing is an indirect way of saying, "You're making me uncomfortable," or "I don't like what you're doing." Instead of saying this, however, the blusher frequently shrinks in embarrassment, often to a kidding by the source of the embarrassment.

Lenita was sitting at her desk typing when one of the insurance salesmen came walking by her desk, leaned over, and whispered, "What were you doing in Mr. Friedman's office for an hour and a half yesterday? Taking a letter, or was there some kind of heavy conference going on?" Lenita's face turned various shades of red. The blush that betrayed her feelings of guilt prevented her from expressing her real feeling at the time, which was, "None of your goddamn business!!"

Occasionally you may find yourself blushing when you're being flattered. The tendency is to interpret this as shyness. Before interpreting it in this way, hold on! Is your blush possibly saying, "I don't believe he or she means it. They're flattering me manipulatively."? Trust the blush as an automatic aversion response that may be saying far more than just "I'm shy."

The next time you blush, try saying, "I don't like . . ." and finish the sentence with the cause of the blushing. In other words, "I don't like you asking me that question." See if that then makes sense in helping you interpret your blush.

## PALING

Individuals pale when they've suddenly or unexpectedly become frightened. Sometimes this is a response to being caught doing something wrong. The paling is often accompanied by other fear responses, such as sweating, nausea, and weakening. It is a response of total helplessness, and as such is self-undermining.

Paul Curtis had become extremely dissatisfied with his job as a city planner for a private consulting firm. He felt he was being overworked and underpaid, but with the difficult employment picture he felt too scared to confront his employer for fear he'd be invited to leave. Instead, he began looking around secretly for another job and was in the process of negotiating a deal with a competitor that involved stealing a client from his present company.

Someone in the office found out what was going on and passed the word along to the president, who called Paul into his office and confronted him. Paul turned white and became nauseous as his boss read him a memo containing all of the details of the secret negotiations.

Because Paul had been unable to deal with his job frustrations and resentments openly and was afraid to assert himself and make his demands openly, he felt his only alternative was to go underground and look around secretly for something else. The paling after being caught was an indication of his guilt, but was also the result of the repressed frustration and anger that he had been unable to communicate originally. When he finally confronted his employer with these feelings, his strength and feelings of well-being returned.

The paling fear response may be unconsciously covering feelings of rage and outrage. You may wish to attack or respond forcefully but have been conditioned not to. It may in fact be inappropriate in most situations to respond with an attack. However, at the same time, the fear response is a self-destructive one that leaves one feeling pathetically helpless. To regain strength and overcome this upsetting feeling, try screaming and stomping your feet, either privately or, if appropriate, in front of the stimulus. If this is not feasible, at least be aware that behind the paling is an enormous strength that is being sapped by the fear.

## NAUSEA AND VOMITING

Nausea and vomiting, though frequently caused by physiological reasons, may also be related to psychological causes. Within family environments, vomiting has been known to appear when there is an inescapable hostile relationship between the vomiter and the family group. For example, one place where such contacts are frequently inescapable is during mealtimes. The vomiting may appear superficially to be related to the food rather than the stressful experience of sitting and eating with individuals with whom the vomiter is in conflict.

In colloquial conversations people talk of somebody who is repulsive as making them "nauseous." Individuals who tend to experience nausea when physiological causes do not seem to be at the root should ask themselves if, in fact, they are caught within a hostile, intimate interrelationship from which they see no escape.

## IMPOTENCE AND FRIGIDITY

Impotence and frigidity may both be forms of physiological withholding. Though basically equivalent responses, the inability to get an erection is usually more frightening to the average male than the failure to respond totally is to the female.

Most men have been conditioned to believe that masculinity means one should be able to perform sexually upon command, day after day and year after year. This is being a "real" man. Consequently, the male who suddenly finds himself unable to get an erection, rather than listening to the message behind this body signal, tends to want to do something about it, like taking vitamins or going to a "shrink." He feels guilty and frightened.

Frigidity is sometimes as theatening to the woman's self-image as impotence is to the man's. The frigid woman is likely to consider herself incomplete or less than a woman for not being able to respond fully.

Both the impotent male and the frigid female are prone to attack themselves as being inadequate and inferior sexual specimens. They see this as a symptom they must try to overcome. Again, we would ask the person to first look at these symptoms as body signals. Knowing, for example, that some cases of impotence and frigidity are selective in that they are present with some partners and not with others, ask yourself first what message this symptom might be giving you regarding your feelings about your partner. Unless it's a chronic condition that is always present with every partner, the symptom may be an expression of some unexpressed aggression. For example, one young man in therapy with Dr. Goldberg for impotence after only three years of marriage discovered under hypnosis that he was very angry that his wife always demanded to be on top during intercourse. While he acquiesced in order to satisfy her, he was really very angry about this. Not being able to experience or express it openly, the feeling came through in the form of a limp penis, which was an expression of his body's refusal to go along.

The impotent or frigid partner should therefore ask themselves: First, am I really turned on sexually by my partner, or am I trying to fake it? Second, is there something about the involvement that turns me off? Am I trying to be someone I'm not? For example, many women play very passive sexual roles because they don't want to seem aggressive, when they really don't feel passive and when they want to be sexually more active. They may become frigid as a hidden protest against this. Third, do I feel under a compulsion to perform on schedule and inwardly resent it? Fourth, am I protesting against something regarding my partner's behavior or physical appearance, such as overweight, repulsive odors, or a lack of sensitivity?

We feel that impotence and frigidity are not always symptoms to be conquered. Rather, they may be messages to be read and seriously explored. Instead of feeling guilty, inadequate, or panicky, and rushing to overcome it, ask yourself what important information regarding suppressed aggressive feelings the symptom may be trying to communicate.

In a highly intellectualized, aggression-repressive society your body signals are the finest paths back to a genuine emotional reality and the reclaiming of your aggressive self. The physical responses we discussed are only a small handful among many similar behavioral manifestations of repressed aggression. They are signals that should be respected and consulted as potential information gold mines, rather than as behaviors to suppress, deny, or apologize for. With your next blush, fart, yawn, itch, paling, or nonresponsive sexual organ, avoid self-recrimination and ask yourself instead what aggressive feeling your body might be trying to communicate to you that you are not consciously admitting to yourself.

# CHAPTER 14

# Fusion: Aggression in the Service of Eros

A major benefit of mastering the art of an assertive lifestyle is the fulfilling and vital quality of such a person's love life. In titling this chapter we have specifically avoided the word "sex," which in our age of pornography and sex-technique manuals has acquired a mechanical and medical aura. Instead, we have chosen the Greek word *eros* to emphasize the *fusion* of sexual and aggressive energy resulting in total, authentic, and joyful erotic fulfillment.

It may at first seem surprising that sex with the deepest feelings of affection and love is less fulfilling than sex that is interwoven and intertwined with aggression. To many, the fusion of sex and aggression conjures up fantasies of sado-masochistic behavior or of a chauvinistic, destructive interaction that is characterized by hostile putdowns, hurt, and manipulation. This traditional perception has resulted in the baby being thrown out with the bath water. That is, the vitalizing dimensions of aggression have been shunned because of the fear and inability to separate out its constructive from its destructive aspects. However, in the course of our work and our investigations into contemporary sexual difficulties—which despite contemporary "liberated" sexual attitudes have by now taken on the dimensions of a modern-day plague—we have repeatedly seen the disastrous effects of striving for sexual competence and fulfillment through "understanding," "sensitivity," and other exclusively "loving" but essentially passive orientations.

Lovers who exclude aggression from their bedroom cheat themselves of a total and exciting experience, and in fact will probably be unable to achieve genuine erotic fullfillment. Those who learn the fine art of utilizing aggression constructively in the service of eros, however, come closer to reaching their erotic potentials. Sexual functioning in our society is too often characterized by inhibited, "nice," relatively passive and guarded interactions in which aggression manifests itself mainly in hidden and indirect forms. Such conditioning in lovemaking has managed to help paralyze a natural, spontaneous, noncerebral, and pleasurable physical activity.

In this chapter we are not concerned with "sex problems" or symptom removal per se. Nor do we see ourselves in conflict with Masters and Johnson and other sex therapists, who have been quite successful in an approach that emphasizes sexual re-education; learning about one's body and the body of one's lover; and the desensitization of sexual anxieties, fears, and repressions. However, theirs is an approach that has not emphasized the integration of sex with aggression. Focusing on this kind of interaction can indeed be a frightening endeavor in a cultural atmosphere that has traditionally taught that the two experiences are incompatible. The fusion of sex and aggression is a new art that has still to be fully developed. Hurried and crude gropings in that direction may backfire, particularly if there has not been a proper prior separation of the hostile, alienating elements from the assertive bonding ones.

## FIGHT FOR BETTER SEX

In our sex education and sex therapy work we have coached lovers in the constructive use of aggression toward the achievement of fusion. We encourage partners to fight for better sex and to separate out sex hindering or sadistic hurting from sexually stimulating, informative, aggressive, and assertive interactions. Toward this end we have developed aggressive play rituals that can be engaged in with good-willed mutual consent. Good-willed consent to behave aggressively allows the love fighting to become rather like a sport than a frightening attack. Aggressive eros is nothing like a street brawl where one person is jumped with the intent to hurt or demolish the other. Rather, it is in the manner of an Olympic event, with a respect for rules, establishment of beltlines, concern for timing, appropriate handicapping, and mutual involvement. Aggression in the service of eros, to achieve a fusion, is more than a clinical form of therapy. It is the development of a total love approach.

Some sex manuals contain instruction, even when authored by highly reputable professional sex therapists and marriage counselors, that renders a disservice to its readers by the teaching of a love orientation that ignores the vital aspects of aggression. It is in fact a distinct possibility that the sex instructions have done more harm than good, by reinforcing sexual anxieties and self-consciousness and raising pseudoproblems and issues regarding orgastic responsiveness. The following is a quotation from an article published in a popularly circulated, reputable, medically edited magazine on sex behavior. This exemplifies the kind of well-intentioned though self-conscious, paralyzing advice regularly being offered to contemporary readers seeking information on how to better their sex lives. The author wrote, "The highly delicate art of lovemaking requires, among other things, sensitivity, skill, ingenuity, and sexual knowledge, as well as an appreciation and awareness of the needs, desires and idiosyncrasies of one's mate. Since these are attributes which have to be learned and developed, and since educational institutions (including medical institutions) did not teach these attributes until recently, it is not surprising that as lovers many males (and females) in our American society leave much to be desired."[1]

Thus to perform the natural and spontaneous act of sex

today it would appear from this advice that one would need the education of a Ph.D. physiologist, the emotional sensitivities of a clinical psychologist, the mechanical agility of a brain surgeon, and the gentleness of a newborn babe. With such advice it is not at all surprising that statistics show that male impotence has reached epidemic proportions, afflicting close to 50 percent of married males who reportedly have a variation of this problem.

These very same so-called impotent married males we have found often have no problems getting turned on by a prostitute or in a casual love affair where they are not afraid to be themselves and to behave aggressively. Nor are they as concerned in these circumstances about being insensitive or harsh. Instead they feel comfortable in behaving assertively and spontaneously and making authentic demands for sexual satisfaction. They do not feel impelled to handle their lovers as if they were china dolls.

## THE INHIBITING SENSITIVITY

A newly married couple, recently arrived from Dallas, Texas, with a 1½-year-old child, came to our Institute for help with their sexual difficulties. He was an attorney and she was working as a dental assistant. They had been living together for two years before they decided to marry. Both were "super-sensitive" and "very gentle" with each other. He couched everything he said in terms designed to avoid getting his "nice" wife upset. He described her as "very fragile." She was quiet and passive. She seemed to withdraw frequently during the therapy session to some secret place inside of herself. She claimed that she was terrified of making her husband angry. But she was most surprised when she heard him describe her as fragile. She told him that she had always thought of herself as a pretty strong person.

During their therapy hours both were soft-spoken, intellectualized, passive, gentle, and fearful of anger, confrontation, and assertiveness. Their sexual complaints were predictable and totally in keeping with their interaction in the therapy session. Both were sexually passive, and consequently they had just about stopped having sex altogether. He reported that at home he would get turned on but would soon give up trying to interest her because she was too "tight," both literally and figuratively. "She just lies there and lets me do it," he complained, "and it turns me off!" His wife admitted pretending to want and even enjoy sex when in reality she wasn't at all interested. Her vagina, which was "tight," was saying "No" for her while she was verbally saying "Yes." She complained that her husband made her feel too self-conscious and joyless with his endless analyzing, probing, and treating her with fear and delicacy.

Their breakthrough to change occurred after she felt sufficiently comfortable and safe to share her sexual fantasies openly. He couldn't believe it was his wife talking when he heard her report the fantasies she had whenever she masturbated, which was at least three times a week. They were peopled with various men she had met only briefly but whom she would imagine were "grabbing me and raping me."

She said she felt too inhibited with her husband because she feared that he would become too "freaked out" by her desires to scream, claw, pound him on the back, lick his body from top to bottom, and in other ways be aggressive with him. Their sex life improved significantly when he was finally able to accept this aggressive side of her and encouraged her to act it out, and also when he was comfortable enough to accept his own aggressiveness with her and not treat her like a fragile flower.

This couple was not so much an example of sexual pathology as they were victims of a socio-sexual ethic that teaches that sex and aggression must be kept separate. Our work and discussion with many people in psychotherapy struggling for sexual satisfaction have revealed that those who keep aggression out of their sexual activity and behave in nicely controlled, "gentle" ways often have elaborate fantasies of what are commonly termed sado-masochistic activities. These fantasies, which we believe are a product of frustrated aggressiveness in sex, have as their repeated themes rape and beatings. In these hostile sex fantasies men see themselves seizing the woman, tying her down, beating her, and then ravaging her sexually. Women, in psychotherapy, typically imagine themselves being held down and raped, often by several men at a time. These are the same people who in therapy also ask, "How come my orgasms with my spouse are not nearly as good as when I masturbate?" One of the pointers we give to clients is, "If you're too nicey-nice with each other in bed, don't be surprised if your sex life dies."

A recently published inquiry with a group of female nudists explored their opinions and attitudes regarding their sexual experiences with men. Typical complaints included:

"With sex I have to be the aggressor almost always, and I don't like it. I feel most men are not aggressive enough."

"Some men get hung up on being sure the woman is satisfied. I find this inhibiting at times. I think there is a point at which a man should let his own sensations take over; when this happens my own response can be freer."

"Unbelievably enough, the thing I dislike most is overconcern. 'Did you have an orgasm, honey?' makes me furious—mostly because it's such an unmale way to react. So sort of weak-kneed."[2]

The men have been victims of a social conditioning that has nurtured a schism in the perception of women; the now familiar "male chauvinist" stance. First, there's the woman you love or the woman who's your wife. She's pure, fragile, docile, passive, and feminine. Sex with her must therefore be had accordingly. Aggressive abandon is only permissible with other women, prostitutes, pickups, casual affairs, or other men's wives.

## THE PIC-BONE: A RITUAL FOR "NICE" COUPLES

We have developed a playful hostility ritual that we call the "pic-bone." We teach it particularly to "nice" couples whose "lovey-dovey" interaction has ruined the challenge and excitement of their sex life. This ritual involves a form of sexual teasing by mutual consent. The partner who does the teasing tries to get the other partner angry and turned off and then accepts this resistance as a challenge to be overcome. In other words, the teaser commits himself or herself to courting and winning back the interest of the partner. This eventuates in a making-up process of sexual intercourse, during which both are aggressively aroused.

The "pic-bone" ritual is therefore an intentional process of conflict creation, particularly useful for mellowed-out couples whose docility, passive comfort, security, and ready availability have reduced the sexual excitement. For example, the man says, "Boy, I really enjoyed dancing and talking with Jimmy's wife after dinner. She was so free and sensual looking—and what a pair of boobs!" At the point when his wife is really getting "turned off" by this comparison of her to their friend's wife, the husband shifts gears and works to overcome her resistance. In this ritualistic way a challenge has been created. Uncertainties and anxieties over rejection, and therefore some of the stimulation of early courtship days are again present. This "pic-bone" ritual is a profound act of love when it facilitates aggression release in a mellowed-out partner and is done with a commitment to overcoming the challenge of rejection.

A troubled portion of our sexually active population does not know how to make and develop intimate human contact except through sex. This brings them close physically but prevents intimacy psychologically. In relationships where sex is the main bond, other dimensions that are a critical part of authentic intimacy may be neglected. Some of the most active sex lives are lived by alienated lovers who use sex as their only holiday and relief from a world of isolation, sometimes splendid in its independence, sometimes despairing in its loneliness. For these individuals sex has also become a powerful tool of aggression avoidance. They are "lovers, not fighters"—so say the stickers on the bumpers of their cars. Outside of the bed they are emotionally inhibited, often detached, and socially incompetent. Our research on spouse murderers, for example, has demonstrated to us the not so surprising fact that the sex lives of these killers is more often than not a very active one. They used sex as a way of avoiding conflict. For them sexual intercourse provided a way of making up without changing or improving a chronic state of interpersonal conflict. Sex was for them a temporary respite from the painful realities of the relationship.

Betty, age thirty-six, an intelligent, vibrant woman, described the role of fighting in the development of her authentic, growing relationship with her thirty-two-year-old boyfriend, Michael. She described the following as "our first sex-connected fight":

"I was rattling on incessantly about my favorite subject: my past experiences with intelligent friends on the subject of ESP. I had been talking for about twenty-five minutes and a glazed look apparently came over my eyes (I was told by him). Finally I noticed he was staring out the window. I asked what was wrong. He said, '*You* have been having a monologue by yourself. You don't need *me*. You could get *anybody* to listen to you. You are obviously not interested in relating to *me*.'

"I became very defensive and began to yell and scream that I had a right to my ideas and a right to be me. 'I am sharing with you what I am interested in, and if you don't like it or me, *get out!!*'

"He just sat there and said, 'Gee, Annie used to throw her shoe at me when I made her angry, but you are really exciting and interesting to fight with.'

"Stunned, I sat there a while and thought. . . . Then he went on, 'I don't want to hear about ESP and other people. I want to hear about you and me and our relationship.' I thought, 'selfish, self-centered bastard!'

"Again silence. He looked at me softly now, and I melted. He wanted to see if I was still angry, but I wasn't any longer as

I realized that he needed me to be interested in him. 'He really cares about me and us,' I thought.

"I came for him, touched his face. We got undressed and went to bed. The sex was *pure* affection—tender caring, passionate, and animal-like all at once. All present anger had been expressed, and it left an opening for love feelings, unadulterated by hostile feelings."

CHAPTER 15

# Sexual Liberation Through
# Compassionate Aggression

It was Kinsey who first pointed out the striking similarities between the physiological responses during sex and the bodily reactions that accompany the experience of anger. These similarities, which are present and true for both men and women, include:

1. An increase in pulse rate.
2. An increase in blood pressure, both diastolic and systolic.
3. Vasodilation (sometimes).
4. An increase in the peripheral circulation of the blood.
5. A reduced rate of bleeding; for example, bleeding from cut blood vessels during fighting as well as during sexual intercourse resulting from clawing, biting, and hitting is significantly reduced. Abrasions and cuts that are received are all remarkably free of extensive bleeding.
6. Hyperventilation (an increase in breathing rate).
7. Anoxia; the facial expressions of the individuals, particularly at the time of orgasm, suggest a shortage of oxygen. This is comparable to the facial expression of the athlete during the peak of his physical exertion. According to Kinsey, the woman's face as she approaches sexual climax bears a striking re-

semblance to that of a runner who is making an extreme effort to finish a race.

8.   Diminution of sensory perception; the body of a sexually aroused person becomes increasingly insensitive to tactile stimulation and even to sharp blows and injuries. The recipient of such behavior may even be receiving considerable amounts of physical punishment without being aware of being subjected to any more than the mildest of tactile stimulation.

Other sensory awarenesses are also diminished. Individuals become decreasingly sensitive to temperature and to extraneous noises.

9.   Adrenaline secretion.

10.   Increase in muscular tension; there is an increased tension in the hands and fingers during both sex and anger, which may result in responses such as grabbing, clawing, and clenching fists.

11.   Increased muscular capacity; individuals, under both the conditions of sexuality and anger, display a significantly greater than usual muscular strength and dexterity. Sometimes this even reaches astounding levels.

12.   Reduction of fatigue.

13.   Inhibited gastro-intestinal activities.

14.   Involuntary vocalizations, which may include groans, grunts, screams, and other noises.[1]

As part of our efforts to liberate the sexual response through constructive aggression, we teach and encourage people to convert their heavy breathing into clearly audible, loud sounds during intercourse. This has a tendency to facilitate the physiological response of aggressiveness.

The fear of making loud noises ("love sounds") is an illustration of how the aggression phobia of our culture has pervaded even the most private experiences. Individuals feel embarrassed and out of control if they emit loud sounds or are confronted with them by others. Polite, well-socialized people in our culture are taught not to raise their voices or to make loud noises of any kind. Consequently, most middle-class people in particular are unnaturally quiet during sex and consider vigorous soundmaking to be "animal-like" behavior.

The biological relationship between sex and aggression has been suggested by brain-mapping studies of animals such as male monkeys. These research studies conducted by physiologists have shown that neural systems for certain sexual and aggressive responses are in extremely close proximity to each other within the limbic system of the brain. The limbic system is a complex set of structures extending downward from the cerebral cortex to portions of the midbrain. The neural systems for certain sexual and aggressive responses may in fact overlap or even be directly linked.[2] One brain-mapping study indicated that the neural structures that elicit immediate penile erections when stimulated electrically are located within one millimeter from the point in the brain that elicits a response of extreme rage.[3]

Research ethics forbid the use of such techniques with human beings. Therefore, one can only conjecture about the existence of a similar physiological relationship between these two responses in the human being. However, there are additional kinds of evidence to support the belief in such a relationship between these two responses. For example, clinical case reports of some human beings who have brain damage that appears to have precipitated violent behavior also have this behavior correlated with a heightened sexual drive.[4]

Psychological research studies have pointed to the relationship between sexual and aggressive arousal. Noted research psychologist Dr. Seymour Feshbach of the University of California at Los Angeles has conducted several studies that have demonstrated that inhibition of the aggressive response results in the inhibition of the sexual response.

In 1970, Feshbach, along with researcher Y. Jaffe, conducted a study with a group of male undergraduates at UCLA. Utilizing an experimental design too complicated to describe here, these undergraduates were broken up into two groups. In one of the groups, angry responses of the males were blocked and prevented from being expressed, while in the other group, these responses were not inhibited. Feshbach and Jaffe found that the group who had their angry feelings and reactions inhibited became less sexually responsive and inhibited their feelings of sexuality more than those whose aggression was not inhibited.[5]

## THE "GENDER CLUB" HOSTILITY RITUAL

Realizing the critical intertwining between sex and aggression and the fact that a healthy erotic response is often blocked because of suppressed aggression, one of the very first aggression rituals we use with couples and unattached singles is the "gender club," a ritual designed to facilitate the unleashing and open sharing of underlying resentments that men in our society have toward women and women against men, but that remain largely unexperienced and unexpressed because of taboos against sharing them.

The early socialization experiences of girls and boys in our culture results in the development of a powerful core of resentment and resistance toward the opposite sex. Girls see boys accorded special privileges of freedom, exploration, aggressiveness, and sexuality. Boys can fight, boys can be openly sexual, boys may roam around the neighborhood, etc., etc., but girls typically may not. Female resentments are bound to build up because of these double standards. This is particularly true in the area of sex, where sexual exploration has generally been considered all right for boys but "bad" for girls. Girls are taught to be wary of the secret sexual designs and motivations of boys. They are also taught to beware of boys who are "only out for one thing." Then they are told about all of the molesters and rapists lurking everywhere. Children's stories are full of wolves in sheep's clothing who ravage girls, not to mention the brutal war stories on TV and in movies that depict the depraved brutality of men.

For the boys, resentment toward women originates in the early relationship to the mother. Typically, she is the one who sets the limits, says "No," makes demands, and does much of the punishing. The myths, fairy tales, Bible stories, and nursery rhymes he hears and reads are full of tales about the evil wiles and destructiveness of the female sex. It was Eve who seduced Adam into eating the apple, thus causing him and everyone after him to lose the Garden of Eden. Samson was brought from superstrength to helplessness by Delilah. Historical recountings are full of examples of kingdoms lost because of a femme fatale. There are also all of the witches in fairy tales such as "Hansel and Gretel" and "Sleeping Beauty" who are evil, destructive, and devouring female figures.

Authentic intimacy and genuine, nonmanipulative, and lasting erotic responsiveness, we believe, can only occur after the underlying hostilities, resentments, and stereotyped images of the opposite sex have been surfaced. The realistic beginning of any intersex relationship should involve an open display of the suspiciousness, resentment, rage, and negative stereotypes the sexes have about each other but tend to block out, particularly during the early courtship phase. These feelings must be shared regardless of how seemingly vicious or irrational they are. Indeed, it is one of the cruel hypocrisies of our culture, destructive both to mental health and heterosexual relationships, that these intersex hostilities are forced by social taboos out of awareness. Much energy is wasted working at being nice to the opposite sex. Men and women alike torture themselves with feelings of unworthiness and inadequacy because they are unable to achieve the purity of love they feel they should be capable of. Relationships are instead launched behind phony smiles and unreal courtship manners. After the early excitement wears off, each spends months, years, or a lifetime struggling to overcome the boredom, anger, and alienation from their partner. The sexual relationships are severely impaired because of the hidden unexpressed aggression that continually contaminates the interaction.

Tom, age twenty-three, stood up to take his turn during a "gender club" hostility ritual, supervised by Dr. Goldberg. The males had first gathered together to discuss all of their stereotypes and resentments toward the women, and so had the women toward the men. Each person in turn stood up, faced the other sex group, and unleashed these feelings. Tom looked at the six women seated opposite him and began: "Women are users—two-faced bitches who'll tell you anything and be anything to get you to marry them—but then, and *only* then, do they show you their real selves. They're so damn jealous of men. They can't stand to see a man having a good time, so they butt in on all his activities. They want to go everywhere with him, football games, fishing trips, even bars, everything! They want to eat him up alive. Then they don't even enjoy themselves. They're materialistic! All they ever think about is shopping and owning things. They drive men to early graves with their demands and then live twenty years in style on the insurance money. They complain that men don't have feelings, but beware the man who cries or shows any fear. They'll humiliate the shit out of him! And they use their bodies and their sex to manipulate men because that's all they've really got to offer him. Then they complain about being treated like sex objects. And they go crazy when "their" man looks at another woman. They prefer him to be a phony and pretend he doesn't notice all the tits and ass being practically shoved into his face by seductive women everywhere. They can't stand a man who acts like a man, and to top it off, they want to be men too. You women want to be liberated. Zap! You're liberated. Now get off our backs."

Tom's outburst was neither logical nor rational, but it was real. These were feelings that Tom himself hardly knew he had until they all came flooding out. And like most single people in our culture looking for a mate, he cherished the illusion of finding a girl who'd be "different" and who he would only feel pure love for. When such a person is supposedly found, the aggression is repressed and replaced by the phoniness of collusion, false accommodation, and imaging. Inevitably, the relationship and the sex turn sour.

Elizabeth, divorced and the mother of three children, stood up to face the men in this "gender club" ritual. Trembling somewhat with anxiety and then resentment, she launched into her attack. "Men are little babies—whining, complaining, and always wanting to have something done for them. They've got to be constantly reassured that they are the boss—the big honcho, the king! They're secretly afraid of women and don't know how to handle them. Then they complain about how they're being manipulated by women. What a laugh! Just show them a little breast or a behind and they start to drool. Horny little toads! But once they've made their pathetic little conquest they run. They don't really know how to handle it. When it comes right down to it, most men stink when it comes to sex. They're only good the first few tines. They meet an honest woman who says she wants sex just as much as they do, and they panic—they call her a castrater and an aggressive bitch! And all you men are so hung up on your pitiful little egos and your success trips. You don't know anything about getting close, being warm, sharing a real feeling or even what a relationship is all about."

## SEX AS A WEAPON

When this aggression between the sexes is repressed, sexuality becomes just another weapon or tool to express it with. Aggression in these instances masquerades as sexual desire. The man who needs to seduce each woman he meets is not being sexual but rather expressing his underlying quest for power and control, and his basic contempt for women, whom he treats interchangeably as objects and with no concern at all for their needs or feelings. Likewise, the man who becomes impotent or ejaculates prematurely may be expressing his resentment or refusal to give satisfaction, stemming from repressed, aggressive motivations.

The seductive woman who tries to turn every man on and becomes indignant or rejecting when she is approached is also expressing her contempt for the male. Just as with the impotent male, the frigid female may be seeking to humiliate her male partner, make him feel inadequate or simply hold herself back from giving him satisfaction.

In an aggression-phobic society, sex becomes a heavily contaminated experience. Sexual involvement becomes just another instrument for control, self-assertion, power strivings, the expression of hostility and contempt, and the desire to humiliate, enslave, or sadistically hurt. Surfacing as much of the underlying hostility as possible and getting people to frankly acknowledge these feelings are the critical first steps in the direction of a meaningful and vital sexual relationship. Though we seem to be in an era of sexual freedom and enlightenment, this liberation is in most cases a superficial one. It is a case of doing it more but enjoying it less. Most sex partners are still frozen by their attempt to live up to standards of sexual behavior that are basically unreal and impossible. Sexual experience is accompanied by an emotionally inauthentic motivation to be inordinately gentle, sensitive, "loving," understanding, and other similar states, which we've been taught are *supposed to be* part of a mature sexual involvement. Eventually each partner has to look elsewhere for real sexual satisfaction. It is only in the casual, spontaneous, outside relationship apparently, that most people will allow themselves to indulge in the aggressive abandon, grabbing, biting, scratching, screaming, and wrestling that is far more real but not usually indulged in in one's marital or other intimate relationships. Men act it out with prostitutes or "girlfriends"; women, with their lovers.

## INTERSEX FEARS

Fear between the sexes is another common unexpressed feeling that disturbs satisfying sexual involvement. Intersex fears include the fear of being rejected, of not performing adequately, of being hurt, exploited, controlled, becoming overly dependent, or being possessed and engulfed. Converting the fear response to a healthy aggressive one requires learning how to defend one's identity, how to tolerate and accept rejection and to persist in the face of it, how to say "No," how to confront, and how to set one's intimacy limits. Early in every sexual relationship authentic self-presentation is important. This involves leveling about and detailing one's real desires and feelings about sex. It includes the open sharing of experiences of past hurts with other partners ("Hurt Museum") and discussing "turn-offs" and "beltlines." Sex partners tend to keep the latter secret (their "turnoffs") and to use them ultimately as weapons against each other. Miriam never told her lover that she hated having oral sex and was particularly repelled by his making such a sexual request before he had bathed. These were sexual "don'ts" that she never shared openly and that caused her to feel repelled very early in their involvement and to react in a frigid manner. She told herself she didn't tell him of these feelings because she didn't want to hurt him.

Tragically, many men and women are so frightened of honest confrontation about their needs that they don't even tell *themselves* what they don't like. They feel embarrassed and ashamed to establish their limits and expectations because of social pressure and often repress these feelings and become consciously unaware of them. For example, many men have a difficult time stating directly or even knowing when they really *don't* feel like having sex. Their self-image of being sexual performers demands that they be *always* ready and eager. This may be equally true of women, particularly in the early stages of a relationship. They feel that they must or should accommodate and enjoy sex with their man frequently. Eventually, this fear of negative self-assertion, this inability to say "No" or to even be able to clearly recognize when one does or doesn't want sex, destroys the joys of sexual involvement. Eventually, individuals are no longer able to differentiate when they are or are not genuinely "turned on." Instead they begin to develop psychosomatic symptoms such as backaches, headaches, and fatigue as every evening becomes a source of anxiety and one partner strategically falls asleep very early or stays up very late "reading" or "working" before coming to bed.

"Beltline sharing" is an important form of assertive self-communication in the area of sexuality that needs to be engaged in early in a relationship. People have personal sensitivities which when offended cause them to withdraw, rage, seek to retaliate, or turn off sexually completely. These may include ill-timed comments about weight, grooming, hair, body odors, comparisons with others, arguments over money, negative references to past relationships such as parents, family, etc. One man, a young married insurance salesman, discovered that his "beltline" was confiding a very personal feeling to his wife and then having her use it against him to belittle or degrade him sometime later. For example, he would confide happily how he had "pulled a deal off" by wining and dining and smooth-talking a customer at a special restaurant. He was at the same time a little embarrassed over his tactics; he had the feeling of having "conned" the customer, and he acknowledged this. Later in the evening his wife began attacking him for being a "con artist," after he himself had confessed his own discomfort over the experience. He saw "red" and wouldn't touch her for days. In another instance, a woman indicated that she discovered that her "beltline" involved any experience of being accused of having hidden motives. For example, she would prepare a special meal or buy a gift for her boyfriend. His joking comment that he wondered what she was "really after," or trying to get out of him, caused her to pull away from him sexually for several days at a time.

Bataca fighting, described in the chapter "Aggression Rituals," involves the use of cloth bats and of handicapping to equalize strength differences to allow couples to safely fight with each other in a sexual relationship. Despite the fact that there are enormous reservoirs of hostility between the sexes, there are no safe, effective physical ways to release them. Traditionally, men overestimate the physical fragility of their women, and the women are afraid to show their real physical strength for fear of seeming to be too "masculine" or aggressive. The supergentle way of relating, particularly in the area of sexuality, ultimately becomes paralyzing and eliminates much of the vitality in a relationship. Bataca fighting, when done constructively, can help to break the passive pattern of relating. It can also act as a sexual stimulus. In particular, it can help each sex partner experience the other more realistically as an aggressive being. Bataca fighting is particularly effective between couples who have gotten into patterns of relating to each other and handling all of their problems in a highly verbal way. One such couple, a forty-three-year-old attorney and his wife, had practically stopped having sex altogether when they joined a creative aggression group for married couples, conducted by Dr. Bach.

They would intellectualize endlessly. He was always trying to be so "understanding," while she was "terribly sensitive" and "afraid to hurt his feelings." Behind their endless verbalizations and ruminations there was intense anger in themselves that neither of them could experience directly. When they were asked by Dr. Bach to engage in a bataca fight, they resisted strongly. They insisted that it was a stupid thing to do, and besides, "What does this have to do with our sex problem?" With the group's encouragement, they finally agreed to try it. After an initial round of holding back, she "accidentally" hit him in the groin area. Although it caused no real pain, he became livid. The fight suddenly became blatantly vicious. Both began to scream at and insult each other. She called him "limp prick" and he called her "ice cold," "uptight" and "dry pussy." Intense rage toward each other that neither had been able to feel previously came pouring out. Behind all of their endless "sensitive" verbalizations, their "fears," and their psychologizing, was a vast reservoir of hidden anger. As this energy was finally released and the verbalizations were transformed into their real essence—namely, aggressive feelings—genuine warmth and caring appeared, and sexual arousal returned.

### "COLD TURKEY" SEX

As we became increasingly aware of the intimate interaction between sex and aggression, we recognized that most couples lose the vitality of their sexual involvement by having sex "cold turkey"; that is, while each is feeling benign and passive. Married couples particularly tend to climb into bed in a passive, relaxed state and both begin to feel there's something wrong with them individually and/or as a couple because they don't become immediately aroused sexually. Then he becomes concerned because his erection doesn't appear instantly, and she thinks something is wrong because she feels "numbed" or anesthetized.

Sexual involvement early in a courtship is usually exciting because aggression is mobilized by the rituals of the chase. The male is trying to "conquer" the female. Her aggressivity is expressed through a certain amount of resistance to him. Most of the aggressive elements, however, are missing in the sexual involvement of long-standing relationships. When there is anger or fighting one or both usually withdraws, whereas in the early stages of the relationship, a fight often served as a stimulus to sexual excitement. Therefore, we now encourage couples to use any device that will mobilize their aggression, even bataca bat fighting. Couples who first use this technique find themselves going from embarrassed laughter to intense anger and often emerge in a sexually aroused state.

### THE NEED FOR CANDOR

Most sexual involvements begin with the mutual expectations between the individuals being either vague or unrealistically romantic. The attitude is one of "Let it happen by itself!" In the early stages the novelty, uncertainty, and lack of commitment provide sufficient spurs. Even relatively inept sex is experienced as exciting. Retaining this excitement, however, will require more active participation, such as assertive signaling, mutual critiquing, confrontation, reinforcement, coaching, and cuing one's partner, providing information about oneself and demanding feedback.

Collusion and divining are two of the major causes of unsatisfactory sexual experiences. Collusion is pretending to like something one actually disapproves of in the desire to please, because one believes the other person likes it. A recent example of the destructive effects of collusion involved a couple that had been together for seven years. The woman, while pretending to be a very "sexual" person, was beginning to compile a catalogue of physiological symptoms that provided her with "legitimate" reasons for abstaining from sex. In the course of her sexual therapy she revealed that while she had always really preferred being on top and straddling her husband during sex because it allowed her to orgasm deeply and frequently, she had pretended to prefer being on the bottom because her husband preferred it. She was sure he would accuse her of wanting to play the "man's part" if she told him the truth.

In addition to colluding with what she believed her husband preferred because of a comment he had made six years prior about "dikey broads," she was "divining" him. That is, she was reading his mind and assuming that he would strongly resent her being on top. When she was finally able to discuss this openly, she discovered that the few times when her husband had been on the bottom, he enjoyed it because he could lie back and let her "do the work." He, too, however, was afraid that openly asking to be on the bottom would mean to her that he was "feminine" or a latent homosexual.

Divining and collusion are particularly common in the process of trying to figure out whether the other person even wants to have sex. It seems to be a source of great difficulty and anxiety for many people to directly ask their partner if they want sex, and to answer such a question honestly when it is asked of them. Some feel that asking these kinds of questions will destroy the "magic" and spontaneity of the relationship. They claim that one shouldn't really have to ask; one should be able to "just know." Consequently, decisions over whether or not to have sex are rife with collusion and divining. Some examples: He decides she doesn't really want to, because earlier in the evening she had mentioned that she had a headache. Or he doesn't want to push himself on her or force her, so he waits for her to make the first move. She doesn't want to be the aggressor, so she waits for him to make the first move. She figures he must want to, because they haven't for four days. But he really doesn't want to. Then she pretends to enjoy it and so does he when neither of them really wanted to in the first place. A pathetic comedy of errors, sure to turn sex into a nightmare, results from this fear of honest communication about sex.

Until recently, women were afraid to tell men what they liked sexually because they weren't really even supposed to enjoy it. Men were afraid to express their preferences for fear of being seen as depraved or animal-like. Until very recently many men didn't even know a woman had a clitoris or where it was. Couples must learn to cue each other assertively during sex, teaching each other about sensitive "turn-on" areas of their bodies. Phase synchronization feedback is also important; that is, a behavior that is exciting during an early stage of foreplay may be a "turn-off" when coitus actually begins. One thirty-three-year-old male loved having his girlfriend nibble him on the neck when they first started kissing but hated her doing this while he was inside of her body.

## POSTCOITAL DISCUSSIONS

Postcoital discussions in which there is absolute candor *not* tempered with tact is important. In the striving for sexual satisfaction, tact spells failure. An honest, leveling approach as to what was enjoyable and what wasn't is a critical dimension to keeping sexual excitement alive.

There are many areas of potential conflict that need to be communicated about openly and assertively. These include:

1. Position: Who's going to be where and at what point?
2. Time: Will we have sex in the morning, afternoon, evening, or the middle of the night?
3. Frequency: How often?
4. Quantity and nature of foreplay: How much time for warming up and what kind?

In this latter dimension, prior assumptions and "shoulds" must be thoroughly examined and often discarded. For example, quick abrupt sex is potentially as satisfying and as delightful as prolonged lovemaking. Many couples, however, feel that they *should* stretch it out or they are not being "sensitive" and "thoughtful" of the other.

Regardless of how sexually compatible a couple is, there will always be some differences in preferences. Partners who deny their differences are in collusion with each other. Others who feel the "magic" will be lost by discussing their feelings openly will see their sexual relationship steadily deteriorate.

## THE SEXUAL CRAZYMAKERS

We have found that two of the most prevalent and lethal forms of repressed aggression in the area of sexuality are playing "Red Cross nurse" and playing the "analyst."

The "Red Cross nurse" is the man who solicitously asks and worries about the woman's orgasm, or the woman who is trying to "help" her man overcome his fears or impotence. Each assumes a very "concerned" attitude, which, however, only serves to intensify the extreme self-consciousness and guilt; e.g., "He's so thoughtful, I must be really frigid and hostile not to come," or "This impotence has got to be my problem. She couldn't be more patient and kind."

The "Red Cross nurse" reaction is not an emotionally authentic one. By being solicitous and concerned, the "Red Cross nurse" is really saying, "I'm sexually healthy but you're not. As soon as you get better our sex will improve." This pose allows the person to hide from his or her part in the problem. The underlying hostility behind the "Red Cross nursing" is seen in its impact. Inevitably the other partner never totally overcomes the "problem," though he or she may "improve" temporarily. The "Red Cross nurse" will naturally assume the credit. However, this will prove to be an improvement of very limited duration, because the "Red Cross nurse" has a stake in the continuation of the problem.

The other pattern of driving one's partner "up the wall" is playing "analyst." This typically upward-bound, middle-class form of repressed aggression involves "helping" the other person find out why he or she can't respond. The "analyst" crazymaker never really expresses emotion. Rather, he or she stands at a detached distance and keeps trying to figure things out and come up with answers. Invariably, this pose goes nowhere except to make the partner with the "problem" feel sicker and more self-conscious. It is a hidden hostile ploy that also allows one to lay the blame on the other.

The writers believe that many of the so-called sex problems of today are the result of the repression of aggression. Consequently, attempts at revitalizing one's sex life through experimentation with new positions, techniques, or mechanical devices are doomed to failure unless the repressed aggressive components are integrated and men and women treat each other fearlessly and assertively rather than through phony accommodations and collusion. Our approach to sex ties in with our ethic, which encourages people to find ways to express themselves aggressively in personal, immediate, direct and constructive ways within their closest relationships. The bedroom can become an erotic playground and a natural setting for the release of one's aggression in safe, nonhurtful, and creative ways.

# CHAPTER 16

# Intimacy Through Conflict

*fight*      *grow*
*To love, ~~honor~~ and ~~obey~~*

Betty and Michael were seen together for marital counseling by Dr. Goldberg. They were on the brink of separation ever since Betty found out that Michael was sleeping around. Even at the time therapy began, he was in the midst of an intense affair. Michael, who was a thirty-nine-year-old dentist, was extremely polite and deferent toward the therapist during the initial sessions and was also very apologetic to Betty. As she cried and screamed, he sat back passively, periodically reassuring her with a pat on the back. When she finally pleaded with him to break off with his girlfriend, he readily agreed to it. Betty said, "I'd like to believe that you really mean it, but I don't." To this Michael calmly replied, "Well, what can I do if you don't want to believe me?" He showed no resentment over her distrust.

During one session when Dr. Goldberg asked Michael what he personally felt was missing for him in the relationship, he replied, "I really don't have any complaints. Betty's a wonderful girl. I'm just a fucked-up selfish bastard." Dr. Goldberg found himself reacting very skeptically to this comment because of the quiet, controlled way it was said. He mentioned this to Michael, but Michael had no response.

Within one month after the initial session, Michael had moved out of the house and was living with his girlfriend. He left Betty a note of apology in which he assured her that she would be much better off without him and that he was doing this for her good as well as for his own. He stated that he was taking full responsibility for the breakup and concluded the letter with, "and I know, sweet Betty, you'll have no trouble finding somebody else to love you." Betty's initial distrust of Michael's promise had been a healthy, intuitively accurate one. His complete lack of anger and resentment over her statement that she didn't believe him was a giveaway indication of his lack of genuine involvement.

The prelude to relationship breakups is often characterized by a similar kind of politeness, passivity, and detachment on the part of at least one of the individuals. That is, breakups are invariably accompanied by a strong resistance on the part of at least one of the partners to "hassling" and "fighting." On the other hand, couples who arrive for therapy in open warfare with each other have, as a rule, a good chance to improve their relationship. Their intense, angry interchanges are a strong indication of genuine involvement and caring.

We think of cocktail party chatter as being polite, superficial, and boring. It evidences a lack of real involvement. The following is a cocktail conversation between a polite, nonconfronting married couple upon the husband's arrival after a day at work:

HE:   Hi honey! Any mail?

SHE:   Mainly junk stuff and some magazines.

HE:   Did the *Atlantic Monthly* arrive?

SHE:   Yes! Would you like to see it? I was reading it in the bathroom. I'll go get it.

HE:   Please. Is there any coffee?

SHE:   Sure. (She gets his magazine and coffee.)

SHE:   Anything interesting happen today?

HE:   Just the same old stuff. How about you?

SHE:   Nothing here either, except that I bought a new outfit at Ohrbach's department store. I hope you're not angry.

HE:   Why should I be angry? I'm glad you found something you like.

SHE:   Do you want to see it?

HE:   Maybe after dinner.

SHE:   Do you want dinner now?

HE:   Right after I watch the six o'clock news.

In this fairly typical kind of exchange between a polite and cordial couple, a crisis of alienation is inevitable. Both are hiding their boredom. They are probably preoccupied with private thoughts and fantasies and resistant to aggressively engaging each other. The "politeness" and "mutuality" are coverups for detachment and the fear of leveling. Individuals in a relationship are, as a rule, very rational and detached when their emotional investment is minimal.

Authentic intimacy is rarely polite or mutual. Genuine involvement means that there are two people openly expressing their unique needs. Because they impact and impinge on each other, they are also bound to frustrate, anger, disappoint, and disillusion each other. Spouses or any couples who rarely clash are probably relating to each other defensively and superficially. They are either afraid of or unable to reveal their real needs.

These polite couples will accommodate each other in phony ways for long periods of time. At some moment of crises, however, the buried resentments and frustrations will burst forth. At this point, the hidden hostilities may be too overwhelming to cope with. Breaking up at this point is far less threatening than participating in healing confrontations.

The traditional marriage vows "to love, honor, and obey" are in many ways cruelly unrealistic. They set a tone and standard that in an authentic relationship will be impossible to achieve. If taken seriously they will induce feelings of inadequacy in couples who care about each other but who find themselves unable to achieve this model of harmony and togetherness they've been taught is possible. They view their conflicts and struggles as indications of personal failure and as reflections of a profound emotional deficiency in themselves. Their anxieties are intensified by the illusion, "Everybody else gets along, so why can't we?"

Areas of inevitable conflict in marriage have been previously discussed in the book *Intimate Enemy* (Bach and Wyden). The following discussion of some of these dimensions will strive to further develop some of these ideas.

## OPTIMAL DISTANCE—"HOW MUCH CLOSENESS?"

Difference in intimacy tolerance is perhaps the core conflict in contemporary marriages. These differences are, however, inevitable because males and females have significantly different early socialization experiences, which help to create these differing intimacy tolerances and the inevitable clashes.

The early male experiences and emotional conditioning in the areas of sexuality, physical and emotional expressiveness (touching, crying), dependency needs, and achievement pressures tend to create in him a tendency to hold back and over-control himself. Touching and emotional display may be seen as being unmasculine, and sexuality may be approached in terms of challenge and conquest. The female, however, is socialized to be more comfortable with her emotionality and her dependency needs. She is not taught to be as competitive or achievement-oriented as the man, which allows her to be more relaxed and open in her relationships. As for sexuality, she is taught to view this experience more as a part of intimacy and a total relationship rather than in the segmentalized terms of challenge and conquest.

In the early stages of marriage or living together, there is a strong tendency for couples to falsely accommodate each other. The husband may spend great amounts of time with his wife when, in reality, he'd rather be off on his own or with friends. Vice versa, a wife might even encourage her husband to do things on his own to show him that he's really "free," but in reality she would prefer him to stay around. When husband and wife stop playing these games and begin to experience and share their real needs, he may begin to feel engulfed and suffocated, while she may feel deprived and abandoned.

The preponderance of intense, destructive marital fights takes place on weekends and during vacations, when the seeds of phony accommodations come into destructive bloom. Quarrels and even violent altercations will be unconsciously precipitated to give one or the other spouse a rationale for expressing resentment or escaping. Disputes of the pettiest nature become the instruments intimates will use to give each other "legitimate" reasons to establish a comfortable optimal distance or to express resentment over feelings of deprivation. Here is a typical Saturday morning dispute:

HE: Where's my toothbrush?

SHE: It was on the sink.

HE: Well, it's not there now. (Angrily) Who the fuck walked off with it?

SHE: I don't know. Maybe one of the kids took it, and please don't curse at me. I'm not one of your office buddies.

HE: Well, the damned kids are into everything. Can't you even control them?

SHE: It's Saturday and we're off to the races again.

HE: Races, bullshit! When are you ever going to learn what it means to be a wife and mother?

SHE: Hopefully never! And if you don't like it, *leave!*

HE: Thanks for the suggestion, I think I will.

The hidden messages in this fight centered around distancing and testing. He unconsciously precipitated a fight to give him an excuse to get away. She unconsciously challenged him to test his desire and capacity to be around her. Had they been able to level about their respective intimacy tolerances earlier, this "petty" argument, which was a mask for the real conflict over distance, could have been avoided.

Intimates trying to get a sense of their differing intimacy needs should ask themselves the following questions: First, when do most of our fights arise? Second, what are these fights telling us about our needs for greater freedom or more closeness? Third, do either of us feel suffocated or deprived in the relationship? Fourth, how often do I enjoy touching or being touched by my partner? Fifth, approximately how many hours can I spend with my partner before I become bored, restless, and easily annoyed? Sixth, do I allow myself the outside friendships and involvements, sexual and nonsexual, that I inwardly know I want?

Couples often feel that they are supposed to enjoy being with each other most or all of the time. Prior to marriage or living together, it was all right and even fun to have many friends and sexual partners. Once the marriage contract is signed, however, couples feel they must satisfy all of their needs within the relationship. This attitude isolates the couple and eventually makes the marriage a nightmare. When each partner depends on the other for the satisfaction of all their primary emotional needs, they set each other impossible tasks and insure failure and frustration. The tragic consequence of this attitude of exclusivity and possessiveness is that the lovers destroy the very thing they so jealously guard. It is no wonder then that many spouses break up their marriage hating each other and exulting in their newly found freedom.

## CENTRICITY STRUGGLES—"WHO'S THE MOST IMPORTANT PERSON IN YOUR LIFE?"

The dimension of centricity refers to the need to establish one's place of pre-eminence in the life of the other person. Invariably in relationships there will be differences in inner feelings of security resulting in statements and demands such as the following: "If you really cared about me you'd give up those group therapy sessions and be at home with us. Aren't we more important to you than that group of strangers?" Or, "You leave for work every morning at 8:00 A.M. Lately you haven't been coming home from the office until seven-thirty. You could certainly leave a little earlier to have dinner with me and the kids. We don't need the money that much."

Centricity struggles are designed to discover the extent of the other person's commitment to the relationship. The questions underlying these conflicts are usually: (1) How secure do I really feel in this relationship? (2) Am I the most important person in his/her life? (3) Am I jealous of his/her activities or friends? (4) If it came down to a choice, what activity or person, if any, would he/she choose above me?

The ideal of a mutual autonomy in which neither spouse experiences a threat to his or her importance as a result of the outside relationships or activities of the other, is a romantic illusion that can rarely if ever be lived up to in an authentic relationship.

## POWER STRUGGLES—"WHO'S ON TOP?"

This dimension concerns itself with the issue of who will dominate the relationship or lifestyle. This struggle is one of the more complex and elusive ones because of the many faces the process of striving for power can take. The following messages, for example, have the same effect, though their content is dissimilar.

SHE:  I'd like you to come home tonight right after work and make dinner for the kids. I don't feel like doing it tonight.

OR

SHE:  Honey, I'm having cramps and feeling really headachy. Would you be a dear and come home right after work and help me out with dinner?

In the first instance, a direct demand was made. In the second, the same demand was made, but indirectly, and softened with a plea for help. A spouse may grab for control and make demands directly through an assertive or dominating style. On the other hand, similar results can be achieved indirectly through chronic illness, emotional symptoms, and manipulativeness.

The power dimension is rife with potential conflicts between any two normally assertive individuals. In an authentic intimate relationship during which each partner expresses these needs to control and dominate openly, overt conflict will therefore be inevitable. In relationships where one of the partners assumes a passive deferent role, there may be few overt conflicts; however, the same need to control will emerge in indirect ways. Concerning this dimension, intimates need to ask themselves: First, am I aware of my needs to control? Second, do I express this need directly or indirectly? Third, how do I express my resentment over being dominated? Do I express it through physical illness, emotional symptoms such as depression or chronic fatigue, or in passive aggressive ways, such as forgetting, withdrawing, or misunderstanding? Fourth, how can I translate my indirect or passive strategies into direct and openly assertive ones?

## TRUST FORMATION—"HOW CAN I BE SURE?"

Conflicts over trust are often the deepest in a relationship. Men and women alike have socially conditioned fears and distrust regarding the motives of the opposite sex. Therefore, trust testing will be a powerful facet in the process of building a relationship, particularly in its early stages.

In their early social conditioning, girls are admonished that "Men are only out for one thing," or "You can't trust a man." Likewise, men are taught to be wary of women, their wiles, hidden motives, and manipulativeness. The seductive female who has the power to destroy a kingdom is an archetypal fantasy.

Alongside these socially conditioned areas of sexually-oriented mistrust are those that emerge as a part of personal emotional traumas early in life, such as abandonment via parental divorce or death of a parent, harsh rejection experiences, parental inconsistencies, broken promises, or the disinterest of detached or busy parents.

Finally, there are the sources of distrust that are culturally conditioned as a result of one being raised in a competitive culture in which individuals are indirectly taught to be suspect of each other's motives.

Trust formation will therefore develop slowly and with innumerable clashes in the following three areas:

THE REVELATION OF "BELTLINES"   This refers to the gradual sharing of critical areas of emotional vulnerability. These may include personal revelations about one's past; sensitivities over one's physical appearance; inadequacy feelings regarding education, achievement, or sexual prowess; and the open discussion of emotional conflicts.

Joan Gibbs had many "beltline" areas. She told her fiancé Richard of only a few. She was particularly sensitive about the heaviness of her thighs and the smallness of her breasts, she said.

Two months later she and Richard had a fight over her refusal to spend Thanksgiving eve with Richard's parents. Richard began mocking her. He said that from the waist up she'd make a fantastic scarecrow, and that the Kentucky colonel could sure make a lot of money frying her thighs.

Joan clammed up and became very withdrawn. She went on like this for several days and never again revealed other "beltline" areas about which she felt even more sensitive. She felt that Richard couldn't be trusted, for example, knowing that she had had an abortion at age sixteen. She just couldn't be sure anymore when that kind of information might be used against her.

The least sensitive "beltline" areas are typically revealed first. If the information is abused by the partner, resulting in embarrassment or humiliation, trust formation will be slowed or some-times permanently destroyed.

BEHAVIOR MANIFESTED DURING A CRISIS   This facet of trust testing may be reflected in questions of the following type: How did she react when I lost my job? How did he react when I became very sick for a month and couldn't take care of his needs? How did she react when I had a fight with her father over my "irresponsible" ways? How did he react during my pregnancy when I was feeling confused, anxious, and unsure? How did she react when I became impotent for several weeks?

Craig Mitchell came home upset and told his wife of two months that he might be getting fired. He had just had a heated argument with his employer over the fact that he had been asked to work overtime four nights in a row without getting paid for it. He was visibly shaken and scared.

His wife Jeannie looked at him coldly and remarked, "That wasn't very good judgment on your part, was it? We've only been married two months, and how do you suppose we're go-ing to eat and pay the rent? All you think about is yourself."

At first Craig felt embarrassed, then guilty. But the more he thought about it, the angrier he got. He thought to himself, "That bitch only likes me when I'm playing the strong man!" It was an emotional turning point in their relationship. Shortly thereafter he told her he didn't want to have any children. The marriage broke up two years later.

IMBALANCES IN PHYSICAL STRENGTH, INTELLECTUAL ABIL-ITY, OR SOCIAL FACILITY   The way a man uses his physical ad-vantage or the way a woman relates to her man in social situa-tions where she may be more facile and smooth; and the way either takes advantage of the fact that he or she is better edu-cated or intellectually gifted are all aspects of this facet of trust formation.

The very thing that Sherry loved most about her college pro-fessor husband was the fact that though she knew nothing about his field of specialization, which was experimental psychology, he would always take the time to explain the research studies he was involved in. He would even ask her opinion of them. Though she knew she couldn't give him meaningful advice, she experienced this as a demonstration of her husband's love and involvement with her and it made her feel very close to him.

## PRESERVATION OF SELF—"I'VE GOT TO BE ME!"

The Gestalt prayer, authored by Dr. Fritz Perls, says in part, "You do your thing and I'll do mine." It has become one of the cultural bywords on how intimate relationships should ideally be. Contemporary spouses are very much preoccupied with the struggle to defend their identities within the relationship against engulfment. Their unique needs, however, will inevitably produce conflict. The dream of a totally nonintrusive, "You do your thing and I'll do mine" lifestyle is, we believe, psychologically impossible to live up to in an involved relationship. Relationships that begin very harmoniously and within which each spouse or lover just happens to like and want what the other one likes and wants, more often than not turn out to be rife with collusion, accommodation, and phoniness. Each person's real needs are being repressed.

Today more than ever, conflicts over the preservation of one's identity are surfacing in the man-woman relationship. Women who have a consciousness of themselves as people with unique needs and rights are increasingly protesting against many of the traditional roles and duties that have typically been assigned to them. Household and child-rearing chores are particularly under attack. While most men until now have tended to be reticent about the ways in which they feel their identities are being violated, we might expect that they will also become more active on their own behalf as women become more liberated.

Conflicts in the area of preservation of self and identity will continue throughout a vital relationship as the individuals develop and change. In a relationship in which these conflicts are not overtly experienced and struggled with, stagnation and repressed resentment will build up.

## SOCIAL BOUNDARIES—"WHOM SHOULD WE INVITE?"

There are many sources of conflict in this dimension as intimates are in the process of deciding on the following: Whom will we seek out and accept as friends? How often will we go out? Where will we go, and when? How much involvement will we have with in-laws and other family? Will there be opposite-sex friendships, and will these be of a physical or platonic nature? May people be brought into the home without notice?

False accommodations are common in the making of these decisions. Individuals give up critical needs, even deny that they have them "for the sake of" the relationship. In particular, spouses often suppress their desires to do things on their own, such as taking weekend trips alone with friends, bringing people home on impulse, or going to certain concerts, sporting events, etc., that they feel their spouses won't like. Even the simple, pleasurable act of talking to strangers or making new acquaintances casually is usually given up because it threatens one's partner.

The conflicts in this area, which are avoided by denying one's real needs, set the groundwork for the downfall of the relationship. This downfall usually begins with feelings of boredom, deadness, and frustration. Standing up for one's real social needs is often fraught with anxiety and conflict because it cuts across the normal possessive and ownership orientation in intimate relationships. However, the price of denial is the devitalization and slow decay of the relationship.

## ROMANTIC ILLUSIONS—"ARE YOU THE PERSON I MARRIED?"

She thought he was so thoughtful and sensitive and is hurt and disillusioned to find him forgetting birthdays and anniversaries. She is also dismayed when she sees her strong, "take charge" husband behave like a frightened pussycat in front of his boss. He, on the other hand, thought she was so gentle and fragile. He is shaken when he hears her screaming and cursing at the driver blocking her car. And he can't believe his eyes when he notices his "pure and faithful" wife flirting and dancing seductively with other men at a friend's party.

In intimate interactions conflict is bound to arise as the partners begin to see each other as they really are rather than as they believed them to be. Spouses often repress the truths they see and remain stubbornly fixated on their fantasy because of their fear of conflict. In the process, however, a reservoir of hidden resentment is built up, which may eventually result in a sudden, violent blowup.

Disillusionments about the other person are an inevitable consequence of the phony courtship rituals most people engage in. Recognizing "dream spoiler" resentments when they arise and discussing them openly are sources of potential conflict that are, however, necessary for the maintenance of a real relationship.

The ideals of peace and harmony in a marriage or any equivalently close relationship are cruel and unrealistic. The attempt to live up to these myths is at the price of repressing conflicts, hostilities, and resentments as they arise, thereby paving the way for an increasingly fragile involvement.

Vital relationships grow in the soil of the conflict-laden dimensions discussed in this chapter. Avoidance and suppression of the conflicts ultimately result in feelings of alienation, boredom, and finally animosity. Some married couples choose to live like this rather than risk the alternatives. For others, however, the relationship simply decays and collapses under its own weight. The tendency to jump in again to find a new and fresh relationship with somebody else, if accompanied by the same conflict avoidance, will simply begin the frustrating, destructive, and alienating cycle again.

# CHAPTER 17

# Stop! You Are Driving Me Crazy!!!

Crazymaking is a form of interpersonal interaction that results from the repression of intense aggression and which seriously impairs its victim's capacity to recognize and deal with the interpersonal reality. We tend to think of the word "crazy" as describing the behavior of a small group of very disturbed individuals. And yet the very same kinds of emotional experiences and interactions that have succeeded in largely destroying the reality grasp of these people are prevalent in milder forms in the lives of all people in our culture. Though the dosage of it in most people's lives is not sufficient to drive them completely crazy, its impact is still sufficiently disturbing to severely harm relationships and to produce emotional symptoms such as detachment and withdrawal, vulnerability to sudden mood swings, violent outbursts, depression and feelings of alienation and isolation.

## THE DOUBLE BIND

The "double bind" has become one of the most widely recognized forms of these crazymaking interactions. In essence it involves the communication of "damned if you do, damned if you don't" emotional messages. The victim is doomed to rejection no matter which way he responds. This process was originally observed and described by the late psychiatrist Dr. Donald Jackson and noted anthropologist Dr. Gregory Bateson.

The double-binding crazymaking mother notices her child Kathy, age seven, sitting alone quietly, perhaps reading or coloring. The dialogue begins:

MOTHER:    "Kathy, you look so sad! Are you sad?"

KATHY:    "No!"

MOTHER:    (out of guilt) "Don't you want to come over here and give Mommy a hug? Show Mommy you love her."

KATHY:    "Well, okay." (goes over and hugs mother)

MOTHER:    (her body tightening up) "You only did that because I asked you. You really didn't mean it. Did you?"

KATHY:    (quiet and confused)

MOTHER:    "Okay, go back to your coloring book—I'm really disappointed."

Kathy's mother was a "good" mother from all surface appearances. However, she had a lot of hidden resentment toward Kathy, who was an unexpected pregnancy and forced the marriage prematurely. When Kathy's mother saw her sitting in the corner looking sad, she felt compelled to be "nice." The "niceness," however, was motivated by guilt over the underlying, repressed resentment toward Kathy and not out of a genuine desire for physical contact with her. Either response Kathy would have made, "No, I don't want to hug you," or "Yes, I do want to hug you," would have met with a rejection response stemming from the underlying, repressed resentment.

Crazymaking messages are never clearly rejecting ones. They are invariably interspersed with "loving" looks or words that seduce the victim into a closeness and then leave him feeling guilty and confused (he sees himself as responsible) when the rejection comes. Kathy will experience herself as "bad" if she believes her mother's message of "You really didn't mean it." The conclusion Kathy will then draw about herself is, "My mother really loves me, and I'm a bad girl because I always disappoint her."

The crazymaking mixture between "loving" and rejecting messages, in no-win combinations, was graphically portrayed in this dinner conversation between father and sixteen-year-old daughter Ellen:

FATHER: Ellen dear, you know your face is getting all broken out from that garbage you eat after school. At this rate boys will never call you.

ELLEN: I bought a cream that Patty told me about. It's supposed to be really good for blemishes.

FATHER: I'm glad you're doing something for yourself, but why don't you ask me before you spend my money on stuff like that?

ELLEN: I thought you'd want me to.

FATHER: I want you to look good, but we have more important things to do with our money than buy cosmetics.

ELLEN: There's a boy in my chemistry class. I think he's going to ask me out, and I was embarrassed about my face.

FATHER: Is that the most important thing to you? Looking good for boys? And do you think beauty is skin deep? It's the person inside that counts, Ellen dear, not the surface stuff.

ELLEN: I really think he likes me as a person, and I wanted to look good.

FATHER: You sound all ga-ga-eyed. I hope you remember you've got school to finish first. If I ever hear that you're pregnant . . .

ELLEN: I promise that won't happen!

FATHER: And I don't want you on the pill!

ELLEN: I thought you wanted me to look good! (almost in tears by now)

FATHER: I do, but that doesn't mean getting all hung up over a boy. Can't you ever worry about anything but how you look and what boys think of you?

ELLEN:   (in tears) I don't.

FATHER:   I know you don't. You can do anything you want. But keep your schoolwork up.

Beneath father's "concern" and "helpfulness" is a need to totally dominate and control his daughter and keep her a little girl. However, he does not recognize these motives at all. He thinks of himself as a loving person. That is, his conscious self-image is of a well-intentioned father with his daughter's best interests in mind. Because he is not consciously aware of his domination and controlling needs, they seep through indirectly and contaminate each "loving" message with a controlling, inhibiting one. On the one hand, father was encouraging Ellen to look good. On the other hand, he was angry because she was doing something on her own to look good. So long as Ellen looked pathetic, which mobilized father's guilt, he was "helpful" and "loving." As soon as Ellen indicated that she might not be all that pathetic, dependent, and lonesome, he started attacking her interest in boys. Father's crazymaking messages to Ellen were good illustrations of that mixture of "love" and rejection that characterizes double-binding. Consequently, anything Ellen does will bring rejection and the feeling that she has failed to live up to her father's expectations.

Sonny and Maxine had been married for 6 years. Sonny, though a rugged, physically impressive, 6 feet, 3 inches and 210 pounds, was still a mother's boy. He married Maxine largely because his mother had told him what a great wife she would make. Basically, though, Sonny was still a boy who wanted to play and be free and was unconsciously resentful and jealous of single friends who went out every night, could go to evening basketball games, "screw around," and get drunk. He was also inwardly jealous of his married friends who left their wives at home alone in the evenings, which Sonny felt too guilty to do. His resentment came through in exhausting and confusing double-bind messages that brought Maxine to the verge of a breakdown.

SONNY: What was your day like, darling? Anything exciting happen?

MAXINE: Nothing sensational. I did teach Timmy how to hold a fork and spoon. Then we went to the park and played catch. I think he's going to be another Roman Gabriel.

SONNY: It's great that you're so into bringing up Timmy, but lately that's all you can talk about. You used to be so much fun to talk with, but now you've gotten to be a big bore— and I hope that doesn't hurt your feelings. But you really *used* to be an exciting person, and I loved you for that.

MAXINE: (raising her voice) I wanted to take a job, and you said you wanted me home with the kids. You said I was being selfish and hostile. Now you say I'm a bore.

SONNY: I didn't mean you were really a bore. But gad, that baby talk is driving me up a wall. There's got to be other things you can do.

MAXINE: Like what?

SONNY: Don't you have any imagination? Then I really pity you! Just forget it. I'm going to watch TV.

Sonny, who really resented being father and husband but could not acknowledge these feelings to himself openly, became a bona fide crazymaker. Everything he said, although loving in intent, was eventually contaminated by the underlying core of unfelt anger. Maxine could never do anything that would please. She became increasingly anxious and withdrawn until she finally had a breakdown and went into therapy with Dr. Bach. During her therapy she discovered that she was actually a willing victim of Sonny's crazymaking. Her self-image was one of helplessness and of being unable to survive without someone like Sonny to lean on. However, she mistook his demanding, controlling manner for strength!

Just as in family interactions, the relationships in most work situations, particularly between employer and employee, contain the basic emotional ingredients for crazymaking double binders. In these crazymaking interactions, the employer becomes a substitute father or mother figure and the employees find themselves behaving like children, eagerly and anxiously searching for approval and reward. The more insecure and frightened the employee, the greater are the chances that he will become the victim of a double binder.

The crazymaking vice president of the sales department of a large garment corporation employing forty-five people became increasingly aware of communication problems in his department, which were being reflected in decreasing sales. He tried firing some salesmen and hiring new ones, but that didn't seem to help the problem. After an initial sales spurt, things would begin to bog down again.

He began reading books and articles on psychological approaches to employment problems. After finishing several of them, he came upon what he felt would be a solution to the morale problems. He had signs placed all over the office and sent out memos to each employee announcing that henceforth he would be available every Wednesday afternoon for private, confidential conferences to discuss any complaints or gripes, no matter how minor. All discussions, he asserted, would be treated as completely off the record.

There was some initial enthusiasm among the employees, although a number of the older ones reacted with skepticism. They remarked cynically that this was probably a trap of some kind. However, some employees began to make appointments. One came in and complained about a lack of adequate secretarial help. Still another complained that the marketing people weren't holding up their end of the business. A few had grievances about lesser issues, such as the length of coffee breaks, the need for more window space, and noise problems.

Initially, they were listened to with great patience, but eventually the vice president would always have a comeback to negate or belittle the complaint. If the employee persisted, invariably the vice president would imply that they were crybabies and perhaps not of sufficient caliber to work for the company. They left feeling insecure and angry that they had taken the bait.

Other employees, less trusting and more cynical, never came in. They would be stopped in the hallways by the vice president and asked why they showed such little concern for improving company morale. He implied that they lacked the necessary company spirit. They too wound up feeling insecure and wondering if perhaps they should contrive a safe but phony complaint to satisfy their boss. Clearly, the employees were being placed in a "damned if you do, damned if you don't" double bind. If they presented a complaint, they were liable to being called crybabies. If they didn't, they would be accused of lacking company spirit.

## COPING WITH THE DOUBLE BINDER

Double binders feed on dependency and feelings of inadequacy. The double binder is applying torture treatment to an unconsciously willing victim who does not feel capable and/or worthy of an openly assertive, autonomous style of life.

In some instances, however, particularly that of parent-child, the child victim is trapped if there is no liberating outside intervention. The double-binding parent overcontrols, blocks out other influences and projects the image of a caring parent, which makes him that much more difficult to confront. The child will begin to signal for help, perhaps by becoming increasingly withdrawn, or going into periodic, sudden, explosive tantrums. Through all this he will remain dependent and childlike, significantly below his age level expectancy. All of these will be indirect pleas for help. A school environment that promotes assertiveness and acceptance of aggressive feelings can have an ameliorating effect. Otherwise, the child may have to enter adolescence and begin to make life sufficiently unbearable for the parents, usually passively, by functioning in a dependent, withdrawn, and noncommunicative manner until the parents are literally forced to recognize that their child is disturbed. The double-binded child is one of the genuine emotional victims with no overt recourses in our society.

In adult relationships a person can sense if he is in the grip of a double binder if he is in a frequent state of anxiety and oscillates constantly between feelings of euphoria ("He loves me.") and depression ("No, I think he'll reject me."). Where one finds oneself always dependent, constantly seeking approval and in general walking on egg shells, one is likely to be interacting with a double binder. The double binder is alternately perceived as benevolent and cruel by the victim, and through all of this, the latter is afraid of talking spontaneously and directly to the double binder for fear of rejection. In general, crazymakers produce confused reactions in their victims, a mixture of wanting to run away and a fear of doing so.

Rooting out and blocking the double binder first requires the awareness that he is feeding on vulnerability and inadequacy. The first major step then is the awakening to one's own capacity to survive independently. The rest is relatively simple, for the crazymaker really needs his victim as much as his victim needs him. He too is afraid of overt aggressiveness. The double binder's helpful and seductive façade needs to be recognized as such with the following awareness. "Nothing I will ever do will really please you. I am not going to let myself be trapped any longer by the fantasy that there is a magic button which, if I press it, will release your love and allow me to feel secure."

Guilt and "shoulds" ("I should enjoy being with him/her.") that heavily color the socialization process for all people in the roles they play in this culture—parent, spouse, teacher, employer, friend, worker, etc.—make potential crazymakers of everyone. That is, as people live up to role expectations that run counter to their real feelings, a core of repressed resentment will form that will cause them to send out double-binding messages. One can however perform in a role while at the same time allowing oneself to experience the resentment and anger one may feel about it. At least with these feelings out in the open, a person can decide whether he really wants to be living as he is living and avoid engaging in the crazymaking dance called double-binding.

## THE MIND RAPE

All the forms of crazymaking have their most lethal effects within the parent-child relationship. Identity denial is a common occurrence between parent and child. Colloquially termed the "mind rape" or "mind fucking," it involves informing another person what they really think or feel because it serves the convenience or need of the crazymaker. In the process, the victim's real feelings are denied validity.

TOMMY (seven years old): I don't want to go to the dentist—I'm scared.

FATHER: You're not really scared. Only little babies are afraid of dentists. You want to be like the big boys, don't you? Big boys like going to the dentist. Isn't that right?

TOMMY: (quietly and uncomfortably does not reply and goes passively along)

FATHER: See, I knew you were a big boy!

For seven-year-old Tommy to defend his feelings was too much to ask. On the one hand, it would mean displeasing Daddy, and on the other, it would mean experiencing his feelings of fear without support. Therefore, Tommy represses his own emotional reactions and accepts his father's interpretation. He has been "mind raped." This begins a process of splitting the child's personality between what he feels and what others inform him he *should* feel. Adults who have been "mind raped" extensively as children, and many have, experience a sense of confusion and uncertainty over what they feel and experience. For self-defense, they might develop intellectual defenses and deal with everything in a detached, cerebral way. This eventually leads to a state of emotional numbness. Spontaneous feelings have been replaced by "should feels" and intellectualizations.

Among adults, mind raping is often done in the name of helping and understanding.

JONATHAN:   My job is really getting me down, and I think I'm going to quit.

MARK:   How can you say that? You work in a beautiful building, you've got great insurance coverage and lots of security. How could you not like it?

JONATHAN:   I feel like I'm wasting my abilities.

MARK:   Why? It can be very challenging. A job is anything you make it!

JONATHAN:   I know, but I've been there for a year now and it's not getting any better.

MARK:   You just enjoy bitching. That's your style. You *know* you really like your job.

The relationship between Mark and Jonathan was basically a friendly one. However, Mark's contention that he really "knew" what Jonathan was feeling, although consciously well-intentioned, was destructive in its impact by creating guilt feelings and confusion in Jonathan regarding his own reactions. On an underlying level, Mark really felt competitive with Jonathan, and did not want him to risk and possibly gain more than he (Mark) was willing to risk and gain. Because the overt acknowledgment of competitive feelings and power struggles are considered taboo between friends, these crazymaking messages ensue.

## COMBATING THE MIND RAPER

Mind raping is a seductive form of crazymaking. The victim hears that the other person is really trying to be "helpful," and it is a comforting fantasy to believe that somebody else knows us better than we know ourselves. Modern-day "pop psychology" has made mind raping under the guise of "analyzing" and "tuning in" a favorite sport. People supposedly read each other's "hidden meanings" and "help" each other recognize "real" feelings without even exchanging a word.

To combat mind rapers, you must always begin with the assumption that a person who tells you what you "really" think or feel is wrong. If he is correct it is probably more by accident than by wisdom. Invariably, the mind raper, who may be partially correct, is oversimplifying a complicated emotional experience. Very rarely, in fact, is there one clear-cut feeling or reason for anything. It is emotionally insulting to be mind read without one's permission, under any circumstance.

In our work in aggression training we conduct an exercise called "mind reading checkout." We train individuals to ask permission of the other whenever they wish to surmise what the other person is feeling or thinking. Individuals quickly learn how often they are sure they know, but are really way off target. This is a very sobering revelation. Some grandiose mind rapers may even *insist* they know you better than you know yourself. This kind of person is toxic to be with and whenever possible should be excluded from one's intimate circle because of their powerfully seductive, destructive crazymaking tendency.

Once one is sensitized to mind raping, one of the most seductive forms of crazymaking, it is fairly simple to recognize. It is frequently accompanied by the word "really."

"I think you really feel . . ."

"What you're really saying . . ."

"I don't believe you really want . . ."

All such messages, as a general rule, should be aborted, even if they might be accurate, and especially if they've been received without your permission. They should be considered to be as insulting as direct slaps in the face. In fact, they are. A polite counter would be, "Thank you for your help, but your reading of my mind only confuses me more."

## THE GUILTMAKERS

Within the context of a parent-child relationship, the guilt-maker parent creates in the child an exaggerated and destructive sense of his impact, generating in the child the fear of self-expression, particularly in the area of aggressive impact.

"Because you don't mind, Mommy gets a headache and feels sick."

"Grandma's old and isn't going to be around that much longer. She counts on you, and if you're not nice to her, something very bad could happen to her."

"You hurt your sister's feelings and ruined her whole weekend."

In each instance the child is receiving a grossly distorted picture of his power and an exaggerated, unreal picture of the fragility of the other person. It may be true that Jimmy aggravated Mother, that Grandma needs positive feedback, or that his sister felt hurt. However, the implication in all of these messages is that the other person is helpless and readily demolished by an aggressive communication. In an aggression-healthy environment we would rebuke the sister for not asserting herself in return; we would chide Mother for allowing herself to be given a headache, and would encourage Grandma to actively pursue positive feedback on her own.

Guiltmakers are passively attempting to stifle the other person's aggressive potential for their own controlling needs. The guiltmaker is an aggression castrater who often compounds insult with injury by a "consoling" message after he has guiltmade. "But I know you really didn't mean it!" is the double dose of crazymaking.

Intimate adult relationships of all kinds are rife with guiltmaking. In each instance this represents a form of manipulation of the other person's aggression phobia. This can be done with words ("Because of you . . ."), with hurt looks, silence, or intentional bungling of something one is doing at the other's request ("I did what you said, and now look at the mess we're in."). Often the guiltmaking is done subtly, in the form of an interpretation such as, "You need to control everything" or "You're always so hungry for attention." Basic, healthy, assertive impulses suddenly become heinous crimes.

## DEFENSE AGAINST GUILTMAKERS

Guiltmakers use others as scapegoats in order to avoid assuming personal responsibility for the things that happen to them. Again, when these occur in the context of a parent-child relationship (i.e., the mother who blames her deteriorating marriage on her child's behavior), they can be particularly damaging. The child accepts these statements as truth and may be frightened and scared by them to the point of extreme passivity and fear of self-assertion.

It is safe to say that within close relationships it is the great exception when one person can truly be held responsible for the life consequences of another. Contemporary psychological-clinical data and thought are increasingly demonstrating the great extent to which people bring unto themselves the things that happen to them. They often, in fact, seek out friends, lovers, employers, and situations that can provide them with comfortable rationalizations for their inadequacies and failures.

The ultimate retort to guiltmakers, therefore, one that will undoubtedly surface their core of underlying hostility is, "I'm not guilty. You got what you wanted, or you wouldn't have gotten involved with me." The extent of the guiltmaker's rage at such a response will serve as a good indicator of his defensiveness and unwillingness to assume responsibility for the things that happen to him. Guiltmaking, even when there is some truth in the accusation, is always counterproductive. As a rule, therefore, guiltmakers must always be resisted and their bullying outbursts viewed as a part of their aggression-castrating repertoire!

## NONENGAGEMENT: CRAZYMAKING BY EMOTIONAL WITHDRAWAL

Few can crazymake by generating insecurity and self-doubt better than the nonengager. The nonengager causes the other person to feel like the heavy, the ogre, the fight starter. It will be recalled that in the chapter "The Myth of the 'Nice' Guy," we described the " 'nice' guy daddy" who never took responsibility for disciplining the children and thereby passively forced mother to become the punitive, disliked figure.

In our aggression-phobic culture, quietness, self-control, and refusal to fight have traditionally been viewed as positive, mature qualities. However, in a relationship of interdependence, these behaviors can create intense frustration. The nonengager gives little feedback or structure, and one is left trying to read the mind of this self-contained person in an attempt to ascertain what they are thinking.

Children of nonengaging, crazymaking parents find themselves forever searching for an ounce of approval. After a certain point they may lose their motivation to be productive or to excel in any way because no matter how well they perform, they get a similarly detached response. Likewise in the marital relationship, the victim spouse eventually gives up in exasperation, knowing that it doesn't really matter what he or she does.

Nonengagement can have a powerful, anxiety-producing effect in the work situation, particularly for the insecure employee seeking to gain some assurance that he is performing adequately. He will begin to interpret the lack of response as an indication that he is doing poorly but that his boss doesn't want to tell him and thus lives in chronic fear that he will receive a termination notice with his next paycheck.

During the workday he may even begin to avoid direct contact with his boss in the magical belief that "If he doesn't see me or talk to me it's another day without facing the bad news." The employee finds himself hanging on for dear life, and this greatly impairs his personal, creative potential. His energy is being drained just trying to maintain himself rather than going toward improvement and greater achievement.

Behind the nonengagement is repressed aggression emerging passively. The underlying message is, "You're not worth the energy," "I don't care enough to get involved," "My head's somewhere else," or "Don't bug me!" The victim of this crazy-maker may expend considerable energy trying to elicit a response and may be unconsciously forced into extreme, provocative, even rageful behavior in an attempt to get a reaction. Invariably, traditional aggression-fearful onlookers will view this victim as disturbed or hostile and sympathize with the quiet nonengager. Thus the victim gets a double dose of crazy-making, one from the nonengager and the second from outsiders who will side with the "nice" quiet nonengager.

## CONFRONTING THE NONENGAGER

Victims of these crazymakers must learn to resist the temptation to label themselves as trouble starters. In general, traditional perceptions of nonengagement as being a desirable quality indicative of depth, maturity, self-control, and peacefulness needs to be altered. Nonengagers must be seen within the context of the relationship in which they hold back and the impact it is having on the other person. In some instances, this form of behavior may be relatively harmless if the interdependent party has a similar style. However, in the instance where the nonengager starves out and drives the victim up the wall, it needs to be seen for the hostile, depriving response it is.

Individuals involved with nonengagers must ask themselves several questions:

1. What am I getting out of this relationship?
2. Why do I remain in it?
3. Are my real needs somehow being satisfied by my partner's detachment?
4. Is there something in my behavior that has shut my partner down.
5. Why do I persist in trying to get blood from a stone when I could be turning somewhere else for emotional nourishment?

One important crazymaking feature of being involved with a nonengager is that the victim's behavior may become more extreme and bizarre in the desperate attempt to get a response. This behavior may be interpreted as neurotic or psychotic by others.

Nonengagers are extremely difficult to impact. They have learned to become comfortable in their detachment. Threats of leaving or ending the relationship may not make a dent. The nonengager is frightened of his aggression, has learned to encapsulate it, and receives relief from anxiety through withdrawal.

Victims of nonengagers therefore need to explore whether they are actually comfortable within the noninvolvement. If they can truly say "No," then demands for engagement need to be made or the possibility of leaving the relationship explored. If one isn't being fed, one must for survival's sake go where food is available.

## "THINGING"

A common crazymaking phenomenon in this aggression-phobic, alienated culture is that of relating to others in the segmentalized way we term "thinging." This dehumanized interpersonal interaction is characterized by the treatment of others as if they were objects to fulfill a specific need or limited set of needs. The person's emotional totality is ignored and even considered a bothersome interference. A man may be seen as a business contact, golf buddy, or car mechanic, or a woman might be viewed by the "thinging" crazymaker as a good lay, a fine mother, or a secretary. In each of these instances, the victim is related to strictly in terms of the specific function he or she performs. In "thinging," the other person's feelings, if not related to the specific function desired of him, are reacted to as intrusions.

For example, the "thinger" takes his nonfunctioning automobile to a car mechanic. The mechanic becomes, in the "thinger's" eyes, an automobile fixing machine. If the mechanic attempts to relate in terms of *his* needs or feelings, the "thinger" becomes impatient. "I don't care about you. I need my car fixed," is the essential message. When this orientation is carried over into close, ongoing relationships at home, in the office, or in school, relationships become cold, mechanical, and dehumanized.

Certain common forms of "thinging" are prevalent in most work situations. Women who assert themselves openly and directly are immediately vulnerable to being labeled "ballbreakers." If a man were to act similarly he would be viewed as showing healthy assertiveness. If a black employee comes to work late, he is immediately vulnerable to being lumped in with a stereotype of blacks that says they are unreliable. A younger male employee who chooses to wear long hair or a beard will almost certainly be labeled a hippie, and it will be taken for granted that he is a political radical and smokes pot.

Another form of "thinging" involves the "disposable" style of relating that is so rampant in our culture. An illusion of love and concern is projected as a form of manipulation to get something out of someone else. These crazymaking "thingers" develop a facile, surface charm and a great sensitivity to the needs and vulnerabilities of others, which disguises their basic underlying attitude of contempt and their motivation to use the other person temporarily in order to satisfy a need. An effective "thinger" out to sell a product, seduce the opposite sex, or get something he needs may receive an unusually positive response:

"I feel like I've known him all my life."

"We really clicked. He's so real."

"He really made me feel special."

When the aim is achieved and the need is satisfied, the "thinger" loses interest, and the victim may be abandoned or discarded. The "disposable" style of relating is prevalent in our culture, in love relationships, between parents and children, in work environments, and in educational settings, among others.

Many an adolescent, brought up in a "nice" middle- or upper-middle-class home, who is now drug addicted, nonfunctional, or coldly cynical, we believe is the product of a "thinging" relationship with his or her parents. These teenagers or young adults were brought up as commodities, status symbols used by their parents to project their own image as heads of a good family. Within that environment there was an absence of sensitivity or awareness of the child's total and individual needs.

"Thinging" parents characteristically relate to their children on a materialistic level. They give them the best money can buy in the anxious pursuit of shaping their child into an image to fit the parents' needs. These are motions of involvement and love, while in actuality the interaction is mechanical, cold, and driven. These parents are too busy with their own ambitions to involve themselves emotionally with their children. They buy their way through relationships instead. Behind the trappings of good parenthood is an absence of involvement. Beneath the "love" is a message of rejection.

## PREVENTION OF "THINGING"

A major clue to the presence of "thinging" is the smoothness and facileness of this kind of involvement. So long as the "objects" being "thinged" perform their functions well, there is no conflict, and everything seems comfortable. Only where the "objects" attempt to project their humanness does conflict ensue.

The human "objects" used by "thingers" are themselves often asking for it. Allowing oneself to be used in machinelike ways is for some people apparently more comfortable than getting emotionally close. In general, victims of "thingers" are individuals who themselves are fearful of the totality of relationships, the aggressive give-and-take, confrontation, "hassle," and involvement of them. To the aggression-phobic victim, the aggression-"thinger" allows him to have an illusion of involvement without the anxiety of real involvement.

"Thinging," when it emerges in the form of stereotyping in

the office or work environment, is among the easiest forms of crazymaking to block or prevent. Persons likely to be stereotyped, such as women, minority groups, long-haired males, etc., need only raise their awareness to the point where they can anticipate what stereotypes they are likely to come up against. At the first indication that they are being "thinged," they need to confront it with a statement such as, "I know that because I'm a woman, you're going to think I'm some kind of castrater or 'ballbreaker.' Actually, I'm really only trying to do an effective job. And just because I'm a woman doesn't mean I want to be catered to or treated any differently than anybody else. If I feel you're doing that, then I'll object."

Relationships easily won, without conflict or hassle, must always be suspect. Since "thingers" are usually effective manipulators, frightened of aggressive involvement, they tend to be difficult to impact or change. Their stock in trade is conflict avoidance. They run away at its first signs.

"Thingers" can be blocked from their manipulations by the recognition of their unreal niceness and smoothness, thereby either avoiding "hooking in" or directly confronting them. The ultimate defense against a "thinger" is through the acceptance and expression of the realities of conflict and aggression in oneself. To the person who is unafraid of these realities in himself and accepting of them in others, the slickness and superficiality of the "thinger" will be seen for what it is; a cold, rejecting, and dehumanized way of relating.

## MYSTIFICATION

The crazymaking mystifier relies heavily on the dependency and ignorance of the victim. The message he communicates is, "If I weren't around to fulfill your needs, you couldn't survive."

The mystifying parent has a particularly cruel effect. Feeding on the helplessness and vulnerability of the child, this crazymaking parent paints images of the world as being a place that is unfathomable, rejecting, and full of pitfalls and dangers. The basic motivation is to retain control and power over the child. After instilling feelings of confusion and helplessness, the parent in effect says, "As long as you're with me, however, everything will be all right!"

Variations on this theme are commonly seen in many different kinds of interactions: husbands or wives who are sure they could not live without the other, employees who become convinced that no other job is as good and no one else would want them, and individuals who are convinced that any style of life except the one that they are leading would have disastrous consequences. All have been mystified either by parents, spouses, or other important figures.

Mystification in the work situation may be an unconscious protective device used by employees who fear a competitive threat from other employees, particularly newer ones. In discussing a project or exploring a particular task, they will present their ideas in such a complicated or obscure way that the other person is overwhelmed by its complexity but too afraid to ask questions for fear of appearing to be stupid. The crazymaking employee thereby succeeds in befuddling his victim, at the same time reducing any competitive threat.

Another prevalent variation of the mystification process was recently noted among a group of aides working in the office of a major political figure. The top aide, who had acquired a particularly favored relationship with this politician, would regularly warn the other aides that the "boss" was temperamental, impatient, critical, and unpredictable. If they wanted to get something done, he informed them, they should communicate through him. By generating this fearsome picture of the politician, the aide was assuring himself that his favored position would not be threatened.

## DEMYSTIFYING THE MYSTIFIER

Only healthy outside forces such as schools or neighbors can offset the cruel impact of the mystification of children. Without positive influences that help these children to see and experience their own strengths and inherent wisdom and capacity to survive, it may take years or a lifetime to overcome the fear and trembling attitude toward life that results from constant mystification.

A sign that one is the victim of mystification is the feeling that "Without him or her I probably couldn't survive, or wouldn't want to live." Invariably, these kinds of feelings contain underlays of hostile dependency and feelings of personal helplessness. In fact, there is seldom another human being so vital that one would fall apart without him. Whenever one has these feelings, one can be sure that one is involved in a mystifying relationship. Aggressively healthy relationships are ones in which each person has a sense of personal strength, autonomous capacity to survive, and the freedom to explore.

In examining the possibility of being in a mystifying relationship, appropriate questions to be asked are:

1.   Do I really experience love *toward* the other person, or am I hiding from the world behind him or her?

2.   Do I really experience love *from* the other person, or does he or she have a stake in controlling me?

3.   What do I really resent about the other person? If I can't think of anything, I know that I'm blocking out a major portion of my feelings in this relationship, the aggressive ones. Why am I afraid to experience my anger and resentment toward him or her?

Mystifying relationships are particularly damaging because in those instances when the mystifier leaves his victim through abandonment or death, the victim often sinks into a depression, develops a deep sense of helplessness or futility, and in some cases develops serious illnesses or becomes suicidal as an expression of his helplessness and hopelessness. Therefore, any relationship based on the feeling, "Without him/her I couldn't survive," are basically destructive and hostile ones, and these underlying feelings must first be uprooted in the process of demystifying the mystifier.

## CRISISMAKING

Crisismaking crazymakers abort communication and instill frustration, fear, and confusion by strategically dropping in threats of abandonment, suicide, divorce, illness, emotional breakdowns, or firing (in an employer-employee relationship) whenever the victim attempts to come to grips with an issue that threatens this crazymaker.

A recent instance of this interaction was observed between Mrs. Esther Grant, age sixty-eight, and her thirty-five-year-old bachelor son, Sam, who was still living with her. One day, Sam announced that he had met a girl and was seriously thinking of becoming engaged. In the middle of a heated conversation in which Mrs. Grant accused her son of abandoning her, she developed acute chest pains and exclaimed that she thought she was having a heart attack, and how could Sam think of leaving her when she was on the verge of death. (In fact, such mothers sometimes outlive their children, whose growth and development they stifle with their crisismaking behavior.)

Victims involved with crisismakers are invariably very guilt-prone and therefore stifle their own needs in order to placate. The crisismaker's typical threats include:

"I'll leave you."

"I want a divorce."

"I'll kill myself."

"I'm going to crack up again."

"I'm going home to Momma."

To the victim the choice seems to be "stifle my needs or face disaster." Either way, the consequences seem to be frightening.

The crisismaking employer creates a work atmosphere that instills in the employee the fear that almost any demand, request, or other form of self-assertion will have dire consequences or may even result in the loss of his job. Increasingly, these employees will tend to avoid any confrontation with their employer because a crisis always ensues. Frustration and resentment will build up within the employees, who will then be prone to seizing on any indirect or hidden way to sabotage their employer.

In a small shoe factory in Virginia, a number of employees had at one time or another requested a raise or a change in working conditions or in the work shifts to which they were assigned. They were immediately called troublemakers and told that there were other jobs around if they were unsatisfied. The enraged employees began to demonstrate their anger by stealing merchandise, neglecting the maintenance of machines, taking long breaks when the boss was absent, and passing the word in their communities that people shouldn't buy the products the factory was making.

## CONTROLLING THE CRISISMAKER

Victims of crisismakers need to see the crisismaking as a form of emotional extortion that is designed to abort attempts at self-assertion. Just as when one allows oneself to be bribed once by an extortionist, the grip begins to tighten, and this powerful tool, once used by the crazymaker successfully, will tend to be used with increasing frequency.

There are two principal approaches to a crisismaking crazymaker. The first involves risking the crisis.

"Go ahead and kill yourself."

"Leave me if you wish," or

"I'm not responsible for your physical well-being," would be appropriate retorts. One may then discover that the threat was, in fact, a hollow bluff. When Sam Grant finally decided to marry and leave his mother, she became quite docile and asked if there were any ways she could help out, by teaching his wife cooking or by helping with the baby they were soon expecting. She never got her heart attack. One approach then is to risk the crisis.

The crisismaking employer feeds on the insecurity and lack

of feelings of self-worth in the employee. In actual fact, replacing employees and training new ones is often as traumatic for the employer as being fired is for the employee. In most cases, employees will discover that they do not get the dire response they anticipate when they make legitimate demands and express their needs. If a legitimate demand, however, does always precipitate a crisis, the employee needs to seriously question if the security of his job is worth the price of his self-respect and mental health.

The other alternative to seriously consider then is whether remaining involved with a crisismaker is really worth it. Crisismaking is an extremely controlling, hostile form of crazymaking. Victims, once they begin to experience their own strengths and aggressiveness, may decide to precipitate their own realistic crisis and leave the crisismaker for good.

## CLOSURE BLOCK OR DERAILING

The seemingly universal human need to bring an encounter, experience, or communication to completion is aborted in this form of crazymaking. It involves shifting the context or focus in the middle of an aggressive confrontation to prevent the resolution of a conflict. It is also designed to throw the victim off guard, moving him from the offensive to the defensive with the use of either counteraccusations or an irrelevant flattery, which derails him.

Mr. Simpson comes into his employer's office to talk with him regarding the raise they had agreed to discuss several months before. Within ten minutes, Mr. Evans, the employer, starts talking about the troubles he's been having with other employees, his conflicts with his wife, concern over the "poor taste" in clothing Mr. Simpson allegedly has and finally stands up saying, "I'm really sorry, Simpson. I can't spend all morning on this. Let's talk about it when I come back from my trip to New York next month."

Closure block or derailing is a fairly common form of crazy-making between intimates. Colloquially, we call it "sidetrack-ing." In essence, it results in preventing the victim from ever get-ting satisfaction of his needs, which the crazymaker pretends not to be aware of. As a result, nothing is ever settled, the same is-sues come up over and over again. Withdrawal and emotional insulation by the victim may become the self-protective responses because of an underlying feeling of "What's the use? I can't make myself heard." Occasionally closure block even takes the form of irrelevant flattery. "I love your face when you're angry," is one such example of derailing with flattery.

## BLOCKING THE CLOSURE BLOCK

This form of crazymaking is among the simplest to counter. Once one is aware of an issue one wishes to resolve, state the issue and then steadfastly avoid being sidetracked by seductive or guilt-making responses. If one avoids "hooking in," the derailer must eventually return to the issue or break off com-munication entirely. Any victim of this form of crazymaking who decides that "We resolve this issue or we talk about nothing else until . . ." can effectively counter this crazymaker.

## THE OCCASIONAL REINFORCER

The crazymaking, "occasional reinforcer" keeps others tied into destructive relationships with occasional crumbs of love, af-fection, flattery, or material reward. He provides enough to keep hope alive but never in a consistent or predictable enough pat-tern to facilitate in the victim a sense of security.

This pattern of crazymaking is an indirect form of sadistic behavior that increases in intensity in direct relationship to the dependency of the victim. The victim tells himself that the crazy-maker "really is" a "nice" guy, "caring," "loving," etc., in spite of his "faults." These so-called "faults" are actually the many cruel, insulting, and destructive things he does in between the occasional positive reinforcements he throws out. This crazy-maker obviously needs his victim as an outlet for his sadism.

## OBSTRUCTING THE OCCASIONAL REINFORCER

It is indeed humiliating to be caught in the ping-pong, excite-ignore, turn-on-decimate pattern of the "occasional reinforcer." He feeds on the vulnerability, feelings of inadequacy, and fantasies of "hope" of his victims. ("She really does care. She just doesn't know how to show it.")

The basic requisite to obstructing the "occasional reinforcer" is to give up the illusion of hope and the belief that under the humiliating messages there beats a heart of gold. Furthermore, one needs also to become aware that only a person of extreme feelings of unworthiness would subject himself to such ping-ponging.

In some instances of an involvement with an "occasional reinforcer" confrontation may help, with a concomitant demand for rewards to be given out more consistently. However, in general, the extreme manipulativeness of this crazymaker makes it an extremely dubious proposition that one will succeed in changing him. The energy spent might best be directed at altering the negative self-image of the victim that allows him to be prey to this kind of crazymaker.

## SOME GENERAL GUIDELINES

1.  Crazymaking is a potential in every relationship in which there is an extreme differential in the power balance, dependency, and vulnerability. To offset this, strive to reduce these disparities by equalizing power, nurturing interdependence, and exposing the anxieties that produce vulnerability.

2.  Crazymaking is a potential in relationships where the power balances are hidden and disguised behind façades of equality. To offset this, try to become aware of and then openly define the exact nature of the power structure of the relationship.

Do not be ashamed to glory in your dominance or your submissiveness if you are aware of and enjoy it.

3. Crazymaking is always a potential in relationships where there is a fear of confrontation. To offset this, demand recognition and openly assert your needs.

4. Crazymaking is a potential whenever either party assumes he really understands and can read the mind of the other person. To offset this, never assume you know what the other is thinking without at least checking it out, and never accept another person's interpretation of you as necessarily being valid.

5. Crazymaking is a potential in relationships encumbered in "shoulds," e.g., "I'm his mother, I'm supposed to love everything he does." To offset this, examine all your "shoulds" and recognize that they do not necessarily have to be held to.

In general, the characteristics of a crazymaking relationship that gives one a clue that one is a victim of a crazymaker are as follows:

1. The relationship oscillates between feelings of euphoria ("He really loves me.") and despair ("He really hates me."). It is a relationship of emotional extremes.

2. The victim is invariably feeling grateful for the benevolence of the crazymaker or feeling unworthy because he "upsets" the crazymaker.

3. Victims invariably have the fantasy that the crazymaker is "special" and that they would not be able to survive without him.

4. Victims find themselves walking on eggshells. They do not feel free to express themselves spontaneously. Rather, they feel the need to choose their words very precisely. They become very anxious if they suspect something they said might be misunderstood.

5. Crazymaking relationships don't grow. The victim continues to hungrily seek approval and security after years of in-

volvement, just as he did on first meeting. Crazymakers never facilitate feelings of security in their victims.

6.    Victims of crazymakers often find themselves clinging to their crazymaker in a cloying type of involvement in which the victim is endlessly proving his or her devotion, adequacy, and trustworthiness.

7.    Victims of crazymakers are prone to quick exhaustion and "butterflies" after being with the crazymaker for relatively short periods of time.

8.    Victims of crazymakers often find themselves in "damned if I do, damned if I don't" binds. They want to leave but are afraid to. Stay or go are equally negative choices.

9.    Victims of crazymakers find themselves fearful of making demands or confronting the crazymaker.

10.    Victims of crazymakers tend to feel that even their due is a gift. They are pathetically grateful for that which they have worked for and is legitimately theirs.

# CHAPTER 18

# The Family Powwow: An Aggression Festival

The standard and traditional model of family life is a contractual one in which each family member is supposed to play a defined role, with the ideal goal being a harmonious, conflict-free atmosphere of peace, love, and quiet. Just as in a Norman Rockwell portrait, everyone will then feel safe and warm within the bosom of the family.

Even though it has become increasingly clear that this is an antiquarian model no longer suitable for today, if in fact it was ever realistic, there is still a tendency for families to remain fixated on this model. Parents in particular tend to feel intensely frustrated over not being able to achieve it. Many feel cheated and disillusioned as the promise of the marriage vows and the fantasies of how family life "should be" fall apart. Much of the contemporary family scene is like a tragicomedy, with its succession of painful emotional disappointments, misunderstandings, and breakups. Consequently, many now are speaking of the demise of family life in America. The overpopulation problems are providing an ideal rationalization for those who are too wary and frightened of family life.

We feel, however, that the traditional family is still a potentially vital, life-sustaining and growth-producing force. Rather, it is the haunting and misleading model of how it "should be," that model that is still being perpetuated on TV commercials, in religious sermons, and in some books on family care and child rearing, which must be discarded. These fantasy images need to be replaced by a real portrayal of family life based on the known psychological realities that nesting, mating, and rearing activities are never harmonious, peaceful, contractable, nor even necessarily hierarchical.

The model that we will be proposing to replace the standard one we term the "family powwow." It is based on a psychologically open foundation that facilitates the expression of the total person, no matter what age, in a climate of candidness and authentic sharing of real feeling. This is suggested in full knowledge that such an approach will more often fan conflict than soothe troubled souls. Peace and quiet are not our goals. In fact, when they seem to reign, we feel, they are usually coverups for noninvolvement, fear of confrontation, or a repressive and authoritarian atmosphere.

Conflict within the authentic family is constant and inevitable. That is to say, each person within a family has differing needs and life rhythms. Therefore, clashes are automatically built in. Father may be tired when seven-year-old Sean wants to play. Julie, who is fourteen and "turned on," wants to blast her cassette player at the same time that mother wants some quiet time. Thirteen-year-old Timothy wants to watch a documentary on space; his sister, who is sixteen, wants to watch "All in the Family," while dad wants to watch the news. In addition, each person has his own privacy needs, social preferences, unique rhythms of energy and fatigue, and resistances against certain responsibilities. Only in the aggression-phobic family will conflict not appear to exist. There it is being hidden behind a façade of rationality and mutuality.

Specifically, some of the major areas of inevitable conflict in the family include *power* struggles, such as who has the final say and who will make the decisions. Struggles over *responsibil-*

*ity* constitute another area of clashing recently intensified by the female demand for liberation. Now more than ever, the whole matter of who is responsible for what has become hazy. Then there are the *territorial* struggles regarding needs for private areas within the home, use of space and objects such as the bathroom, televisions, telephone, and other mutually owned things.

Struggles over *social boundaries* constitute still another rife source of conflict, though one that may not be readily observable. Father may stay glued to the television rather than asserting his needs by going out with his buddies or inviting them over to the house. He probably reads *Penthouse* or *Playboy* rather than having a sex adventure or going to see a pornographic movie, as he may really want to do. Similarly, mother may fill her schedule with responsibilities so that she doesn't have to face the fact that she is basically friendless or that her "friends" are all neighborhood mothers who talk babies, prices, and school, and bore her to death. In general, the desire to invite people over spontaneously or to go out alone often remains unexpressed to avoid overt conflict.

Typically, in struggles for *attention,* mother wants to talk about her day, while father wants to withdraw behind the newspaper and mail, or father is distressed because he is being ignored in favor of the baby. One child may complain because the other is getting help with homework while he or she is being ignored.

In segmentalized families and authoritarian ones, these kinds of conflict may appear to be absent. In the segmentalized family, which is the one most commonly seen today, the family members "play alone together." Much as in the social style of little toddlers, they share a physical space, but emotional and interactional contacts are minimal or absent. Children who come from this environment of "strangers," in which everybody goes his own way and "does his own thing," often emerge aimless and unmotivated. They had neither resistance to grow against nor support to grow from.

In the authoritarian home, on the other hand, there is peace out of fear. Confrontation is met with threats of punishment and retaliation. The quietness, docility, and passivity of the children are not indicative of harmony or peace but of control by dictatorship.

The family is a model for the child in the development of his deepest attitudes toward the management of aggression. Whether he will dread it or see it as a normal form of vitalizing communication will depend on how the family conflicts are handled. He will learn by watching what happens when individual family members assert themselves or confront each other. Where each confrontation escalates into a destructive outpouring of hate, despair, withdrawal, and alienation, the child learns that it is safest to keep aggressive feelings hidden.

## THE PRICE OF SUPPRESSING OPEN AGGRESSION

Parents who obstruct the child's aggressive self-expression with admonitions such as "Don't talk back!," "Show some respect!," "Go to your room!," or "Don't raise your voice or you'll be sorry!," are teaching them that self-assertion and feelings of anger are a part of "being bad" and that these feelings must be hidden or at least denied. The price for this is that such open aggressive expression is driven underground and will re-emerge in indirect, unmanageable, and unrecognizable ways. Both parents and children lose contact with the original feelings and conflicts, resulting in a complicated and chronic situation that may only be unraveled at an expensive price in long-drawn-out psychotherapy.

As an example of this, Tommy was seven years old and an only child when his sister Cindy was born. Tommy was enraged. He had become very comfortable as king of the household, being adored and catered to. His parents reacted very negatively to his resentment toward his baby sister. They called him "selfish" and "spoiled" and told him he "should feel ashamed." "Besides, we know that you're not like that deep inside. You really love her!," his parents would tell him. On several occasions within the first few months after the baby's birth they punished him, something they had never done before. Tommy finally got the message! He began behaving "sweetly" to his baby sister. His rage was now repressed. His parents were pleased at this change and very proud about Tommy's new helpfulness.

However, unexpected problems began to emerge. Tommy became a bedwetter. He also began to have nightmares. One of his parents would be forced to sit with him for at least an hour every evening while he was trying to fall asleep. More than once, while helping his mother with the baby, he dropped her. Indeed, all of Tommy's conscious expressions of rage and resentment were gone. He was now a "good" boy. His parents, however, were suffering with a host of problems that were draining their energies and driving them up the wall in frustration.

There is always a heavy price to be paid by a family that suppresses open aggression. The children may appear to be "good," but their repressed aggression will manifest itself as they become underachievers in school, behave in passive, surly, and withdrawn ways, or develop psychosomatic symptoms such as allergies and gastro-intestinal problems. Or they may displace their repressed feelings against targets outside the home. They will behave cruelly to smaller children or animals. In extreme instances they may become philosophically and morbidly preoccupied with death, sickness, or evil and begin to behave in bizarre or self-destructive ways.

The "family powwow," which takes a positive approach to family conflict, is based on a number of premises. The one that underlies all others, and is the major thread already mentioned in this chapter, is that conflict within the vital, interactive family is an inevitable reality and that there is no such thing as resolving conflict permanently and emerging into the dream state of constant family peace.

The second premise is that aggressive self-expression in the family is just as natural and healthy as are expressions of warmth and affection. In fact, the aggressive feelings, if repressed and therefore not openly expressed, will contaminate and eventually make the experience of genuine love and caring impossible. On the other hand, the scream of frustration and outrage, if accepted and given full play, will facilitate a deeper, more authentic love.

Third, we believe that parents are equally as entitled to the free and open expression of their anger and frustration both between each other and toward their children. In the aggression-phobic model under which most people have been brought up, it is immediately assumed that families are in serious trouble and the marriage is on the rocks when there is fighting and yelling. Therefore, too many parents out of shame and fear unnaturally force themselves to be models of peace and self-control for the sake of their children. However, clinical evidence suggests that parents who repress their anger and resentment toward each other will be more prone to use their children as targets for hostility and blame. That is, they will tend to overreact to their children's behavior with inappropriately harsh punishment and unrealistic demands and expectations for good behavior. The "family powwow" model sees it as the parents' role to be models for constructive, open conflict-resolution with unashamed, unembarrassed sharing of anger, resentment, and frustration.

Because it is within the family matrix that a child learns how to live with and handle aggressive interaction, it is the family's obligation to help children learn how to stay with their aggressive feelings and see them through to a positive conclusion. The child who is taught to confine his aggressive feelings to people and situations he doesn't like outside the home is also being taught that intimacy and aggressive self-expression are incompatible.

The ultimate modeling a parent can do for his child is to become an intrinsic authority figure rather than controlling by dint of role authority. That is, parents need gain their children's respect not by demanding but rather by developing an orientation toward aggression that is compatible with and emerges directly from the reality, confidence, and strength of their own being.

## THE FAMILY POWWOW

The "family powwow," constructive family fight training, was originally developed by Dr. George Bach within the context of family therapy, marathon therapy, and weekend training programs in aggression management.

The family fight techniques taught at these festivals are learned in the presence of other families who join together to coach each other and provide each other with mutual support. A professionally trained fight trainer in fair fight techniques is also present in the early training stages to help families avoid collusion, premature giving up, and the trauma and confusion that result from using these techniques inappropriately.

Learning to fight in the presence of other families is also useful for the purpose of desensitizing family members from feelings of guilt, embarrassment, shame, and the sense of being "different" (i.e., "How come all other families seem to get along so well except us?"). The presence of other families allows the participants to see how common most family battles are. Sharing these experiences with other families turns the "family powwow" into a genuine festival, filled with laughter and fun as well as constructive conflict resolution.

The exercises and techniques we will be describing are designed to provide a holiday from the usual hierarchy, status, and power definitions that govern the everyday interactions in family life. They also provide opportunities for the traditionally rigid lines of authority to be dropped. Children, for example, are allowed for a given period of time and under specific conditions to openly command, insult, and even reject their parents or other key relatives. At the same time, parents too are freed from their usual responsibility of playing the strong, commanding, take-charge roles.

In other cultures, in fact, days have traditionally been set aside each year for leveling festivities, during which time people in the streets can openly make fun of and insult their leaders and authority figures. All over India, for example, during the festival of Holi, which occurs during the spring saturnalia (between March and April), traditional lines of authority are broken down. People spray public figures, ministers, bankers, the police chiefs, even the maharaja, with colored water or colored powders. These public figures, who of course can counter with insults, can be openly insulted and called names such as "ass" or "son of a bitch."

On the occasion of the Fasching, a spring festival held in the Rhineland in Germany for centuries, people have been allowed to display hostility openly toward each other. Leaders and other persons of importance can be teased and made fun of in public.

In America, our holiday of Halloween perhaps comes closest to being such a leveling festival. Children can "trick or treat" the homes of neighboring adults. Basically, however, America is ritual poor, particularly in terms of rituals through which aggressive feelings can be safely expressed. During the "family powwow," which we are proposing in this chapter, the weak are given a chance against the strong as roles are reversed and power is equalized.

A note of caution! The "family powwow" is not a substitute for psychotherapy. Aggression training is for families where there are no severe individual or family problems. While many of the techniques can be usefully employed by a trained psychotherapist, they might prove destructive if incompetently used by amateurs to solve severe emotional problems that exist within the family.

The "family powwow" is divided into three major phases. The first involves a series of exercises, techniques, and rituals designed to desensitize anxieties over acknowledgment of aggressive feelings in oneself. It also gives family members an opportunity to try on role behaviors that they would not normally assume. For example, dominant members play passive roles for periods of time, and vice versa.

The second phase involves learning the use of rituals. These rituals are structured vehicles for the expression of anger and rage in everyday interactions.

The third and final phase involves learning how to use the "fair fight for change." This is a structure designed to develop the communication skills of family members toward the resolution of specific, concrete issues.

## PHASE I: AGGRESSION EXERCISES FOR FAMILIES

The following is a description of a "family powwow" conducted by Dr. Bach, Dr. Goldberg, and several trainers with twenty-two families at a University of California campus.

Initially we separated the children from the adults and taught each group some of the exercises separately. This helped to offset initial feelings of self-consciousness and anxiety that children experienced in front of their parents, and vice versa. As a warm-up procedure for the children, very young ones as well as teenagers, we gave them paper, crayons, or paint and asked them to depict a typical family fight and then to give a verbal description of their drawings.

Eleven-year-old Jeffrey began: "Here I am with my hands over my ears so that I don't have to hear my mother yelling. Her face is red, and she looks like she's going to have a heart attack. There's my father standing at the door ready to run outside. Our dog is hiding under the couch, and my younger sister is fiddling with the transistor radio to make it louder."

In another room the adults sat in a circle and were asked to share with each other a description of their most recent experience of conflict that involved family members. Ms. Holloway, recently divorced, spoke of her resentment toward her oldest daughter, who had forgotten to come home and babysit with her younger brother the previous evening. Ms. Holloway was forced to cancel a date her attorney had arranged with a man. They were supposed to go to a private screening of a new British film.

Dr. Goldberg asked her what she had said or done about this incident. Ms. Holloway replied, "Oh, nothing. What's the use? I know she's angry at me about the divorce, and I guess she's just paying me back. I don't want her to hate me even more." Dr. Goldberg suggested that she talk to her daughter as if the daughter were present in the room, and to be as candid as possible about her feelings. After initial resistance, her rage emerged in the following outburst. "Goddamn you, Penny! You sure do demand your clothing, your money, and your meals on time. That's your birthright, according to you, because you didn't "ask to be born." If you don't get them immediately, then I'm a bitch. Well, it may come as a shock to you that I've got needs too! I asked you to babysit with your younger brother so that I could go out for just one night, and you conveniently managed to forget. It makes me so angry I could kill you!" At first embarrassed and ashamed by this outburst of feeling, she began to realize that despite her divorce she still had the right to get angry and to communicate her feelings and needs to her daughter.

It was particularly remarkable to see the number of parents who either had great difficulty recalling recent experiences of anger or simply could not remember a single recent episode in which they experienced resentment or conflict toward a family intimate. These parents were not intentionally covering up. However, the anxiety and shame surrounding the open revelation of family conflict caused them to repress these memories.

After this initial desensitization procedure, both groups were taught a series of aggression exercises and rituals and were then brought together to participate in them.

## THE SLAVE MARKET

For a period of five minutes each child and his or her parent alternated in the role of "slave" and "master." Whoever assumed the role of the "slave" was permitted to establish limitations, but only *before* the exercise began. For example, a fourteen-year-old girl said to her father, "Don't ask me to sing." One father said to his eleven-year-old son, "I don't want to crawl on the ground." Once the exercise was officially started, however, the "master" was given total control over his "slave." The latter was obligated to fulfill each command immediately and without question. After the five minutes were up, roles were reversed. "Masters" became "slaves," and vice versa. The same rules applied.

This exercise served many important purposes. For five minutes the traditionally rigid and persistent power relationships were transformed. Each family member could experience himself as totally dominant and totally submissive. Ordinarily timid children could be tyrants. Domineering and overpowering parents had to be submissive. Some even enjoyed themselves in their passive, subservient role.

For both the parents and the children, this was also an opportunity to show the other "what it's like." One eleven-year-old boy in a group conducted by Dr. Bach had his mother pretend she was a child. Then he barked at her, "Brush your teeth! Clean up your room! Go find your younger brother. Now show Grandma how your piano playing is coming!" She had to pretend to do all these things. A mother of a hyperactive, overly talkative child had her son sit still and silently for five minutes while she was "master."

In a light, humorous atmosphere, considerable learning was taking place. The learning was reinforced by a postexercise discussion of what it felt like to be in total control as opposed to being totally controlled.

## LEARNING FROM REJECTION

The entire family did this rejection exercise together. One family member at a time was asked by the others in the group to leave the room. He or she was being "rejected." The rest of the family then discussed the reasons why they were rejecting that person. The reasons were often numerous. "He's too pushy," "He never listens!," "She's always too busy to do anything that's fun," were some of them.

When the rest of the family had discussed at least ten reasons why the person was being rejected, they formed a closed circle, and the rejected person was invited back into the room. He was then asked to guess at least three reasons why he was rejected, and he was only readmitted into the circle when this task was accomplished. Once he succeeded, the circle opened and he was allowed in with a family hug.

Rather than utilizing the traditional group therapy confrontation approach, this exercise compelled each family member to appraise himself objectively from a negative standpoint, seeing himself in the way the others saw him.

## ROLE SWITCHING

Family members doing this exercise could communicate to each other the way they saw each other. The awakening was often surprising and somewhat painful. The exercise lent itself to humor through hyperbole.

A typical family scene was chosen such as "getting ready to leave in the morning" or "going to Grandma's on Sunday."

For a period of five minutes each of the roles was switched. Daughter played mother, son played father, etc. The exercise was continued until each person had portrayed each role.

Through this imitation process individual family members were able to directly see and experience how they looked to the other family members. Particularly emphasized were the most irritating and provocative behaviors. Discussion of this exercise afterward was used to pinpoint the various annoying behaviors and to discuss new role expectations within the family.

## PUSHING DADDY OR MOMMY AGAINST THE WALL

Gross inequities in power, both physical and psychological, tend to create rigid and lopsided patterns and interactions between and among family members. Certain family members only know what it feels like to come out on top. Others are always having to take it from someone else.

"Pushing Daddy or Mommy against the wall" is an exercise in equalizing physical differences through handicapping procedures. It can be done by any two family members, and is particularly meaningful where there are significant physical disparities. In this exercise any weaker member of a family can challenge a stronger one and try to push him or her across the length of the room to the opposite wall.

"Arms limitations" or handicapping is the process by which the participants have to search out ways to equalize their strength. The exercise is meaningless and patronizing if the stronger person handicaps himself so much that he or she becomes a pushover. Rather, the equalization process is designed to allow each participant to use his full strength once the limitations are set. If, for example, father accepts the limitation of keeping his hands clasped behind his back, he should then be able to resist his son's or daughter's attempt to push him across the room with all his strength. The more equal the balance, the more meaningful the experience.

It was a challenge to see how creative the participants could be in equalizing their differences. The exercise stimulated discussion afterward about ways in which power could be equalized in other areas of interaction so that the weaker or more vulnerable in the family could feel safe enough to fully release his or her aggressive feelings and interact in honest, nonmanipulative ways without the threat of extreme retaliation.

## FEEDBACK TRAINING

Feeding back is a form of active listening that requires the listener to repeat the essence of what he has just heard, to the total satisfaction of the person whose statement is being fed back. The recipient is instructed not to interpret or read into the statements any interpretations of his own.

At the "family powwow" we combined feedback training with another exercise, the "attraction-reservation." "Attraction" requires focusing on a facet of the other person that has positive impact, followed by a statement of its effect. The "reservation" requires stating a negative, or "turnoff," and describing its effect.

Coached by Dr. Goldberg, Jerry, age sixteen, did this exercise with his father.

JERRY:  The thing I like most about you is your generosity. You always offer to help me financially when I need something. That gives me a sense of security and safety.

JERRY'S FATHER:  (*feeding back*) What I hear you saying, Jerry, is that you like me for my money and that it makes you feel good knowing that I'll always give it to you when you need it.

JERRY:  No, you didn't hear me right at all. When you said I like you mainly for your money, you distorted what I said.

Jerry's father had to feed back several times until Jerry felt he had been heard correctly. His father seemed stubbornly stuck on his own interpretation and feelings about being used. Consequently he persisted in mishearing.

Jerry then communicated his "reservation."

JERRY:    The biggest thing that turns me off about you is that you're always busy with your work. It makes me feel like I'm an annoyance whenever I want to talk to you.

Again Jerry's father was required to feed back what he had just heard Jerry say. When this was successfully completed, it was his father's turn to communicate his "attraction" and "reservation." The "attraction" was done easily. Then his father stated his "reservation."

JERRY'S FATHER:    I'm annoyed most by your incessant answering back. You never do anything that's asked of you without first challenging it. It makes me feel very angry and frustrated.

JERRY:    I hear you say you're annoyed with the fact that I stand up for my rights. That makes you feel angry and frustrated.

This time Jerry's father pointed out the distortion in the feedback. Jerry changed "answering back" to "standing up for my rights," which significantly altered the message. It took several trials for Jerry to feed back this "reservation" accurately.

Despite the seeming simplicity of this exercise, family members typically experienced great difficulty in listening and restating the essence of what they had just heard. Instead, there seemed to be a strong tendency to interpret, shade, and distort the messages according to what they believed the other person "really meant."

## PERSISTENCE-RESISTANCE

This exercise is useful in teaching the "soft touch" in the family how to say "No," and helping those with low frustration and rejection tolerances to learn how to persist and convince others of their demands creatively, rather than walking away in disgust if gratification is not immediately forthcoming.

Any two family members can participate in the exercise. The "persister" is asked to make a request. Then the "resister" is asked to provide a reason why he doesn't want to fulfill the request. The "persister" is then asked to come up with a different and convincing reason each time. The "resister" is asked to search out all the possible reasons he might have that would be real cause for saying "No."

Both participants are instructed never to fake their replies merely for the sake of persisting or resisting. Their persistences and resistances are to be legitimately believed and felt. The exercise ends at any point at which either the "resister" says, "You've convinced me," or the "persister" says, "I'm losing interest in trying to convince you. I've decided it's a waste of time, and I give up."

Considerable learning can take place by using this exercise in the home routinely. Too often a premature "Yes" leaves one with the feeling that one has been manipulated or used. In the same vein, a "No" leaves the no-sayer feeling like a culprit or depriver. By engaging in a "persistence-resistance" encounter, each person can explore the positive and negative ramifications of any transaction before entering into it.

The following "persistence-resistance" exercise took place under Dr. Bach's supervision between fifteen-year-old Susan and her mother:

SUSAN:   Mother, I'd like you to extend my Saturday night curfew to one o'clock.

MOTHER:   No. You're only fifteen. You've got plenty of time for that.

SUSAN:   I've proven to you by the way I've taken care of my little brother while you're away working that I am very responsible and mature for my age.

MOTHER: That's all the more reason why you should know better and not let yourself be vulnerable to something you might regret.

SUSAN: If you agree to extend it to 1:00 A.M., I promise to tell you where I'm going ahead of time so that you can always contact me.

MOTHER: I don't feel comfortable about your coming home late in our neighborhood. There have been too many muggings and attempted rapes lately.

SUSAN: I promise to have my date take a taxicab right to our house.

MOTHER: Truthfully, I'm concerned about you becoming sexually involved and getting pregnant.

SUSAN: If I wanted to get sexually involved I could do that before nine o'clock. I don't have to wait until midnight. Anyway, I promised you that I wouldn't go all the way at least until I'm seventeen.

MOTHER: Okay, you've convinced me. I'll extend your curfew to one o'clock.

An important aspect to be noted about the interaction was that Susan did not argue against her mother's resistances but rather focused on pointing out all of the positives. This is an important part of this exercise in creative self-assertiveness. By avoiding the immediate "Yes" or "No," which seems to be the traditional way of dealing with requests within the family, the "persistence-resistance" exercise allowed Susan and her mother to fully explore the positive and negative factors until they had arrived at a comfortable resolution. The basis for many family hassles lies in contaminated "Yes's" and "Nos," in which one person gives in too readily and then feels resentful and manipulated, or arbitrarily says "No" to everything as a defense against being "pushed."

Persistence-resistance is equally useful between siblings, and between parents and their children, with the latter in the role of resister countering their parents' demands creatively and forcing their parents to meaningfully justify their requests rather than ruling by arbitrary power.

## PHASE II: FAMILY RITUALS

Aggression rituals within the family provide temporary holidays from the harness of the rational, controlled, noncomplaining stance that so many parents seem to strive for; the "We've got everything under control!" illusion.

Rituals have many values. On an empirical level, people report that they make them feel good. By providing structures for the release of pent-up, free-floating, and irrational hostilities, they allow family members to safely and temporarily experience the awesome, horrific "volcano" of rage that exists within each of them. Furthermore, the rituals, by facilitating expression of the underlying rage that accumulates and is constantly being fed by the frustrations, disappointments, and rejections of everyday life, also allow individuals to develop a sense of mastery over these frightening feelings that lie within them. It is a process of learning how to live with aggressive feelings; to scream, curse, and protest in open, nondestructive ways rather than by pretending that these feelings don't exist, only to be victimized by their indirect and crazymaking forms of expression later. By constantly and openly communicating these feelings, we feel families will be able to avoid the usual "hooking in" syndrome, which involves waiting for someone to do or say something wrong and then using that as an excuse to launch a donnybrook. We have also found that the positive experiences of warmth and love will be able to emerge more fully and with far less contamination if the aggression rituals are engaged in regularly.

## THE "VESUVIUS"

The "Vesuvius" is a structure for a one-way blast, an angry eruption or tantrum in which individual family members can express their pent-up feelings of rage and outrage accumulated during the course of the day. The feelings may or may not originate within the family.

Family members are trained to have a two- or three-minute "Vesuvius," in front of the others, upon first gathering in the evening. It can replace the usual lifeless greetings of "Hello," and "How was your day?" Listeners are taught not to "hook in" or in any way respond or react personally to the "Vesuvius."

In Dr. Goldberg's group, Martha, age sixteen, had her first experience engaging in a "Vesuvius." Facing her parents and older sister, who sat listening attentively, she began to shout. "Being sixteen years old stinks!! Wow!! Everybody tells you what to do, but they also expect you to be an adult. That really pisses me off! It's the goddamn decisions they want you to make all the time. What college to go to? What to major in? What guy to date? And there's never enough money to buy things. And you, mother, there's always the damn strings you attach when you give me something. And when I go crazy or want to get stoned, everybody tells me its part of being an adolescent. Thanks for nothing!"

When she was finished, Martha felt drained. Rather than being irritated, she found her family surprisingly accepting. Her older sister remarked, "For the first time I think I know what you're going through."

Typically there are resistances from family members when they are first asked to do a "Vesuvius." They assert that it's "irrational" and couldn't be useful. We won't counter this with a rational justification. Rather, we simply see these feelings of rage building up within people as being a reality. Out of acknowledgment for their continuing existence, we feel that they should be expressed in a structured, nondestructive way.

We feel that the model of man always striving to be rational is unhealthy. Therefore, we allow for the expression of the irrational within the playful framework of the ritual. Yell and scream because *you feel like it!* That's justification enough.

## THE "VIRGINIA WOOLF"

The "Virginia Woolf" is a ritualized insult exchange that can be engaged in between any two family members. Traditionally a barrage of insults would be considered an act of disrespect on the part of the child, and demeaning and destructive for the parent. We feel quite the opposite about it. A toe-to-toe insult exchange, with neither party trying to suppress, bully, or withdraw, is a sign of supreme trust and love. Family members who can share the worst feelings in themselves about each other, we feel, can also experience great warmth and closeness.

This ritual is engaged in with mutual consent and with a rule of no physical violence. The understanding is that everything is "off the record" and not meant for later discussion. It is time limited and engaged in for a maximum of three minutes.

The participants are encouraged to insult each other as fully, loudly, and dramatically as possible, using sarcasm, exaggeration, and vulgarity. Ideally, each will speak the unspeakable. This will pave the way for a more realistic and profound love by allowing the individuals to overcome fears of each other's fragility. It also functions to destroy the belief that individuals who love each other don't also harbor hostile, destructive feelings and fantasies toward each other.

Here is the partial transcript of a "Virginia Woolf" between two brothers, Michael, age twenty-seven, and Jimmy, age twenty-one, and coached by Dr. Goldberg. Both were shouting at each other simultaneously and heard very little of what the other was saying.

| Michael | Jimmy |
|---|---|
| You passive piece of shit, still living at home sucking off your mom and dad, and | You phony manipulator with your vest and your asshole ties and white shirts. You |

expecting everybody to feel sorry for you, and take care of you. When are you going to act like a man? Instead of sitting around, why don't you get a job or at least go out and get laid instead of watching TV and jerking off or eating candy all day? No wonder you're always tired. Your brain is rotting—get off your ass and let it breathe!!

think you're hot shit because you're a Beverly Hills lawyer. I thought you were going to save the people in the slums and the ghettos—now you're saving the rich boys. Mr. Rebel! Mr. Rebel! Mr. Idealist! Oh, yeah! It's Mr. Bullshit!! Fastest tongue in the West!!

Immediately after this interchange, during which they were both becoming red and yelling at the top of their lungs, there was a moment of quiet and then an outburst of laughter from the group and from Michael and Jimmy. Both experienced a lessening of a long-standing tension between them. They had shared some of the "unspeakables," had survived, and could now begin to talk more rationally and less heatedly with each other.

Parents are encouraged to teach their children to engage in these insult exchanges in a structured way, much like a boxing match, rather than threatening to punish when such a natural exchange begins. When conducted in a structured way it becomes a constructive, playful, and satisfying way of expressing hostilities that might otherwise result in endless rounds of teasing and bickering.

## THE "HAIRCUT" WITH "DOGHOUSE RELEASE"

The "haircut," and the "doghouse release" are among the most readily understood and easily learned of the rituals. The process of telling someone off is a very ancient procedure. These rituals give this process a new twist by including a mechanism for release and forgiveness.

The "haircut" is a ritual scolding for behavior that has caused hurt or disappointment. Its purpose is to re-establish mutual good will by allowing the offender to accept responsibility and do penance for the offense. This then facilitates the re-entry of the offender into the good graces of the offended person.

At the "family powwow" Ronald, age fifteen, informed his mother that he wanted to give her a "haircut" regarding her behavior the previous Monday evening while his friends were over at the house. She agreed to accept his "haircut," and a time limit of ninety seconds was set for giving her this ritualistic scolding.

RONALD: "Last Monday I said I wanted to go out with my friends. You said I should invite them over and that you'd close off the living room and not interfere. At least three times during the evening you came in asking us if we wanted food or telling us that the TV was on too loud. Everybody was getting so uptight that the evening turned sour and my friends went home early."

Ronald's mother listened quietly without responding. The ritual requires that she not counter the "haircut" with a defense. At most she is permitted to request clarification if the communication is unclear. Ronald's mother acknowledged responsibility and requested a "doghouse release." This is the penance set by the person giving the "haircut," which the offender agrees to perform in order to re-establish themselves into the good graces of the offended person.

RONALD: "One Saturday night this month I'd like to have the house all to myself and have my friends over for a party. I'll take care of all the arrangements for food and drink, and I don't want you or Dad to come home before 1:30 A.M."

MOTHER: "Yes, I'll agree to that."

Ronald and his mother hugged and felt good about each other after this airing.

The "haircut" is a comfortable structure by which any person in the family with a grievance can air it in a structured way rather than holding it in and building up a reservoir of unspoken hostility and mistrust.

### "MUSEUM TOURS"

Invariably when families first enter into fight training each member harbors a long list of hidden items of past disappointments, hurts, and rejections against the others. Therefore, early in the "family powwow" each family member is given the assignment of writing his family museum list of negative memories. These lists are then shared. Each participant reads his "tour" to the rest of the family while the others listen silently. Private items regarding one particular individual can be shared on an individual basis. Using the procedure already described in the chapter on rituals, some of the items on this list are buried, others bartered, some enshrined, and those that are concrete issues that may continue to cause problems are reserved as "beefs" to be handled within the "fair fight for change" structure.

The following is a partial listing of the "museum tour" engaged in by Mrs. Strickland and her twenty-four-year-old daughter Joanna, who was single and still living at home with her mother.

*Mrs. Strickland's list*:

1.   The time you came home from a psychology class and informed me that I was a classic neurotic and had turned you into one too.

2.   The time you started screaming at me in front of your boyfriend for asking you where you were going, even though I was just trying to be friendly and wasn't snooping on you. I felt humiliated.

3. Last Mother's Day when you went away to Palm Springs for the weekend after you had asked me a month before if I wanted to go out to dinner with you on that day.

4. Accusing me of being the reason why you're not married or on your own. I'm tired of being your scapegoat.

5. Just a few weeks ago when you told Daddy how you don't understand how he could have married me or stayed with me all these years.

*Joanna's list*:

1. The time when you compared me to my sister Julie, saying she was brighter and prettier and telling me that she was a winner and I was a loser.

2. Two years ago when I was in a really down period and asked you to lend me money to go to Las Vegas for the weekend. You called me a parasite because I wanted to use "other people's money" to take "fancy" vacations.

3. The time when I was sixteen years old and found you taking a letter from my boyfriend out of my desk drawer and reading it.

4. A year ago when you called me a prostitute because I went to San Francisco with Manny for a weekend, even though we'd been seeing each other for five months.

5. This one's ongoing. One day you tell me to move out, and then the next day, when I go looking for an apartment, you scream at me for wanting to leave home and be on my own. That drives me up a wall.

The above is just a partial accounting of their two very long lists of buried resentments. Mrs. Strickland and Joanna agreed that No. 2 on Mrs. Strickland's list and No. 5 on Joanna's would be excellent issues for a "fair fight for change." Mrs. Strickland agreed to burn No. 3 in exchange for No. 3 on Joanna's list. They bartered Nos. 4 and 5 on Mrs. Strickland's list for Nos. 1 and 2 on Joanna's list. They gleefully enshrined

No. 1 on Mrs. Strickland's list and No. 4 on Joanna's. Mrs. Strickland remarked, "I always want to remember that infamous day when you officially diagnosed me as a classic neurotic." Joanna countered, "And I'll cherish your description of me as a prostitute."

## BATACA FIGHTING

The purpose of this ritual is to give family members an opportunity to express their angry feelings in a nonhurtful but physical way. Bataca fighting as described in the chapter on rituals is ideally suited for this objective.

Family members must first establish equalizing handicaps to even out strength differences. For example, in one bataca fight between an older brother and his younger sister, he fought standing on one foot. This balanced out the strength differential. A small child could fight with her mother, for example, while the mother was on her knees holding the bat with three fingers.

An all-out bataca fight for a predetermined period of time such as two minutes, allows family members to express resentments that arise from relatively undefined issues.

## THE BATACA LASHING

This ritual is sometimes used to supplement the "haircut" or is given in place of the "haircut," as also described in the chapter on rituals. The "bataca lashing" is a spanking ritual. However, unlike the sadistic beating practices of old-time schoolmasters, who would use wooden paddles, this ritual is done by mutual consent with a cloth bat and is choreographed to allow the person administering it to express his hurt and pain over the behavior of the offender. That is, a child who is angry at a parent for betraying a promise may need to give him or her a "bataca lashing" before the child can really feel comfortable.

The person who agrees that he has offended and will accept a "bataca lashing" establishes a time limit such as thirty seconds, during which time he remains erect so that the other person can hit cleanly. The person giving the lashing is also encouraged to express his anger verbally by shouting out his feelings along with each stroke.

After the "bataca lashing" the receiver may negotiate a "doghouse release," if the offense warrants it. Most partners find that the lashing itself is so satisfying that they are ready and able to forgive and forget after administering it. Parents in particular could helpfully get over the notion that it is humiliating or disrespectful for a child to "spank" his parents. This feeling is a residual of the traditional definitions of "respect," a part of the repressive orientation toward aggressive expression. A parent does not lose his dignity by engaging in this ritual. Rather, he enhances it.

Any of the other rituals discussed in the chapter on rituals can be adapted to the "family powwow." The development of aggression rituals is a new art, and families are encouraged to invent their own. The basic rules are that they require mutual consent, handicapping to equalize strength differences, time limits, and the presence of a coach or third party to help maintain a fair interaction.

## PHASE III: THE "FAIR FIGHT FOR CHANGE"

The "fair fight for change" is a structure developed by Dr. Bach for conflict resolution. Fights over curfews, household responsibilities, privacy, use of automobiles, etc., are all fair game for "fair fights for change." The specifics or "how to" of the fair fight are discussed in the chapter on "Office Fights for Change." The family setting is ideally suited for this process, because children and parents are readily available to serve as coaches and scorers of the fight.

The process of constructively resolving an issue, of listening and being listened to, and of obtaining helpful critique regarding one's style of communicating can significantly raise the level of aggressive communication in the home. The "fair fight for change" is also a structure that can abort the hostility escalation and frustration that characterize most family fights. When used in conjunction with the rituals, it can put aggressive confrontation within the family on a constructive and vitalizing path.

While we suggest that rituals be used daily and "fair fights for change" be conducted whenever there is a dispute over a concrete issue, a "family powwow" or all-day aggression festival could usefully be held every two or three months. Our experience with it is that it is preventative and a revitalizing force. It can help to abort the buildup of hidden and crazy-making forms of aggressive interaction and significantly reduce the alienation and lack of communication that are so prevalent among family members today.

# CHAPTER 19

# Enemies at Work: The Management of Office Aggression

The bulk of the American working population spends almost as much time with their employment, if not more, than they do with their intimates. Certainly a significantly greater amount of energy is commonly expended there than at home. The typical working person arrives home in the evening to eat dinner then plops in front of the television, on the verge of falling asleep. And for many men in particular, the prospect of losing a hard-fought-for job or being usurped from a position of importance and power is more frightening than a threat to his personal life.

Because of this pervasive involvement with one's job, the average office or work environment generates great amounts of frustration, anger, conflicts, and anxieties. Despite the emotional intensity of the work environment, in which eight or nine hours of each day are spent, there is no structure or constructive means with which workers can deal with these emotional experiences as they arise. As a result, the typical office setting is a hotbed of indirect and hidden forms of aggression. This is costly to the employer in terms of productivity and to the employee and the employer in terms of their emotional and physical health.

Several years ago Dr. Bach conducted a marathon for a private dental clinic located in a small northwestern city. The marathon was requested by the director, who had heard of our work with office aggression, because he was becoming increasingly concerned about a communication breakdown in the clinic that he felt powerless to change. Everyone from the clinic, including secretaries and clerical workers, was asked to attend this weekend-long marathon, and most came. Even several spouses were present. There were twenty-three people in all. Participants were instructed not to make any secret contracts ahead of time about what to say or not to say.

The atmosphere for the first nine hours was unusually tense. It became clear that muzzling contracts had indeed been made. The dam finally broke when the male spouse of a secretary told of an affair he knew his wife had had with one of the dentists who was present. Shortly thereafter another "secret" girlfriend of the director began to tremble and ran out to the bathroom to vomit. Stories of trysts, double standards, and secret agreements then began to pour forth.

Further, it was revealed that several of the dentists were sabotaging the clinic by siphoning off clinic patients privately to their own secret private practices. The director himself confessed that he had been siphoning off the well-to-do clients and was building up a private practice he was eventually planning to sell to the clinic.

By the end of the marathon it became clear that the clinic was so corrupt with cliques, secret agreements, and sabotage that gradual dissolution was the favored solution of those present. It also became clear that each of the dentists really only wanted his own private practice and that they couldn't work with each other anymore. Many former antagonists, even a wife and a secretary, who had been going to bed with her husband, became good friends. Confrontation led to authenticity, and although in this case the group agreed to disband, the marathon brought many destructive interactions out into the light.

The indirect and hidden aggression emerges outwardly in the form of mutual undermining, pettiness, rumor mongering, suspiciousness, distortion of other people's intent, and a stereotyped, "thing"-oriented way of relating. "Thinging" is a form of relating to individuals as objects measured in terms of position and power rather than as human beings with unique needs and personalities. Those of higher status are afraid to reveal any humanness or spontaneous emotion, particularly to those who are "under" them. Typically, it is only in times of tragedy such as a death or a severe illness when plans are being made for a gift or collection, or at the annual Christmas party that there are moments of spontaneous intimacy.

## THE AMERICAN CASTE SYSTEM

The typical office and work setting is perhaps the closest America comes to having a caste system. In unspoken ways everyone knows his place—who to socialize with, smile at, greet in the morning with a "Hello!," and whether to do it before or after the other person has spoken first. A walk into the cafeteria, nearby restaurant, diner, or by the lunchwagon readily reveals who is who. Administrators sit together in one place, higher-paid employees or professionals are in another, and secretaries and clericals are at a third, while maintenance workers and other unskilled laborers may be huddled together somewhere else. The boundaries are invisible but very clear. "Trespassers" are greeted with impatient, uncomfortable, and cold reactions.

A recent Gallup survey revealed that nearly 20 percent of the nation's work force admits *openly* to being unhappy with their jobs. One psychiatrist described the way many working people felt as "cornered, trapped, lonely, pushed around, and confused by a sense of meaninglessness."[1]

The employee who feels himself unable to affect people

and bring about change will express his frustration passively and indirectly through chronic absenteeism, lateness, long coffee breaks, office "ripoffs" in the form of petty thievery, the making of long personal phone calls, psychosomatic complaints such as headaches, poor-quality work, diminished productivity, critical errors, forgetfulness, and lack of company loyalty.

Employer and employee both suffer from this state of repressed aggression. That is, employers are often as frightened of their employees as the employees are of them. They are overly careful in the way they speak to their secretaries, and hesitate to confront highly trained employees for fear of losing them. In spite of their positions of power, they suffer from being cut off from genuine feedback, never getting a truly honest or spontaneous response from their employees, and by a sense of being constantly pressured or misunderstood. They fall prey to executive maladies such as ulcers, depression, alcoholism, and heart attacks.

Being equally as unable as their employees to aggress and impact openly and directly, employers also develop a repertoire of automatic, indirect strategies of expressing aggression. Theirs are more subtle than those of the employees. They include a poker-faced unresponsiveness, arbitrariness, confusing communications, veiled threats, and unpredictability. The result is a climate whereby both the employee and the employers find themselves boxed into a world of plastic smiles, phony mutuality, and empty, safe dialogue that cloaks the underlying alienation and hostility.

## WITH FEAR AND TREMBLING

The hunger for communication and authenticity is there, but the fear and confusion over how to get there are more powerful inhibiting forces. Yet our experience in working with the office milieu suggests that behind the "fear and trembling" of the employee and employer are similar anxieties, concerns, and conflicts. However, despite the volumes written on employee-employer relationships, management by objectives, and sensitivity training, we have been amazed at the lack of techniques and tools for dealing with aggressive interaction on an ongoing basis.

Employees *can* learn to deal with intolerable situations directly while still protecting their job security, and employers *can* come out from hiding behind their role-playing games and communicate honestly without threatening their status or losing control. However, our experience in working with office environments is that the opening of communication first leads to the unearthing of vast histories of unresolved conflicts. The "patient" at this point may think it is far sicker than expected and want to withdraw back into phony, safe interactions. We do not underestimate the anxiety-arousing aspects involved in this process. Aggressive interaction that makes people uncomfortable in private settings may be even more anxiety-arousing in work settings where job security is at stake. Although the styles of indirect and hidden aggression are ultimately destructive in many ways, they are still comfortable and familiar habits for individuals conditioned to avoid open confrontation, exchanges of anger, and assertive protection of one's identity. However, as the museums of buried hostility are unearthed, here and now examples of anger and conflict can be dealt with. Slowly, then, the issues can become more germane and realistic. The old issues will no longer contaminate and distort, nor will they engender indirect and hidden techniques of aggression. For purely pragmatic reasons, apart from any broader humanistic concerns, the development of constructively aggressive styles of communication can then be to the benefit of all. Open confrontation can reverse the sense of isolation and alienation.

The fruits of enduring this transitional stage of anxiety are many. It can begin to make the work setting one that is personally satisfying rather than one in which the worker's orientation is focused on the paycheck, vacation times, and retirement. This is the clearest manifestation of the tragedy of today's sterile, passive, emotionally unsatisfying work environment. Employees nurture and sustain themselves on escapist fantasies centered around getting *away* from the work setting.

In an environment that stifles assertive confrontation, genuine closeness becomes impossible, and therefore relationships and situations readily become confusing and threatening. Mickey Reynolds, a graduate engineer from the 1950s, was a department head at a major California aircraft company during the time of the recession in the late 1960s and early 1970s. He became anxious and insecure when he found out that Joe Finch, head of an equivalent department, had been assigned a personal assistant. His immediate conclusion was that he had fallen from favor with the program manager, who was his immediate supervisor. He began to fear that he was to be eased out when he further noticed that the program manager never attended his department's meetings, although he did attend those of the other department.

His interpretation of these signs was that his job might be in jeopardy or that his department was going to be disbanded. If he were to go to his boss for clarification, he felt he would be demonstrating a lack of self-confidence and doubts about the effectiveness of his department. In fact, Reynolds expected that this kind of confrontation would initiate a close, hard look at his department and bring about what he feared.

Fortunately, Reynolds had close associates working with him who noticed that he was becoming increasingly withdrawn and depressed. They urged him, for everybody's sake, to assert himself in terms of a "checking out" of what was really going on. When he finally did check it out with his program manager, Reynolds found that he was not given a personal assistant because the performance of his department was considered to be more than adequate. His supervisor's lack of attendance at his meetings was really a vote of confidence. Later, in talking with Joe Finch, he found that Joe had been experiencing great anxieties of his own. Joe had interpreted the assignment of an assistant as the company's lack of trust in his abilities. He was particularly depressed about the fact that the program manager *was* constantly present at his meetings.

In an atmosphere of insecurity these kinds of interpretations and distortions become rampant. All signs are interpreted negatively. Anxiety over confrontation and the fear of "checking it out" become the causes of lowered morale and increased suspiciousness.

## THE DESTRUCTIVE KINDNESS

The fear of giving honest critique, especially negative feedback, is another major communication obstacle in office settings. Politeness reigns until the last minute, when the bomb is dropped. Julie Rice, a secretary working for a public utility, had a habit of coming to work late and spending long periods of time either in the bathroom fixing her makeup or talking on the phone with her boyfriend. Her boss was reluctant to confront her. He didn't want to get the reputation with others in the office that he was a "bad" guy. Consequently, he handled his resentment passively by withdrawing and avoiding personal contact with her. Instead of confrontation there were long periods of quiet aggravation and secret wishing that she would become pregnant or ill and would go away on her own.

Julie didn't recognize her boss's indirect way of expressing his anger. She continued blithely along in her pattern, convinced she was doing a good job. She appreciated her "nice" boss for allowing her to "be herself" and organize her work the way she wanted it. Meanwhile, her boss's hostility intensified until one day Julie was informed by the personnel department of her transfer to another department without even being told why.

The new secretary, having been told by the others in the office of Julie's sudden and unexplained transfer, began her job with apprehension and fear about her future. This insecurity, of course, made her uptight and impaired her adjustment to the new job and her performance. Julie's boss, by not confronting her with negative critique, caused her problems to be inherited by the other department and, in addition, paved the way for a whole new set of problems with her replacement.

Ed Corwin attended a weekend training seminar in office aggression. He was a "dropout" from college who was now making his living as a bricklayer. While at first he enjoyed this work because he was agile with his hands, he soon began to hate it. His foreman, Buzz Roberts, was the immediate cause. He related to the workers like a sergeant in the Marines. He was a slavedriver who would drive Ed crazy by asking him to do one thing one minute, such as squaring and cleaning a ditch, then within a few minutes he would tell him to stop to do something else, such as getting the steel tied. All the while he would also put time pressures on, such as telling him a job had to be completed by 5:00 P.M.

Inside of himself Ed felt he knew his job and knew that his foreman was ruining things, in addition to making him uptight with these superfluous, unnecessary directions. However, Ed would always accommodate and say, "Yes, Buzz!," "I get you, Buzz!," until he was on the verge of quitting from frustration. During the weekend training session Ed was taught the importance of confrontation. Whereas his fellow workers on the job had always told him, "Brush it off!" or "Just do your job and forget it," at this seminar he was taught just the opposite. He learned to communicate his feelings and how they affected him.

The next time it occurred at work he confronted his foreman, "I really want to do a good job, but I've only got two hands. You tell me to do one thing, and then five minutes later you want to make a change. It bugs me because there's no way I can really do my best under those circumstances." The foreman seemed somewhat startled and a little irritated at first, but he began to give Ed more respect. Each time after that, if a similar thing occurred, Ed would confront Buzz until the message finally got through. Instead of alienating him, the job became easier and more pleasant for Ed. His foreman got to respect him and even began allowing him to run some of the jobs.

The fear of giving negative feedback in time to have a constructive effect, before a situation severely deteriorates, is always an important source of bad feelings. While it avoids conflict in the short run, a much more difficult situation results in the long run. In fact, this fear of giving negative and personal critique can traumatize an entire industry, as was dramatically illustrated during the period when large government contracts to private defense industry were drying up. Many engineers suddenly found themselves being laid off.

During this period, department heads of a defense corporation on the West Coast had the habit of writing very positive reports for each employee on the semi-annual personnel evaluation forms. They reasoned that this would keep morale up. But it also reflected their fear of offending the professional members of their staff. This pattern had evolved during the many years of high employment when engineers and scientists were hard to find and hence were treated with kid gloves. The policy, however, was retained with the rationalization that it would help keep morale high in the face of continuing layoffs.

The head of personnel protested against these uniform and undifferentiating reports. He asserted that the reports were designed to guide the employee toward a realistic self-evaluation and needed therefore to incorporate negative information for this purpose—but to no avail. With each subsequent layoff due to lack of funds, another severe personnel crisis ensued. Those who were laid off were shocked at the apparent arbitrariness of their selection as the "victim." All along they had been receiving most favorable evaluations, and suddenly they learned that they were expendable. It also turned out that department heads, for fear of offending, had secretly been using three kinds of favorable evaluation reports, some of which were actually lukewarm or negative reports in disguise. Out of the originally good-willed desire not to hurt, employees never really knew where they stood. Some of the more competent personnel also left the company in self-defense, further weakening the company's capacity to survive. The end result was the emergence of an atmosphere of rank distrust and apathy, where no one knew what to believe or whom to trust.

## THE EMPLOYEE WHO CAN'T SAY "NO"

Employees eager to please are often afraid to say "No" to a demand that is beyond them. Their fear is that saying "No" will threaten their position by being interpreted as hostile or uncooperative behavior. This is one critical form of aggression phobia that often winds up putting the employee in an untenable position. The "No" that is left unsaid emerges indirectly. The employee who can't set limits appropriate to his capacity finds himself overloaded and turning in a poor performance. Recognizing this situation, he may then attempt to protect himself by passively avoiding further demands on his time and energy, thus engendering a reputation for being uncooperative or apathetic. He thereby succeeds in precipitating an effect even worse than originally feared.

The following conversation is an illustration of just such a dilemma and the way one department store buyer who had been trained in constructive aggression techniques handled herself in this situation.

MR. TIPTON: Mrs. Farber, I've decided to promote you to buyer for my department. You'll be working directly under my supervision. Sales in our department have been expanding at a fast pace, and we're trying to keep that pace going. I come in a half hour early, before work starts, for breakfast meetings with our supervisors. I'm sure that you'll be sharing our enthusiasm and will want to join us at these meetings.

Mr. Tipton's good news contained some hidden messages that if not confronted in time, would be sure to cause Mrs.

Farber trouble later on. One such message was the implicit demand that she be as highly motivated as her boss and arrive to work early. An interwoven implication was that if she didn't come in early, she wouldn't be considered a team player as highly involved and highly motivated as the others. Mrs. Farber, who was sensitive to the dangers in these hidden implications, replied:

MRS. FARBER: I'm really excited about the promotion. I have to tell you, though, that I need to spend some time in the morning with my son. I won't be able to participate in the breakfast meetings on Tuesdays and Fridays. However, I'll get my reports to you for those meetings, and I'll check with the managers about what happened. I'm really excited about the new job, and I'll do all I can to keep the department growing.

The inability or fear of saying "No" in self-defense over realistic limitations and capacities can turn office life into a nightmare. This equally holds for the "nice" guy employer who says "Yes" to everything and everyone. Both reflect their insecurity, and each is afraid of jeopardizing his standing.

This fear of saying "No" is intimately tied to a fear of being aggressive. Saying "No" is experienced as an attack on someone else's feelings, an act of rejection. But the resentment that builds from being imposed upon, overloaded, and over-committed creates its own form of aggression. The poor guy who, even though willingly and with good intentions, allows himself to be used, will act out his resentment indirectly. He may procrastinate, he may misinterpret the instructions, or he may out-and-out forget the whole thing. The ultimate payoff is far worse than the anguish of saying "No" at the outset. That is, the person who compulsively says "Yes" or is fearful of saying "No" will begin to avoid his coworkers, seeing them as added potential for further impositions. His solution, avoiding contact, turns any time at the office into a dreadful experience. One important aspect of constructive office aggression, then, is the ability to say "No" in critical moments and the general recognition that "No" is a form of communication and *not* necessarily a sign of noncooperation or hostility.

## THE "NICE" EXECUTIVE AND THE HATCHET MAN (Not So Strange Bedfellows)

Our work with "nice" guy type top executives indicates that they frequently and privately complain that they are being taken advantage of by those working under them. Indeed, their employees often do have a tendency to become slipshod and irresponsible in carrying out their jobs. Eventually, this gets the "nice" executive into not-so-nice trouble.

Rarely, however, does the "nice" executive personally take the responsibility for warning the employee or terminating the employment. Instead, this dirty work is assigned to a lesser executive, a hatchet man who is given the task of putting on the pressure or doing the actual job of firing the employee.

As fight coaches to these "nice" bosses we work to free them from their phony "nice" guy syndromes which hide their aggression phobia. We teach them to fight fairly with their employees, to stop pretending to be buddies and to make open, clear-cut demands. As they learn to give up their styles of phony accommodation, to openly assert themselves, to increase their tolerance for conflict and to assume personal responsibility for their role as boss, they also learn to get along without a hatchet man. Invariably this frees them to function in their executive roles more comfortably and to relate to their employees more authentically, creatively, and with deeper satisfaction.

## THE PERSISTENCE-RESISTANCE EXERCISE

One of the most helpful learning devices in this area of negative as well as positive self-assertion is the "persistence-resistance" exercise discussed in the chapter on rituals. Of all of the exercises used in our seminars on office aggression, this is the one often rated most useful. It is designed to counteract the tendency in office situations to give up immediately in the face of a refusal. With this exercise, individuals are also encouraged to experience and express all of their resistances, saying "No" as long as it feels right. The persister is encouraged to find different and creative ways of asking and to replace the whining or complaining types of pleas, which are the kinds most commonly refused.

Cecilia wanted a new-model typewriter. She went to her employer, Lila Graham.

CECILIA:    Mrs. Graham, I'm wondering if it would be possible for the office to get me a new IBM Selectric.

MRS. GRAHAM:    Not now. We're really behind budget, and I'm sure we couldn't justify it.

CECILIA:    The Executive typewriter I'm working with is old and always getting out of alignment. Also, I feel my typing has improved to the point where I could really take advantage of the speed of the Selectric.

MRS. GRAHAM:    I can't really see it now without shifting some priorities. We've been overloaded, particularly with the expenses of our part-time help.

CECILIA:    I tried my girlfriend's new Selectric over in Mr. Bryant's office. It was actually fun, and I really feel the strain of using my old typewriter.

MRS. GRAHAM:    I'll think about it.

CECILIA:    You know, the cost of our part-time help? If you get the new typewriter I could get more work out and save the company some of that money.

MRS. GRAHAM:    I see what you're saying, and I think that's an important point. Maybe we are being pound foolish. I'll see if there's a way I can push it through.

Cecilia had learned to persist in the face of several rejections. She made her points, and each one used a different approach. Mrs. Graham, of course, did not give in immediately. She knew it would be difficult. Not until she saw a way, creatively pointed to by Cecilia, did she feel comfortable in accepting the demand.

The process of creative persisting and resisting facilitates more meaningful decisions. Consequently, as a rule we encourage office workers; employees, coworkers, and employers to use this device and initially to always say "No." This is not to encourage negativism. Rather, it allows the resister, the person of whom something is being requested, to surface all of his underlying resistances and negative feelings. The process then also forces the requester to build a meaningful case, to explore whether he really wants what he is asking for, and to give substance to his request. Consequently, whether a request is granted or denied, there will be less of a chance for lingering resentments over having been rejected, steamrollered, or manipulated.

## THERE IS NO MAGIC KEY SOLUTION

The overriding belief in and commitment to "rational" solutions in modern-day management is, we believe, the single most devastating obstacle to the development of an authentic, satisfying work atmosphere. That is, for years management has sought its answers to personnel problems in what we term "magic key" solutions. At one time or another these may mean increasing the length of coffee breaks, improving the lighting, changing the color of paint on the walls, longer vacations, greater worker autonomy over schedule, piped-in music, a casual employer attitude toward the clothing worn and the social behavior of the employee; perhaps even a weekend encounter or sensitivity group experience for interested personnel.

These are all in a sense, on management's part, ways of manipulating the external environment. And while these manipulations may indeed have short-term beneficial effects, in the long run, matters go back to where they were and the same personnel problems continue to haunt the work setting. This situation exists partially because underlying, irrational forms of indirect aggression such as jealousies, competitiveness, hostilities, and frustrations have not been directly or meaningfully dealt with, *within* and *among* the members of the office family. This repressed aggression consequently continually sabotages management's well-intentioned attempts to improve the work environment through rational techniques and "solutions."

For example, in one Midwest factory where auto parts are manufactured, workers arrive to work with transistor radios plugged in their ears, a newspaper under their arm, and lunches with large amounts of sandwiches, snacks, and desserts. During lunch, workers are seen sitting each in his own car eating, listening to the radio, and reading the paper. Management is tucked away in locked offices, sleeping, drinking, or watching TV. We feel that this is a typical example of the isolation that exists in many work settings throughout the country every day. We view this alienation as being, in large part, the result of contamination by repressed aggression, although it is only experienced as boredom and apathy. The underlying emotional life is rife with frustration, suspiciousness, petty jealousies, and resentments. But most of all, the fear of revealing these aspects of one's emotional life makes detachment and withdrawal the safest way of handling these forms of hostility. The end result is impaired performance, high absenteeism, and abuse of privileges. The frustrated employer and employee may even contaminate their union-management negotiations by using this medium for impersonally venting their built-up, unexpressed resentments.

This can be equally as true in a factory setting as it is in a university setting, where supposedly greater critical and rational capabilities are expected to prevail. Here we might assume that communications would be more meaningful. This is a myth. If anything, these ivory-tower settings are even more prone to deterioration of communication, because the fear of overtly expressed aggression is intensified by status anxieties over being perceived as undignified, illogical, out of control, or anti-intellectual.

In the psychology department of a large, highly respected East Coast university that employs over forty full-time psychology professors, there was a growing rift in the department. The experimentally oriented research psychologists looked down upon the applied clinical psychologists. They saw themselves as the only "real" scientists. The clinical psychologists, in return, viewed the experimentally oriented professors as "mechanics" who were isolated from human reality. They avoided each other's seminars, ate in separate parts of the dining room, and passed each other in the halls with barely a nod of recognition.

A crisis was finally precipitated by the retirement of the department chairman. Rigid factions developed over the selection of his replacement. Each side feared that the other's candidate would make life intolerable, cut their budgets, reassign office and lab space, deprive them of graduate assistants, sabotage promotion, and withhold tenure. Even among this group of eminent and sophisticated college professors, there was resistance to and anxiety over aggressive confrontation. The fear of exposing hostilities was so intense that finally a total split resulted in the creation of two separate departments, using separate facilities, and each with its own chairman.

Similar factions develop in many work settings. For example, the "young rebels" pit themselves against the "old guard," the blacks isolate themselves from the whites, and the women rally against their "male chauvinist" coworkers. Characteristically, as each of these factions further isolates itself, the inbreeding of resentment and hostilities flourishes and intensifies. The growing absence of communication between factions prevents the testing and checking out of each other's attitudes and opinions.

Tearing down these barriers after communication has become severely contaminated becomes nearly impossible. "Good will" has long since eroded. Concerted "good will" efforts to bring the isolated factions together often brings about only guarded discussions filled with evasion and pseudocordial mouthings of short-lived resolutions for change.

## AIRING THE HOSTILITIES

The traditional approach to conflict resolution has stressed the need for attacking specific issues rationally. In our approach, this is the very last step, preceded first by the airing of the underlying individual and group hostilities and mutual stereotypes. Rather than widening the gap, as is typically assumed would happen, the structured exchange of open hostility seems to foster intimacy and lay the ground work for communication.

Therefore, the stage must be set *not* for rational attempts at resolving the issue, but for open discussion, by one group at a time, of its position, feelings, frustrations, and hostilities toward the other group. Each group remains silent while listening to the other's venting of hostilities. Interaction is limited to listening only. This cuts down on the tendency of developing a "case" in defense of the silent group's position rather than listening. Once listening occurs, once the other group can be viewed as a collection of people facing their own problems, once trust has been built by sharing and listening to the very worst each group has to say about the other, and once the stereotyping and close-minded misunderstandings are recognized, then the littlest symbols of intended good will can also be recognized. Once each faction has fully aired its resentments and position, then the fragile roots of communication have a chance to break through.

When hostilities simmer and intensify but no constructive outlets are available, and the individuals involved are forced to remain on the job for economic or other reasons, as is frequently the case, these feelings take the increasingly lethal indirect forms we have termed crazymaking. The ingredients for this lethal form of interaction are ever-present in all work situations. Specifically, there are unequal power balances and economic dependence, and there is emotional vulnerability rooted in the ego involvement with status and performance.

## HUMILIATING THE EMPLOYEE

Demands are made by an employer that are structured so that the employee emerges feeling ineffective or incompetent. Instructions are given that humiliate the employee or decisions are reversed arbitrarily, leaving employees confused and worker pitted against worker. Though the employer's intent may not be consciously malicious, the mental health of the employee requires that these messages of indirect hostility be recognized and confronted.

One such form of communication is the "double bind," in which the employer is making incompatible demands and creating a "no-win" situation for the employee. For example, a senior attorney gave a recent law school graduate employee a critical assignment to be done in five days' time. In this instance, the job could not be done up to the law firm's standards in that short a period. The assignment was given, however, with the subtle implication that if the new graduate did not accept it, he would be admitting incompetence. If he accepted the job without protest, he would be doomed to failure. Either way he would lose.

The "mind rape" is another form of office crazymaking. The boss who is solicitous to his female employees may express well-intentioned concern for what he considers to be their special needs for guidance and protection. This imposition of stereotyped assumptions is a common form of "mind rape." Margaret Rogers, recently hired as one of the first policewomen in a small county precinct, was informed by her sergeant that, "We'll be giving you day shifts only because we *know* that you won't feel comfortable working at night, since you'll probably want to be home evenings to care for your family." Regardless of whether or not his assumptions were correct, he was guilty of a "mind rape." What he was doing in effect was stereotyping her. He acted on what he "knew" she "really" wanted and needed and did not bother to check it out. The "mind rape" is a common but often subtle form of crazymaking because it frequently comes under the umbrella of well-intentioned helpfulness. Consequently, it is often left unchallenged because the person whose mind is being "raped" is reluctant to challenge or confront such "thoughtfulness."

## THE GROUP "MIND RAPE" OF AN EMPLOYER

A group "mind rape" against an employer was the crux of a profound communication problem in a large New York-based CPA firm. The senior partner of the firm arranged for a marathon therapy weekend because he was becoming increasingly frustrated over the fact that things went on continually without him knowing about them. At meetings with various accountants in charge of the different departments, he felt that he was given only formal, perfunctory reports, but that many of the major problems were kept away from his awareness unless and until a major catastrophe occurred.

The marathon was scheduled over a two-day weekend in July. The session began very formally and with mild general complaining about having to give up the weekend to attend. Eventually tremendous resentment surfaced against the senior partner. The staff, it became clear, saw him as inaccessible and as someone who didn't really want to be bothered by them. They said he usually made them feel stupid.

The senior partner couldn't believe it and was deeply hurt. He said he worked long hours, neglected fun and his golfing, and always kept his door open.

A huge fight erupted. One of his staff screamed out, "It isn't that your door isn't open but that your mind is closed." It turned out that all of the staff felt awed by his brilliance and dedication and also threatened by it. They all felt that if they said too much around him they would only make fools of themselves. The staff had been "mind raping" him by assuming all along that he didn't want to be bothered by their petty problems. When they saw his door open they always saw him reading and felt sure he didn't want to be bothered.

The senior partner was given an assignment by Dr. Bach of "Project Free Communication." This meant that he would have to make contact at least once a day with one staff member, but without papers or a project to talk about. This was called "proximity time," just making contact. In addition, all members of the staff were taught to not mind read but to mind ask whenever they had concerns in relation to him. They now felt free to do this.

Vague expectations constitute another form of crazymaking communications. A demand or assignment is made or given in which it is unclear as to what is really expected. Employees who are fearful of appearing stupid allow these demands to be left unquestioned. They agonize silently on their own, trying to figure out and fulfill what they believe to be the real expectations.

Mr. Edwards, newly employed in a private consulting firm involved in city planning, had prepared his first formal proposal on a plan for redevelopment of a ghetto area in South Side Chicago. The proposal was referred to him on a Wednesday with the cryptic comment, "Close but weak. Won't sell as is. Please have revised report ready for me by Friday." Mr. Edwards was frustrated by the lack of specifics in the review, but being new to the company, he wasn't certain what to do about it, and was reluctant to ask questions for fear of appearing incompetent.

Such vagueness commonly appears on employer review forms. Comments about an employee such as, "poor attitude," "needs improvement," "not enough company spirit," "something missing," or any other criticisms that are leveled but that lack specifics as to what behavior elicited these comments or needs to be changed can be labeled as vague, hence crazymaking.

The attempt to confront these crazymaking styles in order to open the lines for clear communication are frustrated by yet another form of indirect aggression, "derailing." Mr. Edwards worked all day that Wednesday revising his redevelopment proposal. Late that afternoon he had become so upset by not knowing exactly what to do to improve its "sell" that he went to see his boss to get some clarification. His boss invited him out for a drink to talk it over. The boss was so concerned about Mr. Edwards' capacity to take the pressure that he tried to put Mr. Edwards at ease by spending the whole dinner hour talking about the excellence of the technical approach. The issue of how to make the proposal sell was completely avoided.

These are but a few of the forms of crazymaking. Other forms of this and techniques for confronting them are described in detail in the chapter devoted to the subject.

## THE EMPLOYERS' OPTIONS

The employer who is concerned with how to keep open the channels of communication has many options. The creative aggression techniques suggested here and discussed in detail in the chapter "Aggression Rituals" can all be adapted and applied to the office setting. The courageous employer can set aside a time each week when individuals can, for example, have a "Vesuvius," give each other "haircuts," engage in bataca fights, and role-play dominance and submission in the "master-slave" exercise.

But a sudden switching of behavior on the part of an employer, particularly to a more aggressively free atmosphere and posture, could at first engender anxiety and feelings of insecurity ("Is he trying to get something on us or make fools out of us?"). This may be followed by an opening of the floodgates of pent-up resentments, and feelings may get hurt. We must emphasize therefore that this development of an authentically aggressive work atmosphere requires the basic underpinnings of good will. Employer and employee must recognize that initially tensions and even crises may develop. Without a commitment to see it through, this condition of good will is *not* being met. Both employer and employee must learn the discipline involved in receiving and giving critique, appropriately expressing anger, and supporting those around them to do likewise.

As a sense of trust is developed, the impact and gains of open communication can be enjoyed. To bridge this difficult period, the employer needs to provide a form of "fire" insurance. This is to establish the secure feeling that the risks taken in open, honest communications will not be answered with termination or other forms of retaliation.

## THE CREATIVE EXECUTIVE

Research psychologists from the University of California in Berkeley selected thirty-seven executives from among seven thousand business managers in Irish industrial organizations as being innovators in their country's economic life. What they learned about the personalities of these individuals is integrally related to the thesis of this book. Creative ingenuity and innovative capabilities were found to be negatively related to the qualities we typically associate with "being nice" such as modesty, mildness, and pleasantness. Instead, they found that originality in business management was correlated with traits of aggressiveness such as forcefulness, toughness, and daring.[2]

Our own experience with supervisors in office environments corroborates this relationship between being "nice" and nonoriginality. The many managers, supervisors, and executives who have made it to the top by playing the game of "nice" are also frequently those who suffer from what we term "innovation phobia." That is, they fear being controversial or making waves through creativity. Consequently, the work environments which they supervise tend to become stagnant, mind-dulling prisons. Enduring eight-hour-a-day sentences in these office prisons is indeed a high price for workers to pay in return for having a "nice" guy boss.

The office setting can be viewed as a second home and family. It is fraught with hidden conflict and resentment. The authentically aggressive communication structure can be used to reduce interpersonal alienation and create a vital, authentic atmosphere. Employers stand to gain by stemming a tide of rampant, indirect, passive, and other hidden forms of aggression. Employees will gain from the atmosphere of humanization and a diminishing of frustration and resentment stemming from feelings of being powerless and exploited in an environment that leaves them with no effective recourse.

# CHAPTER 20

# Office Fights for Change

---

Executives strained by office tensions would prefer to pay a psychiatrist fifty dollars an hour to ventilate their frustrations rather than interacting more honestly and freely in the office. Workers drown their resentments and anxieties in alcohol and resign themselves to their "fate." Both look for outside arenas to discharge their office-generated anger and conflict. Typically these are the golf course, handball court, the nightclub or local bar, or weekend and vacation recreation.

Other professionals are drawn in to handle the conflicts when they arise. Industrial psychologists, management consultants, sensitivity trainers, and attorneys are paid thousands of dollars to do the "dirty work." The structure is lacking *within* the organization to deal with the myriad of specific issues and conflicts that arise out of the everyday work interactions. Furthermore, these problems are often seen as too hot to handle by those who are personally involved in the organization.

In the previous chapter we explored the hazards of repressed aggression in the office and what could be done to deal with this phenomenon. In this chapter we will be exploring the next step, which involves a formal structure for requesting specific changes in others, making specific changes in oneself, and improving the quality of interpersonal communication, relationships, and the work environment.

## THE FAIR FIGHT TECHNIQUES[1]

The fair fight techniques that we will be describing are designed to effect specific changes and to keep relationships active, positively involved, and functional. This is *impact* aggression—the good-willed motivation to create change in others and to be open to making changes in oneself in order to improve conditions. This is part of our philosophy that indeed we do have a responsibility to effect changes in the work environment, in order to improve it for *ourselves* and not for some amorphous humanistic reasons. It *is* our responsibility to design, develop, and change relationships and situations and to make them more satisfying and pleasurable. We reject the fatalistic notion that says, "If you don't like it, leave!" Or the belief that relationships are a matter of chemistry; if they're good, that's great; if they're lousy or painful, that's too bad, it can't be helped!

The "fair fight for change," which has been found to be so helpful over the past five years for structuring the creative resolution of conflict between intimates, is now being applied in the office setting. It is a structure that provides a nonmystifying, straightforward, and rational approach to the resolution of specific, concrete issues and conflicts. However, because it is a basically rational form of aggressive interaction, it can only be used effectively after the expression and release of the more generalized and less rational expressions of aggression. This is accomplished through the rituals, exercises, and techniques previously discussed in this book.

The fair fight system is the epitome of constructive and assertive communication in our approach. It provides a foundation for sustained self-assertion and for learning from conflict rather than withdrawing from it. It can also be used to transform vague, everyday feelings of distress and unhappiness experienced in work settings into concrete and negotiable issues. Thus it provides a vehicle to overcome alienation and cynicism by blocking passive, indirect, and destructive forms of aggression.

A salesman complained that his boss's secretary had become so protective of her boss's time that it was becoming impossible to get to see him. A manager of an apartment complex complained that his comanager was not carrying an equal share of the workload. And an employee of a public service organization was becoming increasingly unhappy and angry because his unit chief treated him like a child, hovering over him and criticizing his work openly in front of others. These are just a sampling of typical conflicts and issues that can be dealt with within the fair fight structure.

The question is often raised, "Why negotiate these issues?" After all, a boss can just send out a warning or a directive, or employees can get together and "unionize" or write formal letters of complaint. We have found, however, that while such one-way communications may effect change, they also tend to erode good-willed communication by polarizing people and setting one person or group against another. The fair fight format encourages a total airing of the issue on both sides and allows individuals to see how they communicate and the ways in which they impair communication. It is designed to offset the traditional way of creating change through use of power, a "pressure" technique that is inevitably alienating in impact.

The only kinds of specific issues that are not negotiable under the fair fight format are disputes over behaviors that are beyond willful control and therefore not open to change by an act of will. These are behaviors that reflect deeply ingrained patterns that have characterological or neurotic roots and therefore require professional intervention. These include smoking, alcoholism, and problems of temperament, such as tendencies to extreme mood swings, depression, and withdrawal. We have labeled these issues "nonnegotiables." However, though the behaviors are "nonnegotiables," the conditions under which the individual expresses these behaviors may still be open to negotiation and change.

Some of the issues that are fought over may appear on the surface to be trivial and mere disguises and coverups for more deeply rooted and hidden emotional and interpersonal problems. The fair fight system, however, is not concerned with such psychiatric speculations. Rather, we have found that by staying with a specific issue, no matter how trivial it seems to be, a *process* of conflict resolution is learned. The fair fight system teaches that the *how,* or the process of a fight, is as important, if not more, than the content, or *what* of a fight.

The presence of other, neutral people from the office whom we call observer-participants is an integral part of this procedure. They act as coaches, score the fights (details are provided later in the chapter), and provide help throughout in the form of constructive critique. Their involvement has also been found to lighten the atmosphere by helping fighters overcome the feelings of anxiety, shame, and humiliation that traditionally accompany the open expression of conflict.

Equally important is the effect on the observer-participants themselves. Individuals in our culture have typically been conditioned to shy away in embarrassment from watching others fight. Through their participation they overcome these hindering feelings and at the same time provide the social support the fighters need in order to stay with the painstaking process of conflict resolution. Fair fighting is not a verbal free-for-all but a controlled technique for assertive communication. In the early stages particularly, it can be slow and tedious in comparison to the volatile, high-pitched excitement of the typical verbal brawl. Observer-participants therefore function as a supportive social group helping the impatient fighters to "hang in."

## THE NINE STEPS IN A FAIR FIGHT

Specific steps in the process of fair fighting include:

### Step 1:   *The Engagement*

The fair fight is implemented by the "initiator" who has a beef or complaint. He requests the other person ("fight partner") to engage him in a fair fight. If the "fight partner" agrees to accept, a time and place for the fight is set.

The "engagement" process is critical for offsetting the tendency to jump right in and have it out on the spot. This would only result in one person being caught off guard, and a rapid spiral of destructive encountering would ensue. A fair fight is therefore always conducted upon mutual consent and under agreed-upon conditions.

### Step 2:   *Open Huddle and Rehearsal*

Huddles are brief strategy conferences with one or more fellow workers who are acting as coaches and observer-participants. These huddles can be requested at any time by either partner when needed. They are held openly so that everyone, including the other fighter, can listen if he so chooses. The process is designed to help the "initiator" define his "beef" and construct a "demand for change" and to assist the "fight partner" to express his resistance to the demand in simple and clear terms.

In general, the function of coaching is to help each fighter to simplify his contentions, translate his questions into statements whenever possible (e.g., "Why do you do such and such?" becomes, "I don't want you to do such and such."), and to take responsibility for his feelings, particularly the difficult ones, such as anger and resentment. The "huddle" is a formal extension of the natural process of talking things over with a buddy.

Step 3:  *Statement of the "Beef" and Its Hurtful Impact*

After the "open huddle," the "initiator" of the fight states his "beef." This is followed by a statement of how that behavior reflected in the "beef" negatively affects, hurts, or hinders the "initiator." For example:

MS. SCOTT (an account executive speaking to the vice president of finance):   My beef is that during staff meetings, whenever the secretary is out, you automatically ask me to take the notes. It makes me feel like a stereotyped female thing.

Another example, but of a more complicated nature, is the following "beef" presented by the comptroller of a Midwestern plastics manufacturing firm to the personnel manager of the company:

COMPTROLLER:   You hired Mr. McDonald to computerize our payroll system. You didn't consult me on this choice. You didn't ask if he was acceptable to me nor whether I felt he had the necessary background to do this job. It makes me feel pressured and overloaded, as I'm the one who's ultimately responsible for that job.

Step 4:  *Feedback*

Once the "beef" has been stated, the "feedback" principle is invoked. It remains unconditionally operative until the end of the fight. This means that neither the "initiator" nor the "fight partner" is permitted to express himself without first having repeated back what he has just heard.

Though the "feedback" process is painstaking and can even be exasperating, it is the critical backbone of the fair fight process. That is, while it slows down the fight, it also forces careful listening. It aborts the usual tendency to inwardly prepare a devastating reply while the other person is speaking, which distracts greatly from accurate listening. It is surprising how difficult it really seems to be for people to accurately repeat the essence of what someone has just told them. It is particularly impressive how many "differences" begin to melt away almost immediately as individuals begin to hear each other and are heard for the first time.

A word of caution! The concept of "feedback" does not mean rote parroting. Rather, it means repeating the sense and essence of what the other person has just said. Fighters who are in a hurry to get on with it will tend to repeat what has been said word for word. This becomes an exercise in memory, not in understanding, and defeats the purpose of the "feedback" procedure.

It is possible and also fairly common for one person to feed back a message in a way that is superficially or seemingly correct but that distorts the spirit of the communication. This may occur through verbal or emotional shadings with gestures or sarcasm. The following is just such a "feedback" given during a fight between coowners of an apartment house:

PARTNER A:   I'm angry that you've been copping out each weekend for the past month. You always tell me that you have to be with your family, and you leave me with the job of fixing up and overseeing our apartment house.

PARTNER B:   I hear you saying that you resent my spending time with my family on weekends and want me to be working on the apartment house instead.

Partner B's "feedback" implies that Partner A resents Partner B's spending time with his family, when in reality Partner A is complaining about the lack of cooperation and sharing of responsibility.

The observer-participants can be particularly helpful in detecting these subtle nuances of communication distortion, often too elusive to be recognized by the emotionally involved participants.

Step 5:   *The Demand for Change*
Now that the stage has been set, the "initiator" is ready to make a specific "demand for change."

In a dispute over carelessness in spending between a husband and wife who owned a photography studio, the wife demanded, "From now on I want to cosign any check over fifty dollars."

In a fight over access to information, an employee demanded, "I want access to anything that's written about me and placed in my personnel file."

Demands for change must relate to actions, not attitudes. These changes, once agreed to, can then be measured in concrete terms. Attitudes, however, always leave room for interpretation. In the previous example the employee's demand was not "Don't be secretive," but rather, "I want access." This was also true in the example of the photography studio. In these cases, a signature or admittance to a file could be used as concrete evidence of change.

Step 6:    *Comeback by the "Fight Partner"*

After the "demand for change" has been correctly fed back, the fighting begins. The "fight partner" now has a chance to respond to the "beef" and "demand for change" by verbalizing his side of the picture.

Step 7:    *Fair Fight Interplay*

The fair fight now moves back and forth. Each participant in turn expresses himself in direct and simple statements. Each statement is fed back before the other person counters.

Step 8:    *Closure*

After a thorough mutual interchange, closure is required. At this point the "fight partner" has either agreed to the "demand for change," rejected it totally, or established specific conditions for partial change. "Closure" constitutes a restatement of the agreement just made. Occasionally, however, exhaustion sets in before agreement is reached, and a later date can be set for continuing the fight.

Step 9:    *Follow-up Engagement*

At this future meeting, the success or failure of the agreement is discussed. Any achieved changes should be recognized and reinforced. This involves the giving of appreciation to the person who has successfully made a behavioral change.

At this meeting the "closure" agreement may be either re-affirmed or renegotiated. Commitments are always kept fluid. In the good-willed aggressive interaction of a fair fight, the fighting is never over.

As indicated previously, the content of a fair fight is of secondary importance to its process. More than anything else, the fair fight procedure is designed to sensitize individuals to their unique style of communication and to help eliminate distortions and evasions that contaminate the conflict resolution.

This is achieved through a system of scoring designed to provide the fighters with helpful critique. The purpose of scoring is *not* for comparison of the fighters but rather to help them evaluate and learn from their interactive behavior. Also, "fair fighting" is designed to avoid a win-lose approach and provide a procedure that results in a mutually comfortable resolution and learning experience.

## EVALUATION OF THE FIGHT

The fight style of each partner is evaluated by the observer-participants. The following dimensions of communication are used to help the scorer focus on the process, *not* the content of the interchange:

1. *Reality*. Are the statements rational and realistic in nature? *Plus* is scored for statements that have the quality of "leveling," the open, clear display of authentic feeling and genuine concern. *Minus* is scored if the verbalizations are contrived, insincere, or manipulative.

2. *Fairness*. Can the other person cope with, integrate, and respond to the statements made? *Plus* is scored if the statements are "above the beltline." *Minus* is scored if the effect is to devastate the other person and impair his motivation and capacity to continue.

3. *Involvement*. Are the statements made with genuine feeling? *Plus* is scored if genuine emotion is displayed. *Minus* is scored if a fighter remains detached, withdrawn, or seems to be faking his concern.

4. *Responsibility*. Does the fighter acknowledge his share of the responsibility for the conflict and its resolution? Willingness to take responsibility is scored *plus*. A defensive resistance to accepting responsibility or placing the blame on outside sources is scored *minus*.

5. *Humor*. Does the humor that is present produce joyous relief and generate a relaxed closeness? This kind of humor is scored *plus*. Sarcasm and "putdowns" designed to humiliate the other person are scored *minus*.

6. *Feedback*. Is the feedback accurate, and does it meaningfully reflect the essence of the communication? *Plus* is scored for remembering to feedback and resisting the temptation to immediately counter with one's own argument. *Minus* is scored if the fighter forgets to feed back; does so in an impatient, sloppy, or distorted fashion; or if he jumps ahead before receiving confirmation of the accuracy of his feedback.

7. *Specificity*. Are the statements clear, and do they contain specific, concrete details? If so, score *plus*. *Minus* is scored for contentions and allegations that are vague and general in nature.

8. *Perspective*. Do the statements relate to the "here and now"? *Plus* is scored for "present-oriented" statements. *Minus* is scored if statements drag in irrelevant issues or complaints and allegations from the past.

9. *Change readiness*. *Plus* is scored if there is a willingness to be flexible and an openness to change. *Minus* is scored for maintaining a rigid position and placing the onus for change onto the other person.

10. *Crazymakers and hidden aggression*. Types of crazymakers and modes of hidden aggression are explored in depth in earlier chapters of this book. In general, a *plus* is scored for

confronting the other person in his use of crazymaking and hidden aggression. A *minus* is scored for failing to confront or for participating in the use of either form of this indirect aggression.

Styles of crazymaking include the double bind, mind rape, guiltmaking, nonengagement, "thinging," mystification, crisismaking, closure block (derailing), and the "occasional reinforcer." Forms of hidden aggression to be looked out for include collusion, passive aggression in the form of forgetting, misunderstanding, procrastination, and "no carryover of learning." Other forms of hidden aggression include "moral one-upmanship," intellectualizing, doubting, nonrewarding, playing "sickness tyrant," "Red Cross nurse," and "helplessness."

## A SAMPLE FIGHT

The following fair fight took place between Mr. Brill, director of the design research department of a large engineering consulting firm, and Ms. Conrad, who was a senior member of his technical staff functioning as an engineering analyst.

Ms. Conrad was engaged in a complex assignment, which was due in five weeks' time. She was becoming increasingly disturbed by the tendency of Mr. Brill to constantly interrupt her work by barging into her office unannounced. He would then ask her to take care of "emergencies" such as incorporating an extra printout from the computer, having the answers on a computer run rechecked, or solving an "east-west" loading condition problem.

Ms. Conrad requested a fair fight, and Mr. Brill agreed to it. They met on a Wednesday morning before work with Dr. Goldberg plus two observer-participants present. Since this was the first "fair fight" either of them had ever engaged in, they were allowed to fight without interruption after being briefed on the basic rules, so that they could get some critique on their "natural" everyday fighting and communicating behaviors. In transcribing the dialogue, the "feedback," which was usually done faithfully and accurately, has been omitted.

MS. CONRAD:   My beef is that you barge into my office unannounced and make requests that you expect me to respond to immediately. (fed back by Mr. Brill)

It makes me feel tense, frustrated and angry to the point that now whenever you come around I get nervous and tight inside, and I don't even want to listen. (fed back by Mr. Brill)

My demand for change is that you ask me for my attention before you barge in with another request so that I can tell you if I'm ready to listen and can then properly respond to your request. (fed back by Mr. Brill)

MR. BRILL:   Hey Kate! You know we've got a job to get done. You seem to be awfully sensitive. (fed back by Ms. Conrad)

MS. CONRAD:   I've just gotten so damn frustrated with always being interrupted. You're not doing either of us any good. (fed back by Mr. Brill)

MR. BRILL:   These tasks suddenly come to mind, and I just want you to know we've got to get to these things. [in joking manner] Maybe it's just that time of the month for you, Kate? (fed back by Ms. Conrad)

MS. CONRAD:   Don't lay your female stereotypes on me. It doesn't matter if I'm male or female. No one could switch from thinking about one thing to focusing on another just like that. Can't you be a little bit patient? (fed back by Mr. Brill)

MR. BRILL:   Yes, but then I might forget what it was I wanted to see you about. (fed back by Ms. Conrad)

MS. CONRAD:   Then write it down and send me a note. Or at least let me know in advance that you're coming in. (fed back by Mr. Brill)

MR. BRILL:   You really are awfully sensitive about this. You remind me of my wife—bitch! bitch! bitch! (fed back by Ms. Conrad)

MS. CONRAD:   Do you do that to your wife too? (fed back by Mr. Brill)

MR. BRILL:   (heatedly) You leave my wife out of this. (No feedback as Ms. Conrad immediately lashed back. She was stopped by Dr. Goldberg and was asked to feed back first.)

MS. CONRAD:   You're the one who brought her up. (Fed back by Mr. Brill. At this point both were clearly getting off the track, and open huddling with Dr. Goldberg and observer-participants occurred before resumption.)

MS. CONRAD:   Look, Jim, this job is my responsibility. I realize you've got a lot on your mind, but I've got more to do than just the items you give me. If you just get off my back a little maybe we can get this job out. (fed back by Mr. Brill after he had told her she had "overloaded" him and asked her to repeat herself, one thought at a time)

MR. BRILL:   You don't have to get so uptight about it. I honestly never realized it was getting you so upset. (fed back by Ms. Conrad)

MS. CONRAD:   I guess it's the pressure I feel. I really want to help you out, but I need some advance warning before you come in. (fed back by Mr. Brill)

MR. BRILL:   How am I going to know when you're ready? (fed back by Ms. Conrad)

MS. CONRAD:   I'll let you know. Just ask me. (fed back by Mr. Brill)

MR. BRILL:   That sounds silly! (fed back by Ms. Conrad)

MS. CONRAD:   Then why don't you buzz me on the phone ten minutes before you plan to come in? (fed back by Mr. Brill)

MR. BRILL:   Okay, I'll agree to that. (fed back by Ms. Conrad)

MS. CONRAD:   Good!

One might be asking at this point, "Wasn't that an aw-fully long-winded way of arriving at a simple solution?" The answer is "No." Mr. Brill and Ms. Conrad had been going round and round on this issue for over a month. Each needed to fully air their respective positions and feelings before they could arrive at what seems, on the surface, to be a rather matter-of-fact type of solution.

The fight trainer scored these two fighters as follows:

## SCORE SHEET

Date: *June 13, 1973*

INITIATOR (**I**):    *Ms. Kate Conrad*

FIGHT PARTNER (**FP**):    *Mr. Jim Brill*

*Beef:*    Barges into office unannounced and makes requests.
*Hurtful Impact:*    Tense and angry. Doesn't want to listen.
*Demand for Change:*    Ask me for my attention beforehand.

| | PLUS | MINUS |
|---|---|---|
| *Reality* | **I**: genuinely concerned | **FP**: initial sarcasm suggested he wasn't taking it seriously |
| *Fairness* | | **FP**: comment about comparing **I** to his wife and **I** comment "do you do that to your wife too?" were "below the beltline" remarks |
| *Involvement* | **I** and **FP**: both displayed lots of feeling and involvement | |
| *Responsibility* | **I** and **FP**: both finally began to see their part in it | **I** and **FP**: both at first saw the other as being to blame |
| *Humor* | | **FP**: putdown remark about "that time of the month" |

| | | |
|---|---|---|
| *Feedback* | **I** and **FP:** except for one lapse feedback was consistently and accurately given | |
| *Specificity* | **I** and **FP:** both expressed their contentions clearly and concretely | |
| *Perspective* | **I** and **FP:** both remained in the present | |
| *Change readiness* | **I** and **FP:** both eventually showed willingness to change | |
| *Crazymaking and hidden aggression* | **FP:** confronted **I** with overloading | **I:** overloaded **FP:** guiltmaker comment about "bitch! bitch! bitch!" **FP:** derailed **I** initially by saying, "You seem to be awfully sensitive" and "You remind me of my wife." **FP:** "thinging" comment about "that time of the month" was a stereotype **I:** failed to confront on derailing, "thinging," and guiltmaking of FP |

## BRIEF SUMMARY OF STYLE FACTORS

| | PLUS | MINUS |
|---|---|---|
| *Reality* | rational and realistic | contrives, insincere, manipulative |
| *Fairness* | can cope, integrate, and respond | devastates, impairs the other |

| | Plus | Minus |
|---|---|---|
| *Involvement* | genuine feeling | detached, withdrawn, faking |
| *Responsibility* | acknowledges responsibility | defensive, places blame |
| *Humor* | joyful | sarcastic, putdowns, derisive |
| *Feedback* | accurate and reflects essence | distorts, forgets |
| *Specificity* | clear, concrete, specific | vague, general |
| *Perspective* | here and now | irrelevant, ancient history |
| *Change* | open and flexible | closed, rigid |

*Crazymakers*

1. double bind
2. mind rape
3. guilt makers
4. nonengagement
5. "thinging"
6. mystification
7. crisismaking
8. overloading
9. closure block (derailing)
10. occasional reinforcer

*Hidden Aggression*

1. collusion
2. passive aggression
   a. forgetting
   b. misunderstanding
   c. procrastination
   d. no carryover of learning
3. moral one-upmanship
4. intellectualizing
5. nonrewarding
6. "sickness tyrant"
7. "Red Cross nurse"
8. "helplessness"

Ms. Conrad and Mr. Brill met again one week later and found that their "closure" resolution was comfortable for both and still being maintained and respected. They also discovered that they were feeling friendlier toward each other and were now more sensitive to each other's needs.

# CHAPTER 21

# The Fight for Growth

*Do not go gentle into that good night.*
*Rage, rage against the dying of the light.*

DYLAN THOMAS

Growth is a process that leads to an emotional transformation and the construction of a new, more total, and real way of experiencing oneself and one's relationship to the world. Because the flow of aggressive energy within most people has been severely blocked, an important first step in this growth process is the release of these energies away from passivity, stagnation, and resignation into an assertive, fluid interactional pattern.

Our culture has traditionally reinforced the passive, resigned attitude toward one's emotional self. This is because personal growth usually involves breaking through stereotyped, predictable, and conforming ways of relating and being. The breakthrough, therefore, inevitably upsets the status quo. Each move away from prevailing modes of responding and relating, which have become safe and comfortable in the way that caged animals are "safe" and "comfortable," comes about through some destruction of the familiar and an accompanying, aggressive movement toward the unfamiliar. Consequently, only movements toward greater social adjustment and prevailing "acceptable" social patterns garner support. In the path to emotional growth, therefore, each individual becomes a lonely hunter, making his way through uncharted territory.

These growth efforts also meet with resistance because they upset the balance of existing relationships and interactions. When one spouse, for example, makes a significant shift in the direction of expressing real feelings and deeply felt needs, the other spouse is pressured to change if he or she wishes to maintain a workable balance. If he or she remains the same, the relationship is bound to deteriorate significantly.

Likewise, this holds true in the occupational areas. The person who realizes and wishes to act upon the awareness that he is wasting his precious life in a monotonous, unfulfilling job will inevitably pose a threat both to those who are personally counting on him to fulfill his role as a breadwinner and to coworkers who will be reminded of their own inert reaction to an unfulfilling job. Society traditionally has not made it easy for the person who wants to change occupational horses midstream. Therefore, the person in his late thirties or midforties who would like to make such a dramatic life change will more than likely find himself facing the wrath of those who will be affected and inconvenienced by the changes.

A person in the midst of a personal growth process or crisis will certainly confront obstacles. He may be labeled "sick" or be accused of having a "problem." The person will also confront guilt-inducing messages. These may take the form of "How can you be so selfish?," "Don't you ever think of anybody but yourself?," and "Look what you're doing to everybody!" Since guilt feelings are such powerful motivators in our society, many people will begin to falter and doubt themselves when they hear their inner voice demanding a change, and will often retreat in fear into self-compromising "adjusted" behavior.

The positive aspects of an aggressive assertion on one's own behalf toward growth have been epitomized in recent years by various oppressed groups in our culture. These groups provide fine models for the healthy changes that are possible when individuals take aggressive responsibility for their existence and their life situation. We are speaking here of groups such as blacks, the Chicanos, the gay population, and women. Analogies from these groups to the individual, need to be made with caution. However, there are important lessons to be learned from their experiences.

For decades blacks used passive strategies to improve their dreadful life situation and their negative self-images. Passive resistance, praying, pleading, and trying to humble their way into a rejecting system were all part of their approach. From time to time social crumbs were thrown their way—just enough, in fact, to placate them and keep their hopes alive and to abort more vigorous self-assertion. Consequently, each gain was a tenuous one that never facilitated a strong forward momentum. In the mid-1960s, however, blacks became militant on their own behalf. In the five-year period immediately following they made greater gains in terms of concrete social changes and enhanced self-respect than had been made by blacks in the fifty prior years.

Militant Chicano groups have been largely responsible for making the Mexican-American population visible in our culture. Until they began to aggressively assert the needs and rights of Chicanos as American citizens, this cultural group was largely ignored and repressed. Today, along with the blacks, Mexican-Americans have become an integral part of affirmative action programs in employment settings and in colleges and universities. Chicano studies, for example, has become a part of the curriculum and even an autonomous department in many educational institutions.

The gay population too has long been legally harassed, socially stigmatized, and psychiatrically defined as "sick." Male homosexuals in particular lived with a repulsive public stereotype of themselves as bathroom-lurking perverts who ravished innocent boys.

In the late 1960s gays began to step forward and assert their rights as human beings and citizens. As they became increasingly aggressive on their own behalf, the public's reaction to them also changed dramatically in a positive direction. Even many professionals in the psychiatric and psychological professions began to alter their theoretical preconceptions radically. They were no longer as convinced that it was important to turn gays into straights, unless in fact the gay person was so inclined himself.

The history of the Women's Liberation movement contains a similar theme. So long as women were pleading for justice from the predominantly male legislators on matters such as abortion or equal rights, little ground was gained. When they stopped pleading and began demanding, they started to receive their rightful place as equals. In the process, the sense of identity and the self-image of many women were also radically altered. They no longer felt they needed to view themselves as sex objects or second-class citizens.

Each of these groups went through a period of dramatic self-assertion before significant changes occurred in their own self-perceptions and in the responses of society. As long as they had accepted the passive, "nice" role, however, their position was essentially stagnant.

This interlocking between aggression and growth is equally as valid for the individual, except that the individual does not receive group support for these personal growth efforts. Therefore his path, as he breaks away and finds his own unique emotional rhythms, is a more difficult, anxiety-provoking, and lonesome one.

In thinking about this individual growth process, we have attempted to define some of the major dimensions within which we believe it takes place, and have come up with the following, which we feel are particularly relevant.

## RISK VS. SECURITY

The search for security is a normal bedrock human motivation. But for many people it also becomes a binding chain, an excuse for passivity. The familiar and known, though experienced as deadening and boring, are preferable to the anxieties and uncertainties of change and newness.

Stuart Arnold had been a business major in the mid-1960s, graduating from college in 1967 in the top 5 percent of his class. In the first months of looking for a job, the employment market seemed bleak. Out of fear that he would never find anything better, he took the first reasonably well-paying job offered to him. It involved researching potential investment outlets for a major insurance company. Along with a good salary, there were numerous fringe benefits.

After a five-year period he had become fairly successful and had received regular raises, but he was finding it harder and harder to get up for work in the morning. He was also by now a chain smoker, and his liquor at lunch and in the evenings was becoming increasingly important to him.

His need for security, which had led him to the job in the first place, and which had worked positively for him during the first few years, was beginning to backfire in its effects. Stuart was receiving no intellectual stimulation or emotional nourishment from his job. He was merely going through the motions, but he was also afraid to quit.

There are many Stuart Arnolds in the working world, individuals who have taken jobs and remain in them purely for security reasons. Eventually they begin to function like robots from nine to five. They nourish themselves on their weekend and vacation plans, or on escape through drink or food after work.

In Stuart's case, even though he was afraid to quit, the growth impulse within him was too powerful to suppress. It took over by itself. His behavior in the office began to change radically. He began antagonizing his supervisor by being abrupt and sarcastic to personnel using his services. He also began handing his reports in late, making occasional gross computational errors and was even coming back from lunch late and pleasantly drunk. In other words, his unconscious growth im-

pulse, the part of him that could no longer tolerate the stifling of himself, was forcing him into behaviors that would result
in his getting fired, which is what finally happened.

In other settings and relationships the growth impulse
may also take over by itself. An unhappy spouse may indulge in
an obvious, embarrassing infidelity, which will precipitate a crisis
that will break up a stagnant marriage that neither spouse
would have the courage to end. The "cheater" in the marriage is
labeled by others as the "bad" one, even though he or she is in
reality doing the dirty work to liberate both spouses.

Even such a frightening experience as a "nervous breakdown" may be the unconscious instrument designed to bring
about a crisis needed for growth and change. The "breakdown"
is doing for the person what the person's own security needs
have made him afraid to do for himself. It forces him to re-
evaluate his life and to make changes.

Tragically, social pressures tend to push the person in the
midst of crisis back into an adjustment pattern, the place where
he was before the crisis, rather than trying to help him find the
truths and meaning in his experience. That is, the vulnerable
person who is made to feel that the marriage breakup means
"sickness" or failure and "betrayal" of the other spouse, may
feel pressured to force himself back into the marriage. Likewise,
a person in an occupational crisis, such as in Stuart Arnold's
case, who is given all kinds of dire warnings by others about
the meaning of his behavior, may attempt frantically to read-
just. At the crisis turning point, therefore, a person who gets
negative, frightening kinds of interpretations of his behavior
from others may find himself sinking into self-hate and an anxious, desperate fight to go backward. His experience has been
interpreted for him by others as being "sick," and he has incor-
porated this definition for himself also.

If, however, one has personal strength and emotional support from others that enable one to see the meaning of his
growth crisis, a meaning that says there's something radically

wrong with the way one is relating to one's life, then a beautiful growing process can begin.

## EXPERIENCE VS. ANALYSIS

There are many today, long-term psychoanalytic and psychotherapy patients, who "understand" themselves well and are able to analyze their own and their friends' behavior skillfully. However, they are still struggling with the identical fears and conflicts they had before their therapy. They are still unable to assert themselves sufficiently to effect the needed changes in their behavior or inner emotional experiences.

In these instances, the process of analyzing and "understanding" becomes the disease in itself, a fortress against movement and experience. Each feeling has been dissected and interpreted into nothingness. Its growth energy has been sapped. And these people always end up with the same resigned plaint of, "Yes, I still have the same problems, but now at least I know the reasons why. I understand myself better."

The current popularity of the growth group movement in our country is in major part a reaction against this sterile process of continuous analyzing. Analyzing is derisively termed by them "mind fucking," which is the empty, endless process of searching for "deeper" meanings and more profound interpretations of one's feelings and behavior in order to effect changes.

Understanding and analyzing are indeed important underpinnings of change. However, when they become ends in themselves, they also become the frustrating illusions of growth rather than growth itself.

## REACHING OUT VS. HOLDING BACK

In a heavily mechanized, impersonal society, the capacity and motivation to aggressively reach out and obtain satisfaction for one's needs are crucial to the achievement of joy, a sense of well-being, and involvement with life. The inability to reach out brings about isolation, suspiciousness, and the search for substitute satisfactions. That is, individuals will search for gratification in impersonally obtainable material things and experiences that can be purchased with money. These might include drugs, escapist activities such as films, television, records, overindulgence in food and liquor, or the conspicuous consumption of expensive, useless luxuries. Even psychotherapy, in these instances, may become merely the purchase of a friendship.

The discovery made by individuals who finally learn to reach out and assertively, openly, and directly express their needs is that they are received with delight by others who have also been holding back the expression of their needs.

## SELF-DISCLOSURE VS. SELF-SECRECY

In the early hours of a recent weekend marathon group therapy session, conducted by the authors, a number of the participants present complained of feeling bored. The interchanges indeed were all of a surface nature. Everyone was busy sizing up the group to see how safe it would be to reveal himself.

During the fourth hour one woman began to speak openly of herself. She was forty-one years old and had recently and suddenly been left by her husband of seventeen years. He had gone off with the young, twenty-two-year-old secretary of a friend.

"I need to tell you about myself," she began. "That's why I came here today. I refuse to hide and play it safe anymore. I feel lonely, unattractive, and desperate. I've had a half dozen relationships with men in the past year. None of them seem to continue past the first three or four dates. Usually the guy disappears after we've had sex for the first time.

"I'm embarrassed to say this," she continued, "but I've even taken to advertising in singles newspapers. Last week I visited a professional matchmaker who specializes in finding unattached professional men. I'm really starting to hate myself for all of this, and I need help."

Her self-disclosure broke the ice, and there was a sudden feeling of warmth and vitality in the room. She had expressed herself truthfully. Rather than receiving negative critique from others, she had reached and transformed the group.

Inhibited growth is always in part the result of a fear of self-disclosure. The fear stems from feelings of shame and a lack of trust in others. Until very recently, crises such as divorces, abortions, alcoholism, school failures, extramarital affairs, homosexual feelings, or even having a disturbed or retarded child were all treated as taboo subjects. People tortured themselves hiding these important aspects of themselves. They saw themselves as freaks or perverts, different from everybody else.

At the moment of breakthrough, when a person is able to openly say, "This is who I really am, and this is what's happening to me," the growth process begins. Suddenly he finds he is able to make an emotional connection with others whom he invariably finds have had similar life experiences.

Secretiveness about oneself intensifies guilt feelings, self-hate, and the sense of alienation from people. One is literally poisoned and paralyzed emotionally by these secret feelings and the resulting sense that one is sicker than or radically different from others.

## LIVING BY ONE'S OWN RHYTHM VS. CLINGING TO AUTHORITY

One prevailing, emotionally destructive by-product of living in a fact-obsessed and statistics-hungry society is the tendency to compare oneself to the norms and standards of behavior set forth by others. Magazine and newspaper articles that purport to contain such information are written about subjects such as sexual and marital adjustment, personal attractiveness, emotional health, and occupational adjustment. These writings can have a very disturbing effect on vulnerable readers who will be prone to compare and rate themselves negatively.

A vital step, therefore, in which aggression functions in the service of growth, is learning to say, "Those are statistics. They are not me. Nobody else in this world is like me. I have my own unique rhythms, and the thing that really matters is whether or not I'm comfortable with myself." Once this point has been reached, there develops a founded sense of self-acceptance rather than an endless, crazymaking striving to conform to the patterns of those mythical "others."

The writers' own life experiences have confirmed this for us. Dr. Bach has long been considered a maverick in the profession of clinical psychology. While others in the profession insisted that people had to be worked with individually, he was working with people in couples and groups. While others were working in fifty-minute therapy sessions, he was experimenting with time-extended sessions that eventually evolved into twenty-four-hour and longer marathons. And while others were trying to find ways that patients could resolve and get rid of anger and hostility, he was searching for ways in which individuals and relationships could be vitalized by their expression.

Dr. Goldberg also found early in his career that traditional modes of functioning as a psychologist were for him numbing and life-denying. Over a ten-year period he moved from experimenting with different modes and arrived at a point where he worked primarily through following and trusting his own intuitive rhythm and emotional responses.

We can only affirm from our own experiences that every compromise with one's own emotional reality eventually results in a negative emotional effect on oneself and one's relationships. The more we personally have trusted our own growth inpulses and remained fluid with our own changes, the more we feel we have been able to help people trust in and grow from their own vital energies, while also moving away from the constant self-deprecating tendency of labeling themselves as "sick." Living by one's own rhythm requires an acceptance of the aggressive challenge of an ever-changing life. It often feels like a perilous route, and it is not devoid of its moments of great fear and self-doubt. The end point, however, is a constant sense of self-renewal. The price, we feel, is easily worth the risks.

# REFERENCES

Introduction

1. FUNSTEN, KENNETH, "100 Books for the Modern Person," Los Angeles *Times* (The Book Review), September 20, 1981, p. 3.

2. BACH, GEORGE R. AND DEUTSCH, RONALD M., *Stop! You're Driving Me Crazy*. New York: G. P. Putnam's Sons (1979).

3. GOLDBERG, HERB, *The New Male-Female Relationship*. New York: Wm. Morrow, Inc. (1983).

4. GELLES, RICHARD J., "Violence Toward Children in the United States" in *American Journal of Orthopsychiatry,* Vol. 48(4) (October 1978), pp. 580–92.

5. NICHOLSON, LUREE, *How to Fight with Your Kids and Win!* New York: Harcourt Brace Jovanovich (1978).

6. BACH, GEORGE R. AND TORBERT, LAURA, *A Time for Caring*. New York: Delacorte Press (1982).


Chapter 2

1. SPITZ, R. A. AND WOLF, K. M., "Anaclitic depression: an inquiry into the genesis of psychiatric conditions of early childhood" in Freud, A. et al. (eds.), *The Psychoanalytic Study of the Child,* New York: International Universities Press, Vol. 2 (1946), pp. 313–42.

2. KANNER, L., "Early Infantile Autism" in *J. Pediat.,* Vol. 25 (1944), pp. 211–17.

3. ZASLOW, ROBERT W., "Resistance to Human Attachment and Growth: Autism to Retardation." San Jose, Calif.: unpublished manuscript (1970).

4. MEGARGEE, EDWIN I., "Undercontrolled and Overcontrolled Personality Types in Extreme Antisocial Aggression" in Megargee, Edwin I. and Hokanson, Jack E., (ed.), *The Dynam-*

*ics of Aggression.* New York: Harper & Row (1970), pp. 108–20.

5. "Toys and Socialization to Sex Roles" in *Ms.,* Vol. 1, No. 6 (December 1972), p. 57.

6. SPITALNY, TERRY, "Battles and Best Friends in the Nursery School" in *Child Study,* Vol. 34, No. 4 (Fall 1957), p. 9.


Chapter 3


1. GOODE, WILLIAM, "Violence Among Intimates" (Appendix 19), Mulvihill, Donald J. and Tumin, Melvin M. (eds.), *Crimes of Violence: A Staff Report to the National Commission on the Causes and Prevention of Violence.* Washington, D.C.: U. S. Government Printing Office, Vol. 13 (December 1969), p. 941.

2. BACH, GEORGE R., "'Thinging': A Subtheory of Intimate Aggression Illustrated by Spouse Killing," presented at the 75th Annual Convention of the American Psychological Association, Washington, D.C. (September 2, 1967).

3. WINNICK, H. AND HOROVITZ, M., "The Problems of Infanticide" in *British Jr. of Criminology,* Vol. 2, No. 1 (1961), pp. 40–52.

4. SARGENT, DOUGLAS, "Children Who Kill—A Family Conspiracy?" in *Social Work* (January 1962), pp. 35–42.


Chapter 4


1. BOSS, MEDARD, *Psychoanalysis and Daseinanalysis.* New York: Basic Books (1963), pp. 259–60.

2. JANOV, ARTHUR, *The Primal Scream.* New York: Putnam (1970).

3. LOWEN, ALEXANDER, "Bio-energetic group therapy" in Ruitenback, Hendrik M. (ed.), *Group Therapy Today*. New York: Atherton (1971).

4. Ibid., p. 286.

5. Ibid., p. 285.

6. BACH, GEORGE R., Unpublished manuscript.

7. ZASLOW, ROBERT W., "Resistance to Human Attachment and Growth: Autism to Retardation." San Jose, Calif.: unpublished (1970), p. 33.

8. BACH, GEORGE R., Marathon Group Dynamics: I. Some Functions of the Professional Group Facilitator II. Dimensions of Helpfulness III. Disjunctive Contacts. *Psychological Reports,* 1967, 20, pp. 995–99.

9. DOUDS, J., BERENSON, B. G., CARKHUFF, R. R. AND PIERCE, R., "In Search of an Honest Experience: Confrontation in Counseling and Life" in Carkhuff, R. R. and Berenson, B. G. (eds.), *Beyond Counseling and Therapy*. New York: Holt, Rinehart and Winston (1967), pp. 170–79.

10. YABLONSKY, L., *The Tunnel Back*. New York: Macmillan (1965).

11. MASLOW, ABRAHAM, H., Impromptu talk given at Daytop Village in *Journal of Humanistic Psychology,* Vol. 7 (1967), pp. 28–29.

12. WHITAKER, CARL A., "The Use of Aggression in Psychotherapy" in Bach, G. R. (ed.), *Proceedings,* Ninth Annual Conference, Group Psychotherapy of Southern California, Inc., Los Angeles (1962), pp. 5–13.

13. SHEPARD, MARTIN, *The Love Treatment: Sexual Intimacy Between Patients and Psychotherapists*. New York: Peter H. Wyden, 1971.

14. DAHLBERG, CHARLES C., "Sexual Contact Between Patient and Therapist" in *Contemporary Psychoanalysis,* Vol. 6, No. 2 (1970), pp. 107–24.

15. CHESLER, PHYLLIS, *Women and Madness*. Garden

City, N.Y.: Doubleday & Company, Inc. (1972), p. 149.

16.   DAHLBERG, op. cit., p. 123.

17.   MASTERS, WILLIAM AND JOHNSON, VIRGINIA, *Human Sexual Inadequacy*. Boston: Little, Brown, 1970.

18.   CHESLER, op. cit.

19.   WHITAKER, CARL A., "The Use of Aggression in Psychotherapy" in Bach, G. R. (ed.), *Proceedings,* Ninth Annual Conference, Group Psychotherapy of Southern California, Inc., Los Angeles (1962), pp. 5–13.

## Chapter 7

1.   The quote from Dr. Edwin I. Megargee was taken from an article, "Undercontrolled and Overcontrolled Personality Types in Extreme Antisocial Aggression" in Megargee, Edwin I. and Hokanson, Jack E. (eds.), *The Dynamics of Aggression.* New York: Harper & Row (1970), p. 108.

2.   Material on Duane Pope was culled from an article, "Riddle of the 'Nice' Killer" by Bard Lindeman, which appeared in *The Saturday Evening Post,* Vol. 238, No. 98 (October 23, 1965).

3.   Material on Charles Whitman was obtained from an article, "All-American Boy," which appeared in *Newsweek* (August 15, 1966), p. 24, and an article, "The Eagle Scout Who Grew Up with a Tortured Mind," which appeared in *Life,* Vol. 61 (August 12, 1966), pp. 24–31.

4.   Material on Mark James Robert Essex was obtained from newspaper reports as follows:

(a)   Los Angeles *Times* (January 10, 1973), pp. 1 and 14.

(b)   Los Angeles *Times* Part 1 (January 14, 1973), p. 5.

(c)   Los Angeles *Times,* Part 1 (January 11, 1973), p. 15.

(d)   Los Angeles *Herald Examiner* (January 10, 1973), p. 2.

(e)   *Time* (January 22, 1973), pp. 20–21.

5.   Material on Juan Corona was taken from:

(a)   *Newsweek* (June 7, 1971).

(b)   *Time* (June 4, 1971).

(c)   Los Angeles *Times* (May 31, 1971).

(d)   Los Angeles *Times* (July 20, 1971).

6.   Material on Charles Watson was taken from:

(a)   "Mother Tells of Watson's Disintegration" in Los Angeles *Times* (September 1, 1971), p. 3.

(b)   "Tex Watson—My Pride and Joy!" in Los Angeles *Herald Examiner* (September 1, 1971).

7.   Material on Leo Held was taken from:

Los Angeles *Times* (October 24, 1967), p. 1.


Chapter 9


1.   MILGRAM, S. AND HOLLANDER, P., "Murder They Heard" in *Nation*, Vol. 198 (1964), pp. 602–4.

2.   ROSENTHAL, A. M., *Thirty-eight Witnesses*. New York: McGraw-Hill (1964).


Chapter 11


1.   GARRITY, JOAN TERRY, under the pseudonym of "J," *The Sensuous Woman*. New York: Lyle Stuart (1969).


Chapter 12


1.   STORR, ANTHONY, *Human Aggression,* New York: Atheneum (1968).

Chapter 13

1.   BASTIAANS, J. "The Role of Aggression in the Genesis of Psychosomatic Disease" in *Journal of Psychosomatic Research,* Vol. 13 (1969), p. 311.

2.   BUTLER, B., Quoted by Le Shan, L., "Psychological States as Factors in the Development of Malignant Disease: A Critical Review" in *Journal of the National Cancer Institute,* Vol. 22, No. 1 (1959).

3.   BACON, C. L., RENNECKER, R. AND CUTLER, M., Quoted by Le Shan, L., in "Psychological States as Factors in the Development of Malignant Disease: A Critical Review" in *Journal of the National Cancer Institute,* Vol. 22, No. 1 (1959).

4.   STRAVRAKY, KATHLEEN M., "Psychological Factors in the Outcome of Human Cancer" in *Journal of Psychosomatic Research,* Vol. 12 (1968), pp. 251–59.

5.   *Human Behavior,* Vol. 1, No. 5 (September/October 1972), p. 27.


Chapter 14

1.   DeMARTINO, MANFRED F., "Mistakes Men Make in Lovemaking—According to 175 Women" in *Sexual Behavior,* Vol. 2, No. 4 (April 1972), p. 18.

2.   Ibid., pp. 18–22.


Chapter 15

1.   KINSEY, A. C., POMEROY, W. B., MARTIN, C. E. AND GEBHARD, P. H., *Sexual Behavior in the Human Female.* Philadelphia: Saunders (1953).

2.  MacLean, P. D., "New Findings Relevant to the Evolution of Psychosexual Functions of the Brain" in Money, J. (ed.), *Sex research: New developments*. New York: Holt, Rinehart and Winston (1965).

3.  MacLean, P. D. and Ploog, D. W., "Cerebral Representation of Penile Erection" in *J. Neurophysiology,* Vol. 25 (1962), pp. 29–55.

4.  Mark, V. H. and Ervin, F. R., *Violence and the Brain*. New York: Harper & Row (1970).

5.  Feshbach, S. and Jaffe, Y., *Effects of Inhibition of Aggression upon Sexual Responsivity."* Preliminary Report, University of California, Los Angeles (1970).

Chapter 19

1.  "Is the Work Ethic Going out of Style?" in *Time* (October 30, 1972), p. 96.

2.  Barron, Frank, *Creative Person and Creative Process*. New York: Holt, Rinehart and Winston, Inc. (1969).

Chapter 20

1.  The fair fight techniques described in this chapter were originally developed as techniques for married couples and described in the book *The Intimate Enemy*.
Bach, George R. and Wyden, Peter, *The Intimate Enemy*. New York: William Morrow and Company, Inc. (1968).

# INDEX